D1595298

The Economic Geography of Barbados

The
Economic Geography
of Barbados

A STUDY OF THE RELATIONSHIPS
BETWEEN ENVIRONMENTAL VARIATIONS
AND ECONOMIC DEVELOPMENT

By Otis P. Starkey

NEGRO UNIVERSITIES PRESS
WESTPORT, CONNECTICUT

Preface

THE BRITISH West Indian island of Barbados provides a significant example of the hidden advantages of environmental handicaps. Elsewhere, it has been noted that the highest degree of civilization does not necessarily develop where nature has been most kind. For example, the history and accomplishments of the Norwegians on their rugged, fiorded coasts, of the Dutch on their marshy deltas, and of the Danes on their sandy islands indicate that the apparent disadvantages of their environments stimulated their activities rather than handicapped them. In Barbados, hurricanes, droughts, and pests seem to have afforded like stimulation.

The Barbadian environment is not lacking in advantages; it offers a fertile soil, much level land, a pleasant, oceanic climate, and an excellent position for world trade. However, this study shows that these favorable features have not accounted for its many periods of rapid economic development. Instead, those characteristics which have hitherto been considered its greatest handicaps—its droughts, hurricanes, and uncertain trade relations—have been the most powerful factors in stimulating Barbadian progress.

The Barbadian environment is sufficiently favorable so that planters and laborers alike have built permanent homes and developed a loyalty to the island. Such conditions might have resulted only in an easy-going life with the outworn methods of the past weighing down economic progress. Such a stagnant culture has been common, for example, in certain parts of the cotton belt of the American South.

But the Barbadian environment has not been *too* favorable. Its droughts, its hurricanes, its pests, and its uncertain markets have generated urgent problems which the planters were forced to solve or emigrate. Although some progress undoubtedly would have occurred without the stimuli of these problems, it might have taken centuries to accomplish the improvements made during a few years of stress.

The example of Barbados indicates that environmental handicaps should not be categorically classified as misfortunes. As will be shown (page 114), even the most devastating hurricanes were not entirely disadvantageous. In fact, it might be reasonably argued that hurricanes have done more good than harm in Barbados, although the immediate results have been disastrous. Nature has not "spared the rod and spoiled the child" in Barbados.

In gathering the material for this study, I have been helped by so many people that to name any here would be discourteous to many others who have been equally helpful. During my stay in Barbados, I received courteous assistance from numerous officials and private citizens. Equally helpful were the many librarians and government officials I consulted in England and the United States.

In the preparation of this study I am under the greatest obligation to Professor J. Russell Smith, of Columbia University. Professor Smith was my first instructor in economic geography. The interest that he aroused at that time was largely responsible for the start of my career as a geographer. His continued helpfulness and friendship have contributed greatly to whatever progress I have since made in that field. I am also indebted to my former teachers, Professors Douglas Johnson, A. K. Lobeck, George T. Renner, O. S. Morgan, and Henry S. Sharp, all of Columbia University, who read this study in manuscript and made many helpful suggestions. This work has benefited by the criticisms of Professors Robert E. Chaddock and Frank Tannenbaum.

My thanks are due to my wife, who assisted me in the preparation of the manuscript and in proofreading, and to Mrs. William F. Christians who edited and typed a large part of the manuscript. I am grateful to Mr. G. Etzel Pearcy, who drew the relief map (Figure 1), and to Mr. Philip Taylor, who helped with the maps and graphs.

Otis P. Starkey

Philadelphia, Pennsylvania
July 31, 1939

Contents

Tables

Maps and Graphs

The Economic Geography of Barbados

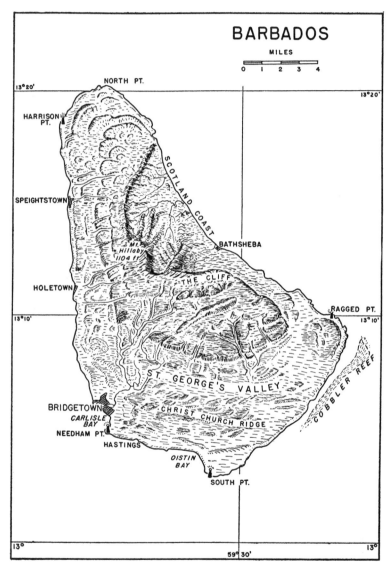

1. A PHYSICAL MAP OF BARBADOS

Source: Generalized from Commander J. Parsons, *Admiralty Chart No. 2485: Barbados.*

CHAPTER I

Introduction

BARBADOS is a small, densely populated West Indian island. Its area (166 square miles) is only one-fourth greater than that of the city of Philadelphia. But in spite of this small size, its fortunate location and fertile soil have enabled it to play a major part in the economic and political development of the Caribbean area. Probably no agricultural area of comparable size has received such frequent mention or entered so much into world affairs. As a result, unusually complete records are available which may be analyzed with profit by the historian, the sociologist, the economist, or the geographer.

The following study is geographic, and is oriented around the variability of the physical environment. The results of this variability have been unusually conspicuous in Barbados, probably because of the one-crop economy which has characterized the island for almost three centuries. However, the writer does not maintain that this is the only important, or even the principal, factor in the development of Barbados. Hence care has been taken to present other factors, cultural and physical, and to avoid the unrealistic consideration of the environmental variables apart from the whole picture.

Barbados is situated at about 13° north latitude, and 100 miles east of the main chain of the Lesser Antilles. It is almost exactly southwest from the Azores (2,100 miles) and from England (3,600 miles). European ships have an easy passage to Barbados since the larger part of their voyage is with the steady northeast trades.

Barbados appears flat as one approaches it and may easily be mistaken for a low-lying bank of clouds on the horizon. Because of the outlying coral reefs, vessels usually approach the island only from the leeward. From this side, the island appears like a garden with its gentle westward slope interrupted by long natural "terraces." Trees are scarcely in evidence except for occasional tall palms, clusters of trees around huts and plantation buildings, and a fringe of trees and bushes along the shore. Windmills of the Dutch type, the tall chimneys of the sugar factories, and a sprinkling of wooden huts are other details which appear as the shore is approached.

There are three harbors which might be used by transatlantic vessels: Carlisle Bay, Oistins Bay, and Speights Bay. All are on the leeward coast, and each has its settlement, but the only important port, at present, is Bridgetown on Carlisle Bay, which almost monopolizes the shipping of the island. Here is a busy scene which far surpasses in activity anything that can be observed at the other ports of the Lesser Antilles. At anchor are usually several large steamers, while in the Careenage (the inner harbor) are tied up numerous schooners and small boats.

Unlike other cities of the Lesser Antilles, bustling Bridgetown has a considerable number of modern shops, a railway station, and busses which leave Trafalgar Square at frequent intervals. A cluster of public buildings on one side of Trafalgar Square is adjoined by several shopping streets and by warehouses on both sides of the Careenage. A few blocks from this commercial core, stone houses gradually replace the outlying shops and offices. The city's residential section is largely occupied by the colored inhabitants, while the homes of the white population are mostly in the suburbs. Most of the buildings around Bridgetown are of coral limestone, two or three stories in height, with gently sloping roofs. Wooden porches and balconies, wooden shutters, blinds, or jalousies are common additions. The characteristic color of the structures is a light buff or some similar tint which, with the dust of the roads and the general plainness of the architecture, suggests a Mediterranean town. In the poorer parts of Bridgetown and its suburbs, wooden shacks replace or supplement the coral limestone buildings.

The hinterland of Bridgetown is not so flat as it appears from the boat. The island consists of a coral limestone cap overlying folded and faulted sedimentary rocks which outcrop only in the northeastern section of the island. If one drives northeast from Bridgetown across the center of the island, the land appears to consist of fertile, well-cultivated terraces, each with a natural retaining wall of coral rock. The road rises gradually, cutting its way through each terrace until the highest level is reached. Here is found a stretch of almost level land, green with sugar cane and ground provisions and extending several miles to the east and southeast. The weather, which was somewhat oppressive in sheltered, dusty Bridgetown, is here pleasant because of the winds and the 1,000-foot altitude. On the eastern side of the upland, "the Cliff," the eastern edge of the coral limestone, appears suddenly. A thousand feet below its summit and a mile to the east, is the windward coast with its high surf caused by the trade winds. On the uplands, the land is level, slightly rolling or gently sloping upward toward the Cliff. Underground drainage has discouraged the growth of valleys and gullies. Below the Cliff is a rugged landscape, carved out by streams from the folded sedimentary rocks. The comparative barrenness and wildness of this district have caused it to be called "Scotland."

A drive of about four miles southward from the Cliff, with a gradual descent of several hundred feet, brings one to the top of another escarpment. Below it spread out the rich, almost level lands of the streamless St. George's Valley, and two miles beyond, Christ Church Ridge rises by low terraces parallel to the valley to a maximum elevation of 400 feet. At the western end of St. George's Valley is Bridgetown, on which converge the roads from the leeward and southern coasts, from St. George's Valley, and from the terraced uplands.

Barbados is a poor place for a hermit, for there is hardly a place where voices cannot be heard. Everywhere the population is dense, ranging from 3,623 per square mile in Bridgetown to 540 per square mile in the inland parish of St. Thomas.[1] Unlike the neigh-

---

[1] *Report on the Census of Barbados, 1921,* p. 15.

boring islands, hardly an acre of Barbados is without some evidence of human occupance. Except in Bridgetown and its suburbs, stone plantation buildings, Canadian pine huts of the Negroes, coral roads, sugar cane, and provision crops appear in every view. The general pattern seems to be universal although, as will be shown later, significant differences appear in detail.

The cultural landscape is tropical in appearance although not so much so as the landscapes of neighboring islands. The whole cultural pattern, however, is essentially English, and the outward material evidences to the contrary are largely a veneer overlaying the cultural core. Although over 93 percent of the population of 170,000 are descended, at least in part, from African ancestors, every Barbadian, white, black, or colored, thinks of himself as a member of an Anglo-Saxon society. The popular nickname for the island, "Little England," is, from this angle, quite justified.

Strategically situated islands are noted for their variety of cultural contacts—witness Singapore, Hong Kong, and Hawaii. Barbados is not an exception, although unlike some of the others, the result of these contacts has been but a modification of the English culture. Other cultures have contributed material features to the island, but these have been merged into an English framework.

The only other culture that has had any great influence is that principal offshoot of English culture, the culture of the northeastern United States and adjacent Canada. These mixed influences can be illustrated most readily by the vocabulary. English terms such as "luggage," "assurance society," "limited company," are common, but along with them occurs the "drugstore," American both in name and in type of service rendered. Government accounts are kept in pounds, shillings, and pence, but the local banks issue notes in dollars. Local prices are quoted in either system, and sometimes both currencies occur in the same advertisement. Small change is the same as that used in England, but a halfpenny is commonly called a cent, et cetera. An interesting result of this system is the tendency to quote prices in multiples of twelve, as twenty-four cents, thirty-six cents. Pronunciation also suggests the mixture of two cultures: The English accent is heard among officials, but many of the planters and shopkeepers use a pronunciation which seems more like that of eastern Canada. The speech of the Negroes varies from a dialect which departs from the King's English as much as does that of Negroes in the American South, to a careful speech, depending on the education, foreign experience, and social pretensions of the individual.

One of the earliest cultural contacts of the first English settlers was with the Arawak Indians, but aside from the crops borrowed from the Indians, and a few names, no residue of this contact has survived.

Almost the same may be said for the African cultural contacts resulting from the slave trade. Negro music, social customs, and religious ideas are mentioned in early accounts,[2] but today almost no African cultural survivals, such as were found in Haiti by Herskovits,[3] have remained significant. Obeah, or witchcraft, and a few proverbs are the only certain nonmaterial survivals, and, of these, the former has been discouraged by the Government, as were many other African customs in the first century of Barbadian settlement.[4]

Certain Negro social characteristics may be cultural rather than physiological inheritances, for example, the Negro tendency to organize into friendly societies, lodges, and the like may be an inheritance from the societies of West Africa. However, there is no evidence of cultural continuity, and the present forms are but copies of European institutions.

Other cultural contacts have been those with the Dutch, Caribs, Spanish, and Portuguese, and with other cultures through English intermediaries. The residue, other than crops and animals, from these sources has been slight. The details of these and other cultural contacts will be deferred to Chapters III–VI.

Even a superficial study of Barbadian history shows that the island has been subject to recurring crises (Figure 2), caused by

[2] Richard Ligon, *A True and Exact History of the Island of Barbados*, p. 49.

[3] M. J. Herskovits, *Life in a Haitian Valley*.

[4] In 1688 an act provided that wooden swords, drums, horns, and other instruments of the Negroes should be destroyed. See *Acts of Assembly Passed in the Island of Barbados, from 1648–1718*, p. 119; also later acts.

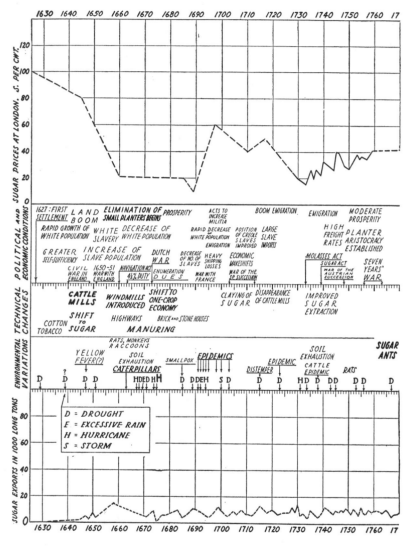

2. A CHRONOLOGICAL CHART SHOWING THE PRINCIPAL VARIABLE
FACTORS INFLUENCING THE DEVELOPMENT OF BARBADOS, 1627–1935

Sources: This chart is based largely on the material presented in Chapters III–VIII.
The principal sources are:

1627–1763: *Calendar of State Papers, Colonial Series;* Vincent T. Harlow, *A History
of Barbados, 1625–1685* (Oxford, 1926); John Oldmixon, *The British Empire in*

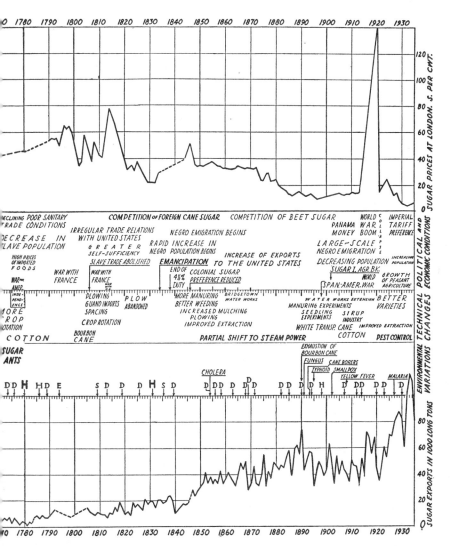

America (London, 1741), Vol. II; Richard Pares, *War and Trade in the West Indies* (Oxford, 1936) ; Frank W. Pitman, *The Development of the British West Indies, 1700–1763* (New Haven, 1917).

1763–1850: Lowell Joseph Ragatz, *The Fall of the Planter Class in the British Caribbean, 1763–1833* (New York, 1928) ; Sir Robert H. Schomburgk, *The History of Barbados* (London, 1848) ; John Davy, *The West Indies before and since Slave Emancipation* (London, 1854).

1850–1935: *Barbados Blue Books, 1850–1935; Colonial Reports: Barbados.*

droughts, hurricanes, epidemics, plant pests, changing social and political conditions, and the uncertainties of the world market. The effects of these variations have been especially striking, first, because since early times the Barbadian population has so thoroughly utilized its physical environment (considering the technical knowledge available at the time); second, because the economy of the island since 1650 has been built on sugar products which were raised primarily for sale abroad rather than for home use. On the proceeds of the sale of sugar, molasses, and rum, the island has depended for purchasing power to import the very necessities of life. These imports include a large part of the food supply of the island, all of the clothing, and the major portion of the building materials used. Let the sugar crop fail, and many Barbadians face not only bankruptcy, but starvation.

Variations of the Barbadian physical environment may be devided into several significant types:

1. Seasonal and diurnal variations which are fairly regular in occurrence, and to which the tempo of life could be adjusted as soon as their regularity and significance were recognized.

2. Secular variations due to the destructive exploitation of resources: in Barbados, notably soil exhaustion and alteration of the flora and fauna.

3. Irregular variations in the environment such as hurricanes, droughts, epidemics, and pests.

Another class of variations consists of changes in human ability to utilize the Barbadian environment. Such changes cannot be neglected, since they interact with, and often accentuate or neutralize, the effect of the variations in the physical environment. This second class of variations may be divided into three significant types:

1. Changes in human knowledge of the presence of resources (discovery).

2. Changes in human ability to use known resources (technological changes), for example, the quadrupling of Barbadian sugar yields since the first cultivation of the cane. '

3. Changes in human ability to exchange the products resulting from

the use of resources (economic changes), for example, the inability of the Barbadian planters to dispose of their crop in 1921.

Although, for analysis, the author will divide the Barbadian environment as much as possible into its constituent parts, nevertheless it should be remembered that the prosperity of Barbados has been influenced by these parts acting in combination rather than by any one part acting separately. Thus a year of low rainfall does not necessarily mean a poor sugar crop if the ground water supply is unusually good or if the canes are unusually free from insect pests and plant diseases. Likewise, a combination of two natural catastrophes may be more disastrous than the sum of the damages caused by each occurring separately.

How may these environmental variations be expected to operate on man? This query is part of the general problem of environmental influences which has been investigated by all of the social sciences. Within recent years essential agreement has been reached by all except the extremists in each science. A few quotations from modern geographers will show the modern viewpoint:

The forces of physical nature are bound to each other in their consequences, in their relations, and in the consequences of these relations. Man does not escape the common law; his activity is included in the network of terrestrial phenomena. But, if human activity is thus circumscribed, it does not follow that it is fatally determined. Because of its connection with natural phenomena it is without question included in geography in two ways: it responds to the influence of certain facts and, on the other hand, it exercises its influence on other facts. . . . That is why we must add to the group of material forces this new force—human activity—which is not only a material thing but which also expresses itself through material effects.[5]

Between the facts of the physical order there are sometimes relations of causality; between the facts of human geography there are usually only relations of connection.[6]

The geographical elements of the environment are fixed only in the narrow and special sense of the word. The moment we give them human associations they are as changeful as humanity itself. That is why modern geography has so definitely steered away from determinism and toward

[5] Jean Brunhes, *Human Geography*, p. 27.   [6] *Ibid.*, p. 593.

a study of types of actually working regional combinations of human and environmental conditions.[7]

Historical geography may be considered as the series of changes which the cultural landscapes have undergone and therefore involves the reconstruction of past cultural landscapes. Of special concern is the catalytic relation of civilized man to area and the effects of the replacement of cultures. From this difficult and little-touched field alone may be gained a full realization of the development of the present cultural landscape out of earlier cultures and the natural landscape.[8]

The common point stressed is the dominance of human activity. Adjustments to the physical environment are made not to get a nice adjustment, but rather to suit cultural aims.

In Barbados, we find English culture entering into an exotic physical environment, changing that environment, and at the same time being changed by it. To this altered English culture have been added from time to time features of other cultures. The resultant represents a satisfactory, but not perfect, cultural adjustment to the Barbadian physical environment.

What has been the effect of the variability of environmental conditions on the development of this cultural adjustment in Barbados? This query is the central theme of this study. In attempting to answer it, the data will be arranged to present the facts rather than to support any preconceived theory of definite relationship. In Chapter II, the Barbadian environment will be described. Chapters III, IV, V, and VI will present the historical evidence which describes the past interactions between cultural forces and the Barbadian environment. In Chapters VII and VIII the present Barbadian economy will be examined with special attention to environmental and economic variables. Finally, in Chapter IX, the conclusions which the writer has reached from the preceding evidence will be presented.

[7] Isaiah Bowman, *Geography in Relation to the Social Sciences*, p. 37.
[8] Carl O. Sauer, "The Morphology of Landscape," *University of California Publications in Geography*, II, No. 2 (1925), 47.

CHAPTER II

The Barbadian Environment

ALMOST no part of the Barbadian landscape has escaped alteration by man. During the first century of settlement the indigenous
flora and fauna were almost completely destroyed, and were replaced by exotic forms. The soil was greatly altered except where
it was too thin for cultivation. Pests and diseases from other areas
were accidentally added to the Barbadian environment by man. It
is also possible that the clearing of the forests decreased both the
rainfall and the sensible temperatures.

A few aspects of the Barbadian environment were either beyond
human control or were but slightly modified by human occupance.
The great fluctuations in the Barbadian weather, especially in
rainfall and winds, have occurred throughout Barbadian history
and have been apparently unaffected by human efforts. The structure and the surface features of Barbados have been altered by
man in minor ways only, such as through the draining of ponds
and the digging of wells. Likewise, the mineral resources have
been only slightly diminished by human use.

This chapter will present a brief description of each major
feature of the Barbadian environment. In addition, a summary
statement of the major human adjustments to each environmental
feature will be included.

POSITION

Most of the Lesser Antilles have a good position for trade, but
Barbados has the additional advantage of being eastward and
windward of the main chain. Thus it was the logical stopping
place for sailing vessels from Europe which wished to transship
cargo for the other Lesser Antilles, and then proceed to Trinidad,

Jamaica, or Colon, without encountering adverse winds or currents. The trade winds and the equatorial currents made it easy for vessels proceeding from eastern South America to North American or European ports, to stop at Barbados for water, supplies, and trade. Likewise, slave vessels from Africa bound for Caribbean and North American ports found it convenient to make their first American stop at Bridgetown. The map (Figure 3) demonstrates these points, and shows that Barbados had a position

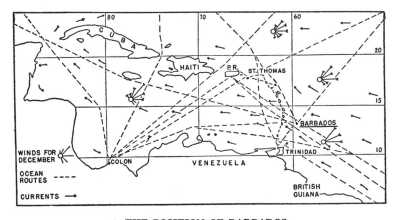

3. THE POSITION OF BARBADOS

at the entrance to the Caribbean unrivaled except, perhaps, by St. Thomas.

Bridgetown lost a large part of these advantages after the growth of Port of Spain, Trinidad. That port, because of treacherous currents,[1] is not so ideally located as Barbados for sailing vessels. For steamers, however, this factor is of minor importance and is offset by Trinidad's advantages of cheap fuel oil and freedom from hurricanes. Nevertheless, the position of Barbados still gives it an important place in the world's trading routes, and many vessels stop at Bridgetown en route to the now busier Port of Spain.

[1] U.S. Hydrographic Office, *West Indies Pilot,* II (1929), 265, 266, 282.

CLIMATE

The favorable position of Barbados must have been all the more attractive to sea captains because the Barbadian climate was more pleasant than most other West Indian climates. Although it seems hot to those accustomed to the climate of England, its sensible temperatures are mild, and it is free from extremes of both heat and cold. Those who adjust their manner of living to Barbadian climatic conditions should have little difficulty in living comfortably in such an equable climate.

Temperature.—The lack of extreme temperatures in Barbados is due to the moderating influence of the surrounding ocean. No part of Barbados is more than five miles from the sea, and the moderating influence of the sea is the more penetrating because of the almost constant winds across the island. Such differences in actual and sensible temperatures as exist among the various parts of the island are largely due to differences in altitude and exposure to the winds.

Accurate temperature observations are not available for many stations throughout the island, for temperatures are so uniform that the relatively minor fluctuations are of little interest and, therefore, are not recorded. It is, however, generally recognized that the uplands are considerably cooler than the lowlands, and that the windward side of the island has more moderate temperatures than the leeward side. The figures in Table 1 support these generalizations.

The seasonal variation in sensible temperatures results from changes in wind and humidity. Thus the coolest and most pleasant weather occurs from January to March when the winds are strong and the humidity is moderately low. The most oppressive weather occurs from August to October when both the temperatures and humidity are high and the winds are only moderate.[2]

Sensible temperatures vary greatly within short distances be-

[2] A month-to-month description of the climate is given in Sir Robert H. Schomburgk, *The History of Barbados,* pp. 28–29; see also *Monthly Weather Review,* April, 1926, pp. 156–57.

TABLE 1 ª

TEMPERATURES AT REPRESENTATIVE STATIONS

PLACE	ALTI-TUDE (FEET)	ANNUAL MEAN	FEBRUARY MEAN	AUGUST MEAN	EXTREMES *Maxi-mum*	*Mini-mum*
Leeward						
Bridgetown	30	79.6° F.	77.6° F.	81.0° F.	90° F.	65° F.
Codrington	181	78.6	76.5	80.0	91	61
Windward						
Binfield	1,063	75.0	?	?	83	67
Joe's River	430	76.2	74.5	77.2	83	69

ª *Monthly Weather Review,* April, 1926, pp. 156–57, gives a summary of rainfall data and gives complete data for Bridgetown and Codrington. Binfield and Joe's River data are taken from *Barbados Blue Book* (1874–79).

cause of different exposures to the winds and different humidities. Thus in October, Bridgetown (relative humidity, 80 percent; wind, seven miles per hour; average temperature, 80.4°) seems much hotter than Codrington House (relative humidity 70 percent; wind, seven and a half miles per hour; temperature, 80.3°) which is only a mile and a half distant.[3]

Except in parts of Bridgetown, the temperatures of Barbados, although hardly stimulating, may be considered as satisfactory for a wide range of human activities. Even when the weather is oppressive, the unpleasant heat lasts only from noon to about four in the afternoon. Temperature conditions are also suited to most warm-temperate and tropical plants, and agriculture is not greatly restricted by the temperature factor alone. The lack of cold weather does have the disadvantage of not killing off germs, pests, and plant diseases during the winter, but this is partly balanced by the sterilizing power of the bright sunshine, and by the ability of the winds and rains to carry away many germs and pests.

The life of the people of Barbados is adjusted to temperature conditions, not so much as a matter of necessity as of convenience. Many of the adjustments seem to have been taken over from neighboring islands where they are more necessary. Thus the mid-

[3] *Monthly Weather Review, loc. cit.*

day siesta is not unknown in Barbados, but is by no means common. Barbadians rise early, and slacken their pace during the middle of the day, but the stores do not close, nor does business cease. Sports and amusements are adjusted to the temperature; for example, strenuous games are played early in the morning or late in the afternoon; football is played in the cooler season; cricket, in the warmer season.

The houses, especially of the middle and upper classes, are now generally well ventilated and provided with porches, jalousies, and other devices for benefiting from the breeze. Likewise, lightweight and light-colored clothing is common, but by no means universal. The temperatures are not oppressive enough to have forced the abandonment of English styles; thus waistcoats, dark formal clothes, and the like are still worn when English etiquette requires them.

Light.—On the average, the sky above Bridgetown is more than half-covered with clouds (from five-tenths covered in January to sixty-seven hundredths covered in June).[4] No accurate observations exist for the higher (and rainier) parts of the island, but it may be reasonably inferred that they are more cloudy. The clouds

TABLE 2

LIGHT CONDITIONS IN BARBADOS, 1929–33 [a]

YEAR	NUMBER OF DAYS WITH NO SUNSHINE	NUMBER OF DAYS WITH LESS THAN TWO HOURS OF SUN	NUMBER OF DAYS WITH LESS THAN FIVE HOURS OF SUN	NUMBER OF DAYS WITH MORE THAN NINE HOURS OF SUN
1929	5	21	49	185
1930	4	13	37	191
1931	4	19	53	194
1932	3	12	45	185
1933	3	21	57	177

[a] C. C. Skeete, "Weather Observations and Weather Records in Barbados, 1924–33," *Journal of the Barbados Museum and Historical Society,* I, No. 3 (1934), 128.

[4] C. C. Skeete, "Weather Observations and Weather Records in Barbados, 1924–33," *Journal of the Barbados Museum and Historical Society,* I, No. 3 (1934), 128.

are most common during the morning and late afternoon and, as the statistics in Table 2 indicate, they intercept only from 22 to 40 percent of the sunlight. Thus light conditions, especially in the drier parts of Barbados, are brilliant. The tropical sun is bright, and entirely overcast days are rare.

The common lack of shade trees in much of Barbados, the glare from the white coral roads, and the light-tinted buildings increase the effect of the brilliant sunlight on the eyes. Several travelers reported that sore eyes were a common Barbadian affliction. Davy [5] and others noted that face-clothes used to be worn to protect the skin from the sun. This custom has disappeared, but white Barbadians still avoid the sun as much as possible, and have surprisingly untanned complexions. Jalousies on the windows, wooden awnings built out over the sidewalks in front of Bridgetown's shops, parasols carried by the ladies, and sun umbrellas carried by the plantation managers on their tours of inspection help to protect white complexions from the tropical sun.

Rainfall.—The most significant statement that can be made about the Barbadian rainfall is that it is extremely irregular in every way. Although averages that have some descriptive value can be made, economically it is the wide departures from these averages which are important. On the average, about 62½ inches of rain fall annually on Barbados, but this average includes stations with 20 inches of rain and stations with over 100 inches. This 62½ inches average of rainfall was obtained by averaging together such extreme years as 1930, when the rainfall for the island averaged 38 inches, and 1896, when the rainfall averaged over 89½ inches.[6] Of the average of 62½ inches, 45 inches fall during the rainy season (June to November), while the remaining 17½ inches fall during the drier season (December to May).[7]

Usually the distinction between the rainy and drier seasons persists. However, in some years, individual drier-season months (as,

[5] John Davy, *The West Indies before and since Slave Emancipation*, p. 67.

[6] Barbados Botanical Station, *Occasional Bulletin*, No. 8, 1897; also U.S. Weather Bureau, *Climatological Data, West Indies and Caribbean Service* (1935).

[7] F. Hardy, "Some Aspects of the Flora of Barbados," *Agricultural Journal*, January, 1932, p. 52.

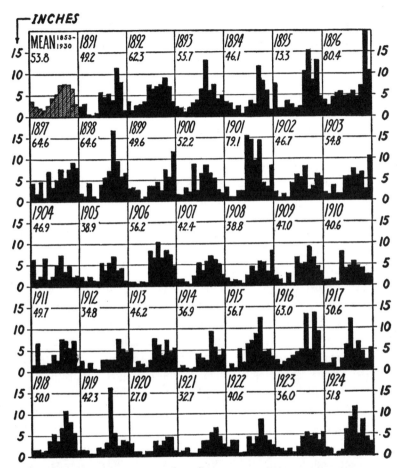

INCHES

MEAN 1853-1930 53.8	1891 49.2	1892 62.3	1893 55.7	1894 46.1	1895 73.3	1896 80.4
1897 64.6	1898 64.6	1899 49.6	1900 52.2	1901 79.1	1902 46.7	1903 54.8
1904 46.9	1905 38.9	1906 56.2	1907 42.4	1908 38.8	1909 47.0	1910 40.6
1911 49.7	1912 34.8	1913 46.2	1914 36.9	1915 56.7	1916 63.0	1917 50.6
1918 50.0	1919 42.3	1920 27.0	1921 32.7	1922 40.6	1923 36.0	1924 51.8

4. THE MEAN RAINFALL AT THE BARBADOS BOTANIC STATION
(CODRINGTON) COMPARED WITH THE ACTUAL RAINFALL
FOR EACH YEAR, 1891–1924

Very few of these years had the same distribution of rainfall as in the
mean year.

Source: "World Weather Records," *Smithsonian Miscellaneous Collections,*
LXXIX (Washington, 1929), 1014–15; *Ibid.,* XC (Washington, 1934), 376.

for example, April, 1904) are rainier than most of the months in the rainy season. A more frequent occurrence is the delayed beginning of the rainy season or its early termination. Figure 4 compares the average conditions with the actual conditions for selected years, and provides additional proof of the above points.

There are three types of rainfall in Barbados. The first type is referred to as general or regional rains, and occurs throughout Barbados and often throughout neighboring islands. The cause of these rains is not known,[8] but it seems to be related to the humidity of the trade winds. From Hackleton's Cliff, the rain-bearing clouds can be seen approaching the island, and the general rains have begun over the ocean before the clouds have reached Barbados. These general rains are especially important to the lowlands of St. Philip and eastern Christ Church since these regions receive very little of other types of rainfall.[9]

The second type of rainfall consists of convectional or "heat" rains. Such rains have occurred during each month of the year, but are almost certain to occur at least once and usually much oftener during each of the months from July to November, when there is a combination of high temperatures, high humidity, and low wind velocities. In the morning the sunshine warms the lower levels of the atmosphere; the heated air rises and forms cumulus clouds. About ten or eleven o'clock these clouds precipitate rain over an area of from one to two square miles. Soon cumulo-nimbus clouds form, and heavy torrential rains may occur over the original and adjoining areas.

With average wind velocity of five miles per hour or less, initial development tends to occur inland. With average velocities of approximately five to ten miles per hour initial development tends to take place over the coast opposite to the direction from which the wind is blowing. Finally with wind velocities exceeding ten miles per hour, initial development takes place, if at all, over the sea at approximately five to fifteen miles from the coast opposite to the direction from which the wind is blowing. . . .

---

[8] C. C. Skeete, "Barbados Rainfall," *Pamphlet No. 9* (Department of Science and Agriculture, Barbados, 1931), p. 5.

[9] *Ibid.*

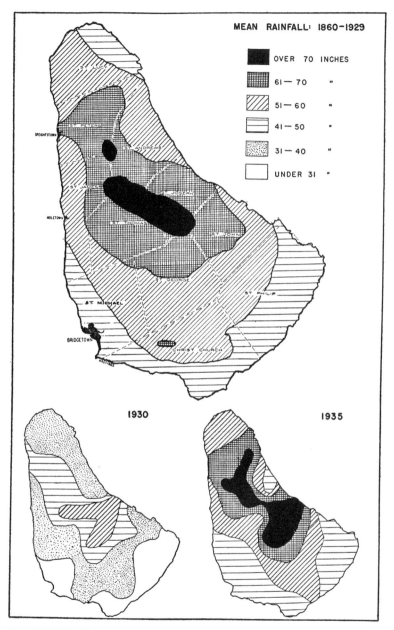

MEAN RAINFALL: 1860-1929

■	OVER 70 INCHES
▨	61 — 70 "
▨	51 — 60 "
▢	41 — 50 "
▨	31 — 40 "
▢	UNDER 31 "

1930

1935

5. RAINFALL MAPS OF BARBADOS: MEAN, DROUGHT YEAR (1930)
AND RAINY YEAR (1935)

Sources: *Report on the Department of Science and Agriculture, 1930–1931;*
United States Weather Bureau, *Climatological Data, West Indian and Caribbean
Service, passim.*

It is noteworthy that in as much as the general wind current rarely moves from west or northwest, heat rain cloud development seldom occurs over St. Philip and eastern Christ Church. These districts are however occasionally reached by rain of secondary development. In contrast, however, in as much as the main air current frequently moves from points between east and south, the parishes of St. James, St. Thomas, St. Peter and St. Lucy are those in which this type of rain most frequently develops.[10]

The third and rarest type of rainfall is the cyclonic type and is associated with the tropical cyclones (including hurricanes) which pass over the island, once or more each season, between July and October. These rains are often heavy and are likely to do more damage (through floods and soil wash) than good. The destructive hurricanes which have visited Barbados have been invariably accompanied by rains of this type.

All three of these types of rainfall are affected by altitude and, roughly speaking, the rainer areas (Figure 5) are those of high altitude. The principal exception to this generalization occurs on the windward coast, where the rainfall is much heavier than would be expected from altitude alone. On the other hand, the convectional rains prevent the development of a pronounced rain shadow on the leeward coasts.

The seasonal distribution of the rainfall results because both the conditions favoring all three types of rain are more common between June and November. At this time of the year, the doldrums are relatively near Barbados, the trade winds are weaker, and the air is more humid. Conditions approach those of the doldrums belt sufficiently to bring heavy rainfall, yet the oppressive calms of the doldrums are unknown.

The significance of rainfall to the Barbadian economy can hardly be overemphasized; indeed, rainfall is the ever-recurring theme in the following chapters. The rains nourish the crops which are the lifeblood of the island's economy. Rainfall is so intimately connected with the underground water supply that a drought year may mean a shortage of well water. Much of the progress which

[10] C. C. Skeete, "Weather Observations, . . ." *Journal B.M.H.S.*, I, No. 3 (1934), 121–23.

man has made in the further utilization of the Barbadian environment has been associated with a better conservation of its water supply.

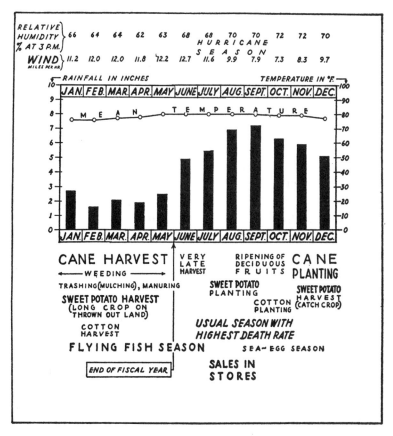

6. THE SEASONAL DISTRIBUTION OF BARBADIAN
ECONOMIC ACTIVITY

Sources: W. W. Reed, "Climatological Data for the West Indian Islands," *Monthly Weather Review,* LIV (1926), 156–57; *Barbados Advocate Weekly* (1932–34), *passim.*

Wind.—As in all trade-wind islands, the wind is an important feature of the Barbadian environment. The average wind velocity is shown in Figure 6.

Actually, the winds vary with the exposure, and are somewhat stronger on the windward coast and weaker in the hollows. Rarely, however, is the air stagnant, except in the gullies and in some of the alleys of Bridgetown. Wind velocities of less than three miles per hour are uncommon, and many a year passes without so low a recording. The maximum velocity recorded in most years is about twenty-five miles per hour, although velocities in hurricane years run much higher.[11]

The winds reduce the sensible temperatures, influence the amount of rainfall, and move sailing vessels and windmills. On the whole, the usefulness of the winds more than offsets their destructive force in hurricanes, and, as will be shown in Chapter VI,[12] even the hurricanes have not been wholly evil in their effects.

It is the uncertainty of the hurricanes which causes the most apprehension. In many years the governors have appointed days of supplication to God for deliverance from the storm.[13] The list of hurricanes below shows the irregularity with which these storms occur (the most destructive have been starred). All the storms occur between July and October, and thus not all the sugar cane is destroyed, since the cane fields harvested in the spring are not replanted with cane until November or December.

OCEAN CURRENTS

Barbados lies in the south equatorial current, and ordinarily is washed by waters which have flowed from Africa across the Atlantic Ocean and along the Guiana coasts before turning northwestward to Barbados. Driftwood, seeds, and even a live alligator on a log have been carried from Guiana to Barbadian shores.[14] Thus it seems probable that much of the indigenous flora and fauna may have been carried to Barbados by the currents. Guppy concluded, after a broad study of the tropical and subtropical

[11] These figures are based on statements in *Colonial Reports: Barbados, passim.* A wind velocity of only half a mile an hour was recorded on July 7, 1908. The lowest wind velocity in 1910 was 3.1 miles per hour. Maximum velocities recorded range from 22.9 (1911) to 26.8 miles per hour (1909).

[12] P. 114.   [13] *Colonial Reports: Barbados* (1935–36), p. 29.

[14] F. Hardy, "Some Aspects of the Flora of Barbados," *Agricultural Journal,* January, 1933, p. 51.

TABLE 3

Dates of Hurricanes and Severe Storms in Barbados, 1666–1918 [a]

August 19, 1666	October 31, 1780	August 11, 1830
October 7, 1670	August 31, 1785	August 10–11, 1831 *
August 31, 1675 *	October 5, 1786	July 26, 1835
August 13, 1694	October 5, 1806	September 31, 1835
October 17, 1694	August 28, 1810	July 9–10, 1837
? ? 1700	July 22, 1815	July 26, 1837
? ? 1702	September 29, 1815	October 6, 1841
? ? 1720	September 15, 1816	September 12, 1846
? ? 1722	October 21, 1817	September 19, 1848
August 13, 1731 *	September 27, 1818	July 10, 1851
August 25, 1756	September 21–22, 1819	October 11, 1894
August 29, 1757	October 13–15, 1819	September 10, 1898 *
August 25, 1758	December 18–19, 1822	August 21, 1918
October 10–11, 1780 *	August 28, 1827	

[a] Schomburgk, *op. cit.*, pp. 37–66, 689–95; E. B. Garriot, *West Indian Hurricanes,* U.S. Weather Bureau, *Bulletin H; Monthly Weather Review,* 1924, Supplement No. 24, pp. 46–47; *Colonial Reports: Barbados* (1880–1936).

North Atlantic, that the flora of Barbados is partly derived from West Africa, due to this current.[15]

According to the *West Indian Pilot,*[16] the current which ordinarily flows from the southeast near Barbados tends to flow from the northeast when the trade winds are strong. This change would bring the waters of the north equatorial current to Barbados, and would lessen the amount of material carried from Africa and South America to Barbados. It has been suggested that this trend has become more common in recent years, and that flying fish and other fish commonly associated with the debris floating in the water have therefore become scarcer.[17]

STRUCTURE AND RELIEF

The simplified geological map and the cross section (Figure 7) give a good idea of the structure of Barbados. In general, it is

[15] H. B. Guppy, *Plants, Seeds, and Currents in the West Indies and Azores,* Chap. I–X.

[16] *West Indian Pilot,* II (1929), 256; H. O. Chart No. 2319.

[17] *Barbados Official Gazette,* Supplement: October 10, 1932, pp. 2–3.

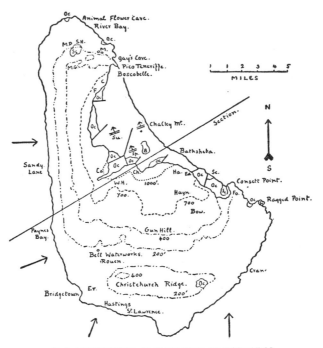

7. *A*. GEOLOGICAL SKETCH MAP OF BARBADOS

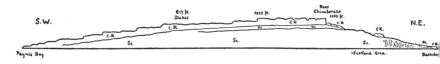

B. CROSS SECTION OF BARBADOS ALONG LINE ON A

The arrows on the island represent the dip of the Scotland Beds. The arrows outside the island indicate the supposed direction of thrusting that accompanied the uplift (according to Trechmann). The following abbreviations represent geological data:

Sc Scotland Beds   Oc Oceanic Series   C R Coral Rock

Source: Reproduced from C. T. Trechmann, "The Uplift of Barbados," *Geological Magazine*, LXX (1933), 21, 26.

extremely simple, consisting of a basement of much-folded sand-stones and shales (the Scotland series) covered unconformably by the soft, chalklike rocks of the Oceanic series. Except in the Scotland district, both of these geological series are covered unconformably with a layer of coral limestone which varies in thickness from a thin veneer to 240–260 feet.[18]

A major structural feature of the island consists of the terraces (benches, platforms, or steps) which are conspicuous even to the transient visitor. According to Jukes-Browne and Harrison:

> Each of these platforms was once a fringing coral-reef like that which now surrounds the greater part of the island, and they now form a succession of steps or terraces of greater or less width, rising one above another from sea level to a height of nearly 1100 feet in the centre of the island, each step in the ascent being of slightly older date than the one below.[19]

Recently Trechmann has proposed a new theory, according to which the coral rock was formed almost entirely before the uplift began. Trechmann believes that the uplift was:

> an oblique or differential one; the higher part of the island has been tilted or thrust towards the east and north, followed by later repeated uprising with slighter tilting, the force extending outwards and directed from the west and south. The southern Christ Church dome is due to later upward bending.[20]

Both theories imply an uplift and recent instability of the earth's surface. Earthquakes have been felt in Barbados on many occasions,[21] but there is no evidence that they have been associated with any uplift during human occupance. The damage caused by earthquakes has been negligible, and there is no reason to suppose that the instability of the rocks of Barbados need be considered in Barbadian construction projects.

Surrounding the island, except along the Scotland coast, are coral reefs which, according to Jukes-Browne and Harrison, are a

18 A. J. Jukes-Browne and J. B. Harrison, "The Geology of Barbados," *Quarterly Journal of the Geological Society,* XLVII (1891), 211.
19 *Ibid.,* p. 209.
20 C. T. Trechmann, "The Uplift of Barbados," *Geological Magazine,* LXX (1933), 45.
21 Schomburgk, *op. cit.,* pp. 68–69.

new terrace in formation.[22] These reefs are best developed on the southeast coast, where they were a constant danger to navigation until the establishment of lighthouses. Along most of the coast, the reefs discourage the landing of all boats except those of very shallow draft.

The coast line of Barbados is unusually regular, and it is the leeward position of the ports rather than any great indentation which protects them from the winds. The windward coast is rarely used for landing except by native fishermen. Landings are further discouraged by the wave-cut limestone cliffs, twenty to sixty feet in height, which extend for nine miles along the northern coast and for twelve miles along the southeastern and eastern coasts.[23]

Aside from the cliffed area, the coast consists generally of beaches of white coral sand which are sometimes as much as twenty yards wide. These beaches serve as landing places for small boats and as bathing beaches. It is significant that some of these beaches are changing in width; for example, near Hastings the beach has almost disappeared, while two and a half miles to the east the beach is becoming wider.[24] These alterations may be attributed to the shift in ocean currents, and thus substantiate the common belief of Barbadian fishermen that the currents have changed in direction in recent years.

Except in the Scotland district, the land rises by steps or terraces, the first of which occurs less than a half mile from the shore. Each successive terrace consists of a rock wall, rising sharply for from five to eighty feet from the preceding terrace, a gentle down slope which terminates in a bottom land, and then rises almost imperceptibly to the next rock wall. Since most of the elevation is attained by sharp rises, almost all of the coralline land is either flat or gently sloping. St. George's Valley, which includes the gently rolling areas between the main upland and Christ Church Ridge, adds greatly to the total level land on the island.

In the Scotland district the relief is rugged, and level lands are

---

[22] Jukes-Browne and Harrison, *op. cit.*, p. 210.
[23] Hardy, *op. cit.*, p. 58.   [24] *Ibid.*, p. 59.

found mainly on the alluvial flats in the broader valleys. The outstanding relief feature is the series of hills which start from the edge of the Cliff and seem to point toward a common center near the mouth of St. Andrews River. Part of the Scotland district (usually the higher part near the Cliff) is covered with rocks of the Oceanic series, which form more gentle and more arable slopes than the rocks of the Scotland series.

The road system is closely adjusted to the relief. The principal roads follow the level lands along the coast and in St. George's Valley. Other roads ascend the terraces either by cuts through the terrace walls or by twists and turns to take advantage of low points or gentle slopes on the terraces. Once the higher level is attained, the roads are fairly straight except where irregular estate boundaries have necessitated sharp detours.

In the Scotland district, the roads are relatively few. Several of the main roads follow spurs from the Cliff down to the valley. There is no road along the windward coast, but a road roughly parallels the coast on the Oceanic rocks. Until 1937, a railroad reached the Scotland district by going through the St. George's Valley, and thence northeastward along the coast.

In an island as densely settled as Barbados, it is not to be expected that the houses will be closely adjusted to several types of topographic sites. Availability of land, gregariousness, the whim of the master in slavery days—all of these factors have influenced the location of the Negro huts. The better type of house, such as was plotted on the British Admiralty chart, seems to be more restricted in its choice of site. A close study of this chart shows that ridges and slopes, where available, were the preferred locations (Table 4, page 30).

WATER SUPPLY

The availability of water is the major environmental factor which influences Barbadian prosperity. Rainfall brings this water to Barbados, but it is largely structure and relief which determine its disposal and availability.

Surface drainage is of minor importance in Barbados except in

TABLE 4

<small>Location of Rural Buildings in Relation to Topography [a]</small>

TOPOGRAPHY	WINDMILLS			OTHER BUILDINGS		
	Flatlands	*Slope*	*Ridge*	*Flatlands*	*Slope*	*Ridge*
Coralline district						
Lowland areas	100	75	73	284	145	178
Highland areas	17	69	53	26	98	85
Scotland district	10	24	19	10	19	15
Total . . .	127	168	145	320	262	278

[a] This table is based on Admiralty Chart No. 2485, *Barbados*.

the Scotland district. There the soil on the hillsides is very thin, as is apparent from the frequent outcrops of bedrock. The heavy rains of this district run off in shallow gullies, carrying with them a heavy load of mud which colors the ocean waters along the Scotland coasts during and after each rain. In clear weather, the gullies are dry or are mere trickles. Even the main stream, called by courtesy St. Andrews River, does not usually carry enough water to reach the sea. Instead, it terminates in a pond located on an alluvial flat just behind the beach.

In the coralline areas, surface drainage is rare and is of importance only after heavy rains. The stream system [25] consists of a series of gullies which radiate from the boundary of the coral limestone on the Scotland district toward the leeward coast and St. George's Valley (Figure 1). The gullies are restricted to the main upland and the leeward coast. Those which flow southward disappear into the deep soils of St. George's Valley. Christ Church Ridge is entirely free of gullies, and depends entirely on underground drainage.

The depth of the gullies varies considerably, the deepest places (about 150 feet) occurring at the edge of the terraces. Usually the gullies are entrenched even where they cross the level areas; thus they are a considerable barrier to overland transportation, and most of the roads are on the interfluves. If crossed, even the

[25] Hardy, *op. cit.*, pp. 61–62.

shallow gullies must be bridged, for their sides are almost perpendicular.

The gullies are frequently dry along most of their course. Some water is received by tapping underground streams, from springs, and from rainfall, but except where the rain has been heavy, these waters do not produce more than a small brook. Very heavy rains have swollen some of these streams into flood proportions, especially in those gullies which flow into the river at Bridgetown. For example, on October 14, 1819:

> The rain fell in torrents, which brought down the gully (the natural water-course from the parishes of St. Michael, St. George, and from a part of St. Philip) with impetuous fury, sweeping before it Constitution Bridge. About nine o'clock in the evening, the new bridge, which had cost the country so much money, was demolished in an instant. The destruction continued, and the daylight of Friday morning (the 15th of October) showed a scene of desolation not witnessed since the great hurricane of 1780. The water had risen in the streets to three or four feet, and in many places as high as five feet. All was confusion and alarm, and every person in Broad Street sought to escape destruction which tottering houses and the rise of the water threatened. As the day advanced, the storm increased, accompanied with heavy thunder and lightning; the rain fell in torrents, and the ground tier of every store which had escaped destruction, was nearly filled with water.[26]

The larger part of the rainfall of the coralline area is first absorbed by the coral rock, and then sinks gradually through it to underground streams which flow between the coral limestone and the older rocks, and discharge as underwater springs off the leeward coast. These underground streams have eroded subterranean caverns from which much of the domestic water supply is pumped. At the bottom of the Bowmanston shaft (water works), "one can walk for miles in either direction nearly up to one's neck in water."[27]

The spongelike characteristics of the coral rock enable it to act as a reservoir which supplies both the soil and the underground streams with water, and thus delays the effects of any

---

[26] Schomburgk, *op. cit.*, pp. 51–52.   [27] Trechmann, *op. cit.*, p. 29.

period of low rainfall. Some of this stored water rises through capillary attraction and moistens the subsoil; other water seeps out at the base of the terrace walls and moistens the soil there or feeds occasional springs.[28]

It has already been noted that the slopes from the terrace walls often descend gently to hollows. Whether these hollows are former lagoons (as has been suggested by Jukes-Browne and Harrison [29]) or are due to faulting (as has been suggested by Trechmann [30]) has not been definitely determined. In any case, the soil in them is deeper than elsewhere on the terrace, and is often swampy in character during the rainy season.

At first, the ponds and swamps which formed in these bottoms were an important source of water; later, as the demand for cane fields increased, the more compact upper layers of the coral rock were cut through by shallow wells known as "sucks" through which the water flowed to the more porous layers beneath. But even after drainage, the bottoms remained places where the plants can tap an unusually good supply of soil water.

The seepage of water is an important cause of landslides, especially where the water seeps out under the coral cliff into the soil of the talus slope on the edge of the Scotland district. The land is very unstable here, as is shown by the 481 breaks reported in the water main from Newcastle to St. Andrews within two years.[31] These breaks usually occurred after heavy rains. Less frequent, but much more harmful, were the actual landslides, the greatest of which took place on October 11, 1785, at Crab Hole, St. Joseph. At that time, an area one mile in length and 300 yards in width moved. The landslide buried the plantation buildings and the crops.[32] In 1900, a slide occurred at Boscobelle, St. Andrews, and part of the coral rock from the escarpment fell and scattered over nearly a square mile of the Scotland district.[33] Many other landslips have been noted in Barbadian history.

[28] Hardy, *op. cit.*, p. 61.
[29] Jukes-Browne and Harrison, *op. cit.*, pp. 223, 200–11.
[30] Trechmann, *op. cit.*, pp. 45–46.
[31] *Barbados Official Gazette*, April 22, 1937.
[32] Schomburgk, *op. cit.*, pp. 67–68.   [33] Trechmann, *op. cit.*, p. 22.

SOILS

The soil is an important limiting factor in the utilization of Barbados, for the bulk of the unplowed land is untilled because of thin, infertile, or exhausted soil. Even the cultivated areas have remarkably thin soils, and would lose their fertility were it not for heavy fertilization. Improved methods of soil cultivation are responsible for a large part of the increase in Barbadian productivity.

The soils of the Scotland district have not yet been studied in detail because of their minor economic importance and great variety. Except over the chalky Oceanic rocks, and on the alluvial flats in the valleys, the soil is too thin for sugar cane and is used for pasture, provision crops, or arrowroot. The composition of these thin upland soils varies with the underlying rock. The thinness of these soils and the desiccating power of the winds cause them to dry rapidly and discourage their cultivation. The better Scotland soils are alkaline and closely resemble the coral limestone soils in most characteristics. However, they contain more fine sand and less clay than the coral limestone soils under similar rainfall conditions (Table 5).

TABLE 5

PHYSICAL COMPOSITION OF BARBADIAN SOILS [a]

	SCOTLAND SOILS	LIMESTONE SOILS Red	Black
Number of determinations	5	8	8
Coarse sand	4.2%	1.7%	2.1%
Fine sand	23.8	8.5	12.4
Silt	24.5	20.0	29.4
Clay	37.5	57.8	40.6
Moisture	4.2	4.5	6.6
Calcium carbonate	4.7	2.2	4.1
Loss in solution	2.2	3.2	2.9
Total of fractions	101.1	97.9	98.1
Total replaceable bases	26.6	28.7	48.9

[a] *Report on the Department of Science and Agriculture, 1930–31*, p. 72.

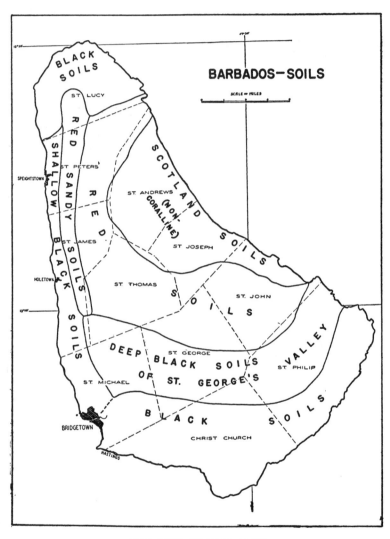

Within the figure:

BARBADOS—SOILS

SCALE of MILES

BLACK SOILS

ST LUCY

RED SANDY

SHALLOW BLACK SOILS

ST PETERS'

SPEIGHTSTOWN

SCOTLAND

ST ANDREWS

(NON CORALLINE)

ST JAMES

HOLETOWN

RED SOILS

ST JOSEPH

SOILS

ST THOMAS

ST JOHN

SOILS

VALLEY

DEEP BLACK SOILS OF ST. GEORGE'S

ST GEORGE

ST PHILIP

ST MICHAEL

BLACK SOILS

BRIDGETOWN

CHRIST CHURCH

HASTINGS

8. SOIL MAP OF BARBADOS

The coral limestone soils are residual soils with the possible exceptions of the red-sand soils and the deep St. George's Valley soils, parts of which were probably washed there from the adjacent uplands. It has been estimated [34] that from fifty to sixty cubic feet of coral limestone would have to decompose to produce one cubic foot of red limestone soil. Thus the former levels of Barbados must have been considerably reduced to produce the present soil cover which varies from a few inches to fifty feet. This cover, however, is extremely uneven, and may vary from a few inches to many feet in the same field. In general, the shallow areas tend to be near the coral walls, while the greatest depths are reached in the bottoms and in "swallow holes." [35] It seems probable that surface erosion and slumping have caused considerable soil movement within limited areas on each terrace, and thus the bottoms of the terraces have been filled.

The coral limestone soils have been divided by color into groups (Figure 8) which coincide roughly with altitude. The boundaries between these groups are not sharp except occasionally where high terrace walls intervene between them. The principal differences in the soils seem to be differences in maturity, the oldest soils (red soils) being on the uplands which have been exposed longest to erosion and which receive the heaviest rainfall.

The limestone soils of Barbados are clay, but their high limestone content gives them qualities of a free-working loam.[36] Mechanical analysis shows that, in general, the clay content of the soils tends to decrease, and the lime content increases in the younger soils (Table 5). Thus the younger and darker soils are better in structure and are somewhat more resistant to drought than are the more mature red soils. It is thought that the red soils may have been acid in their original state, for the subsoil is usually acid.[37] If this be correct, then the slightly alkaline condition (pH 7.5+) of the red surface soils is due to heavy applications of marl by early planters. On the other hand, the black soils are alkaline

[34] J. B. Harrison and A. J. Jukes-Browne, *The Geology of Barbados* (Bridgetown, 1890), p. 52.
[35] *Agricultural Journal,* III (1934), 1.
[36] *Ibid.,* p. 36.   [37] *Ibid.,* p. 35.

(pH 8.1-8.5) in all horizons, and were probably in good physical condition when first exploited.[38]

Moisture is the major problem in Barbadian soil utilization, and intensive cultivation, mulching, and cover crops are used to maintain the soil-water supply. The favorable physical structure combined with the tapping of the underground water by capillary attraction favors the maintenance of favorable water conditions. The greatest difficulty arises when "during the season, the soils gradually dry out until, by the end of March, cracks are beginning to appear which, by the close of the dry season, may be large enough to take the leg of a horse." [39] A crisis is reached when in severe droughts the underground water supply becomes depleted.

Barbadian soils have always been described as very fertile. However, it is extremely difficult to determine the natural nutrients in Barbadian soils because of the heavy and continuous fertilization which has been carried on for nearly three centuries. Almost all Barbadian soils at present are rich in lime and adequately supplied with phosphates.[40] Potash deficiencies are common, especially in the red-soil areas, but this deficiency varies greatly from plantation to plantation according to past manuring practices.[41] Nitrates and organic matter are the principal needs, and these needs are greatest on the black soils because of the smaller production of cane trash and similar organic materials produced on, and turned back into these soils.[42]

Adding marl and mould from the gullies was the earliest form of manuring practiced in Barbados. However, the large number of cattle brought to Barbados to operate the cattle mills produced a large supply of manure which soon became the major fertilizer of the island. In fact, when the cattle mills were displaced by windmills about the first half of the eighteenth century, the cattle were still kept for their manure.

Cattle manure was applied as pen manure which supplied organic matter to the soil, acted as a mulch, and provided nitrogen,

[38] *Agricultural Journal,* III (1934), 35.
[40] *Ibid.,* pp. 10–12.   [41] *Ibid.,* p. 12.
[39] *Ibid.,* 2.
[42] *Ibid.,* p. 6.

phosphoric acid, and potash to the plant. The methods of making pen manure were well described a century ago:

A movable pen is made of light railings tied together, and to posts fixed firmly in the ground, enclosing a piece of ground proportionate to the number of cattle to be turned into it; at the end of the week it is shifted, by leaving one side standing, and moving the other three sides on the opposite face of the remaining side, thus enclosing a second piece; into this fresh enclosure the cattle are turned for another week. In this manner it is moved every week till the planter gradually goes through his whole estate, and follows it up by turning up the soil for tillage. This is considered a very advantageous practice; indeed, some overseers entirely trust to it, and give the ground no other dressing. . . . In Barbados the practice is to tether cattle to stakes driven into the ground. The spot is covered with good mould, and then well littered with dry and green vegetable matter, which, with the animal manure from the cattle, makes a compost heap sufficient for a certain space of ground. When this is completed the stakes are withdrawn, and placed in another part of the field, in which the same process is renewed . . . but as much labour is required to bring mould and dry and green vegetable matter to form successive layers, some planters adopt the Jamaica plan of movable pens already described.[43]

Barbadian practice today is the same as in this description of nearly a century ago.

Recent experiments of the Barbados Department of Science and Agriculture indicate that mixtures of ammonium sulphate, sulphate of potash, and superphosphates are cheaper and more productive than the excessive applications of pen manure hitherto used in Barbados. Green manures and additional mulching have also been recommended, as a result of these experiments, to provide additional organic materials needed by Barbadian soils.[44]

FLORA [45]

When Barbados was first visited by Europeans, it was reported to be covered with forests and thickets. The nature of this in-

[43] George R. Porter, *The Nature and Properties of the Sugar Cane*, p. 32.
[44] *Report on the Department of Science and Agriculture, 1930–31*, pp. 60–68; *1929–30*, pp. 86–93.
[45] This section is based almost entirely on F. Hardy, "Some Aspects of the Flora of Barbados," *Agricultural Journal*, January, April, July, and December, 1932; January, 1933.

digenous forest can be judged by considering the only large surviving area of virgin forest, Turner's Hall Wood, and the vegetation of isolated gullies. This evidence indicates that the Barbadian forest was not so dense or so varied as tropical forests elsewhere. For example, the rain forest of Dominica contains at least 176 species of trees, compared with only seventeen found in Turner's Hall Wood.

The trees in Turner's Hall Wood include the locust (*Hymenaea Courbaril*), used for making rollers for the early sugar mills, and the West Indian cedar (*Cedrela odorata*), used for building and cabinet-making. The fustic (*Chlorophora tinctoria*) was exported during the early days of the colony to be used as a yellow dyestuff; it was also used for building. Likewise, the bully tree (*Diopholis salicifolia*) was used for its hardwood. In addition to these useful trees, the macaw palm, Spanish ash, and poison tree were common species.

The indigenous flora of Barbados was probably brought there by ocean currents, by winds, and by birds. The arrival of European colonists soon revolutionized the plant associations, and today most of the island is occupied by artificial plant associations. The indigenous associations are limited to the rocky areas, the gullies, the beaches, the roadsides, and those few stretches of forest which have been permitted to survive. Aside from these remnants of indigenous flora, the plant cover of Barbados consists largely of the following: cane fields, gardens, sour grass pastures, guinea and para grass pastures, dry pastures, and orchards and isolated cultivated trees.

The cane fields.—Nearly half of the acreage of Barbados is occupied by cane fields, and, since two successive crops of cane overlap, fields of waving cane are always a conspicuous feature of the Barbadian landscape.[46] The common method of cultivation has been well described by Hardy:

[46] According to the 1937 cane census reported in the supplement to the *Barbados Official Gazette*, February 18, 1937, the acreage was:

	Reaped	
Plant canes	16,919	
First ratoons	10,662	

In Barbados, plant canes are grown chiefly from pieces of stem ("joints" of cane), and in certain districts (such as the red soil districts of the uplands), ratooning is practiced to some extent. The date of planting a new crop of plant canes from cuttings is usually about November, i.e., towards the end of the rainy season. The plants require about 18 months to reach maturity, so that the time of reaping lies in the months of March to July in the year but one after that in which the canes were planted.

It is possible and customary to weed cane-fields in Barbados up to the end of the seventh month after the date of planting. The operation is made troublesome, however, by the presence of "trash" (i.e., dry cane leaves) which is spread over the ground at the expiration of three or four months from the time of planting, to prevent excessive loss of soil moisture. At the trashing period (January to March), plant-canes are generally about one to two feet tall, and have reached the critical period in their growth, since dry weather prevails in these months and danger from drought is not inconsiderable. It is a matter of some surprise that in Barbados young cane plants can successfully live through the dry season, especially during certain years in which the rainfall is abnormally low. The explanation of the fact might more reasonably be sought in the peculiar condition of the sub-soil and of the underlying spongy and porous coral rock (which undoubtedly store up much water in the rainy season, and yield it up again by capillarity in the dry season), than in the drought-resisting propensities of the cane plant. No doubt, also, the occasional showers that fall during January and February assist the cane plants in tiding over the dry season.

Manuring with artificial manures is carried out in Barbados at the commencement of the rainy season (in April to June). Soon after this date, the canes are of such a height that efficient weeding becomes impossible.[47]

The weeds of the cane fields are plants whose seeds are blown from the pastures, roadsides, and gullies into the fields. There are two groups of weeds: those which can survive frequent mutilation by the hoe of the weeders; and those which grow up after the cane

---

Second ratoons	3,865
Others	820
Total	32,266
Add plant canes to be	
reaped next year	16,919
Grand Total	48,185

[47] *Agricultural Journal,* October, 1932, p. 31.

is too thick for weeding (roughly, the last half of the eighteen-month growing period). It is interesting to note that many of the most persistent weeds (for example, *Cyperus rotundus* or nut grass) are believed to have been introduced by man.

The cane is harvested in the spring and is not planted again until the following late fall. In the interval, it is customary to grow catch crops, such as sweet potatoes, yams, eddoes, beans, and, more rarely, guinea corn, Indian corn, and various vegetables.

Gardens.—A large part of the garden crops are raised as catch crops on cane lands. However, many householders and planters maintain small permanent vegetable and flower gardens for home use. In addition to these, a considerable number of market gardens are found on small holdings near Bridgetown.

Orchards.—Orchards are rare in Barbados, and the tree crops are generally produced on isolated trees around the planters' homes. The more common fruit trees, in order of their importance, are: mango, hog plum, chile plum, Jamaica plum, golden apple, lime, dunk, Barbados cherry, sugar apple, sour sop, custard apple, guava, avocado pear, pomegranate, Barbados or Otaheite gooseberry, genip, papaw or papaya, mammee apple, and shaddock. In addition to these, the following are grown in shady, moist, and protected localities: grapefruit, orange, tangerine, sapodilla, spice guava, French guava, star apple, cashew, and akee.

The seasons are pronounced enough in Barbados to produce a definite periodicity in the fruit trees of Barbados:

In the case of the *deciduous* fruit trees, (i.e. those that completely shed their leaves once a year) the leaves begin to fall at the commencement of the dry season, so that during the months of December to April, the trees are bare. At the beginning of the rainy season, (i.e., in May or early June), the deciduous fruit trees put out their flowers. Soon after this, the new leaves make their appearance, and by the middle of the rainy season, these are fully expanded. The fruits, at the same time are ripening. Thus the fruits of the deciduous fruit trees of Barbados come into season between the months of August and December.

e.g. Plums, Golden Apple, Sugar Apple, Sour Sop, Custard Apple.

In the case of the *evergreen* fruit trees the leaves are never altogether absent from the trees, but most of the old leaves are shed in the dry season, and most of the new ones are produced in the wet season. The

flowers of the evergreen fruit trees are usually put out during the dry
season, and the fruits ripen in the early part of the next rainy season;
i.e., the fruits of the evergreen fruit trees come into season chiefly during
the months of June and November.

e.g. Mango, Avocado Pear, Citrus, Mammee Apple, Cashew.

The distribution and intensity of the rainfall during the wet months
of the year, however, greatly influence the time of flowering and fruiting
of the evergreen fruit trees. In many instances, these irregularities cause
the production of more than one crop of flowers and fruits in the rainy
months or of none at all.

e.g. Cherry, Dunk, Gooseberry, Guava, Genip, Sapodilla, Star Apple.[48]

Other trees.—Trees are no longer an important element in the
Barbadian landscape. A large proportion of those visible are ex-
otics which have been planted along roadsides or around houses
for shade. The most important of these shade trees are: [49] ma-
hogany (*Swietenia mahagoni*), introduced into Barbados between
1780 and 1800; tamarind (*Tamarindus indica*), introduced about
1650, fruits are exported; evergreen (*Ficus nitida*), introduced
from India before 1750; white wood (*Tecoma leucoxylon*), South
American and probably indigenous; sand-box (*Hura crepitans*),
probably indigenous; cabbage palm (*Oreodoxa oleracea*), indigenous; casuarina or mile tree (*Casuarina equisetifolia*), introduced about 1870; and silk cotton (*Eriodendron anfractuosum*),
indigenous.

Artificial pastures.—These pastures play a major part in the
maintenance of the cattle which, since the seventeenth century,
have been an important part of Barbadian agriculture. Lands
which had been planted in cane and which had become too exhausted or too thin for cane were planted with grass. During the
last century, by far the most important of these grasses has been
sour grass (*Andropogon pertusus*). The origin of this plant is unknown, although it has been suggested that "it is a hybrid derived
from an indigenous species . . . and an Australian or Indian
species introduced into Barbados before 1830." [50] Sour grass is a
vigorous, drought-resistant perennial which grows to a height of

[48] *Agricultural Journal*, January, 1933, p. 37.
[49] For a more complete list, see *ibid.*, October, 1932, pp. 53–63.
[50] *Ibid.*, January, 1933, p. 48.

two and a half feet. Generally, the pastures are cut for hay several times a year. Until recently it has not been customary to manure these pastures, but recent experiments [51] have shown that such manuring is extremely profitable, and the practice is expected to become common. Artificial pastures of guinea grass and para grass are also found in the better-watered locations.

Dry pastures.—These widespread areas include a variety of grasses (including the introduced devil's grass, *Cynodon dactylon*), numerous prostrate and erect plants, and a few shrubs. Usually these pastures occupy small areas of waste land near dwelling houses or along roadsides which do not have deep enough soil or an adequate water supply for cultivation. These pastures serve as feeding grounds for the domestic animals of the planters and peasants, and thus the sour-grass pastures can be saved for hay.

FAUNA

The indigenous fauna of Barbados was extremely limited, and the present fauna, including pests and domesticated animals, has been largely introduced by man. So far as can be determined, the indigenous animals consisted of the Barbados monkey (*Cepus capucinus*), the raccoon (*Procyon lotor*), eleven species of indigenous birds, forty additional species of birds seen during migrations, one specie of snake, ten species of lizards, and numerous insects.[52] To these should be added the numerous species of fish, turtles, shell fish, and crustaceans which inhabited the waters surrounding the shore.

The aquatic fauna has been an important source of food for Barbados, but the terrestrial fauna has been important mostly as pests. Flies, mosquitoes (yellow-fever rather than malarial type), cockroaches, and ants have annoyed man throughout Barbadian history, although they have not been so numerous as in more humid tropical areas. More serious have been the numerous in-

[51] *Report on the Department of Science and Agriculture, 1929–30*, pp. 93–94.
[52] Schomburgk, *op. cit.*, pp. 635–83.

sects which have attacked the crops at various periods in Barbadian history,[53] and which are still a constant concern to the planters.

The introduced terrestrial fauna has, like the introduced flora, largely supplanted the indigenous species. Cattle (European, zebu, and mixed) are found on every estate, and pigs, horses, mules, goats, poultry, dogs, and cats are fairly widespread. The woolless sheep, introduced from the savannas of West Africa, are common in the drier areas and provide much of the local mutton.[54] Less fortunate acquisitions have been the mongoose,[55] the rat, the sugar ant, and numerous plant pests and disease germs which have been brought into the island.

MINERALS [56]

The mineral resources of Barbados are limited to those commonly associated with sedimentary rocks, and are of small importance to the Barbadian economy. The coral limestone has provided building stone, building lime, and lime for fields. The Scotland series has provided clays for claying sugar and still provides the clay from which the local pottery is made. Oil has been known for some time to exist in the Scotland series, and a bituminous deposit (manjak or glance pitch) has provided a small export for many years. Small quantities of petroleum have been obtained within the last decade, and further explorations are expected to uncover other deposits.

[53] *Sugar, a Handbook for Planters and Refiners* (London, 1888), pp. 84–103, gives a summary of the then known sugar pests. More recent sources are: R. W. E. Tucker, *Notes on Insect Pests of the Sugar Cane* (Barbados Department of Science and Agriculture, 1930), Pamphlet No. 3; R. W. E. Tucker, *Control of Field Crop, Garden, and Fruit Pests in Barbados* (Barbados Department of Science and Agriculture, 1931), Pamphlet No. 7; also frequent references in *Agricultural Journal.*

[54] W. R. Buttenshaw, "Barbados Woolless Sheep," *West Indian Bulletin*, VI (1905), No. 2, 187–97.

[55] The mongoose was introduced into Jamaica in 1872 and shortly thereafter into Barbados. See D. Morris, *The Mongoose on Sugar Estates in the West Indies* (Kingston, 1882).

[56] Harrison and Jukes-Browne, *op. cit., passim;* Edward G. Sinckler, *The Barbados Handbook; Barbados Blue Books.*

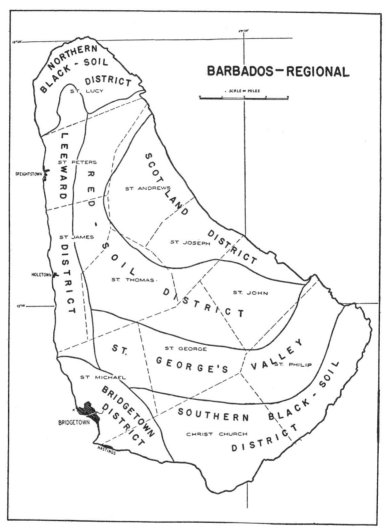

BARBADOS—REGIONAL

SCALE ∞ MILES

NORTHERN BLACK - SOIL DISTRICT

ST. LUCY

LEEWARD DISTRICT

ST PETERS

SPEIGHTSTOWN

RED - SOIL DISTRICT

SCOTLAND DISTRICT

ST ANDREWS

ST JAMES

ST JOSEPH

HOLETOWN

ST THOMAS

ST. JOHN

ST. GEORGE'S VALLEY

ST GEORGE

ST. PHILIP

ST MICHAEL

BRIDGETOWN DISTRICT

BRIDGETOWN

HASTINGS

SOUTHERN BLACK - SOIL DISTRICT

CHRIST CHURCH

9. REGIONAL MAP OF BARBADOS

Except for the division between the Scotland district and the coralline areas, there are few sharp boundaries which may be used for dividing Barbados into regions. Although such regionalization (Figure 9) as is here attempted is arbitrary, it provides a useful summary of the Barbadian landscape.

The Bridgetown district.—Although this section is less favored in soil and climate than several of the other regions, the leeward position of Carlisle Bay and the configuration of the topography led to the choice of this site for the principal town of Barbados. To the Barbadian, Bridgetown is a metropolis, with its combined features of stores, amusements, business offices, and easy communication with the outside world. For the Negro especially, to live in or near Bridgetown means close contact with the bustle of society and with the outside world. Economically, residence in this district offers an opportunity to hear about odd jobs around the port and town, or even in Panama, Cuba, and the United States. So strong is the attraction of the metropolis that the population of the Bridgetown district has continued to grow even when the Barbadian population has been declining sharply.

The Bridgetown district suffers from a long dry season, relative lack of breeze, and thin, relatively sandy, soils. Hence it is not surprising that in times of depression many of its plantations were subdivided and sold to the Negro population. The demand for this land, especially on the part of Barbadians returning from employment abroad, was so great that exhorbitant prices were usually asked and received. For example, Goodland plantation, just north of Bridgetown, was subdivided and sold for from $600 to $2,400 per acre. Obviously, at such prices, peasant farmers can hardly hope to make a living from farming alone. Only the attractions and opportunities in Bridgetown allow the land to bring such a price.

[57] The conclusions in this section are based primarily on personal observation and on: F. Hardy, "Some Aspects of the Flora of Barbados," *Agricultural Journal,* January, April, July, December, 1932, and January, 1933; C. C. Skeete, *The Condition of Peasant Agriculture in Barbados;* Harrison and Jukes-Browne, *op. cit.*

The general condition of the land in the possession of small holders in this parish is worse than in any other parish, and a considerable portion of this land is entirely neglected and lying waste. The close proximity of Bridgetown serves to attract occupiers of small holdings to seek work in the town in preference to agricultural work, with the result that the land is neglected. [58]

When the land is farmed, it is used for vegetable-raising for home or Bridgetown consumption, for raising sugar cane for fodder or chewing, and for pasturage. Petty theft is common; and certain crops, therefore, are often favored because they cannot be easily stolen.

The business center of Bridgetown is located close to the port, which, compared with most Lesser Antillean ports, is well equipped for commerce. The outer harbor, Carlisle Bay, is an indentation half a mile deep and one and a half miles wide with adequate anchorage for ships of any size. Steamers are generally unloaded by means of twenty- or thirty-ton lighters handled by Government-owned tugs. The lighters and schooners (less than 14.5 foot draft) can enter the Careenage, which is equipped with cranes ranging in capacity from two to twenty-five tons. Close to the Careenage are the warehouses of the leading commission merchants and plantation suppliers. The port is also equipped to provide ships supplies, coal, and fuel oil, and to undertake minor repairs. Almost all of the foreign trade of Barbados is handled through this port.

The commerce of Bridgetown consists of the exportation of local products, largely sugar and molasses, the re-exportation of foreign products landed for transshipment, and the importation of plantation supplies and a great variety of goods sold through the retail shops.

Although small stores which handle staple commodities such as flour, salted fish, and rum, are found throughout the island, almost all of them are owned by, or are affiliated with Bridgetown dealers. A variety of goods is only to be obtained at Bridgetown. Even the stores in Bridgetown carry relatively small stocks of many commodities. Advertisements announcing the arrival of the rarer types

[58] C. C. Skeete, *op. cit.*, p. 25.

of goods (especially imported foods and clothing) appear from time to time in the newspapers.[59]

Manufacturing in the Bridgetown district is largely community manufacturing. There are two biscuit factories, a tobacco factory, two cotton factories, an ice factory, a gasworks, an electric company, an oil refinery, two foundries, a fertilizer factory, three rum refineries, and a number of very small factories which are hardly more than shops. A few of the manufactured products, especially biscuits, jams, rum, and soft drinks, are exported to neighboring islands.

The financial affairs of the island are concentrated in Bridgetown. All the banks (Royal Bank of Canada, Barclays Bank, Canadian Bank of Commerce) and the insurance companies have their offices there, and the attorneys and accountants who handle the business of the sugar estates have their offices in Bridgetown. With a few exceptions, all of the Government offices are also located in the Bridgetown district.

The social life is concentrated at Bridgetown. Large social functions are commonly held at the Marine Hotel, the Aquatic Club, and other halls to the east of Bridgetown. The cinemas and such amateur entertainments as are occasionally arranged, are held near Bridgetown. Moreover, the large churches, clubs, lodges, and friendly societies are in Bridgetown, and are important social centers.

The residential sections are located along the roads which lead out of Bridgetown. Negro areas and white areas are closely intermixed, although the whites generally occupy the broader streets and the cooler and breezier sites. Busses, patronized by all but the wealthiest, traverse the principal roads of the residential districts. The Bridgetown district is the only portion of Barbados which has cheap and frequent public conveyances available from early morning until ten at night.

[59] See, for example, quotations from advertisements in the *Barbados Advocate,* August 5, 1932: "Chinese shantung silks, new shipment at 2/6 per yard." "Fresh arrivals ex 'Lady Drake' Canadian Hams." "Malt and cod-liver oil—a fresh supply to hand." "We are receiving today: Dutch rolled sausages, Edam cheeses, Gouda cheeses. Call early and secure your share!" "Notice of arrival of Schooner 'Minnie M. Mosher' with shipment of DEEP SEA FISH."

St. George's Valley.—Directly east of Bridgetown is the prosperous region of St. George's Valley, which is easily accessible to Bridgetown by good roads. A close network of plantation roads connects each field with the two arterial roads which traverse the valley from Bridgetown to the windward coast. The contour varies from flat surfaces to gently rolling lands, which makes it possible to use more machinery here than elsewhere on the island. The black soil is deep and fertile; the sugar factories are large and efficient. Consequently, few of the estates have been subdivided into peasant farms. Rather, the tendency has been for the plantations to come under the control of the sugar factories. The rainfall is only moderate, but the deep soil and high standard of cultivation enable it to be used effectively. In every way, this area is the best of the black-soil regions.

The red-soil district.—This inland region is even more prosperous than St. George's Valley. Although its soil is often shallow, it produces luxuriant crops because of the heavy rainfall. The plantations here manage to make money even when the black-soil plantations are suffering heavy losses, since it is estimated that it is possible for the red-soil plantations to produce and deliver a ton of sugar for £1 5s. 9d. less than can the black-soil plantations.[60] None of the plantations in this area have been subdivided recently; the peasant villages are generally long established. In addition to the economic advantages of this district, its altitude of from four hundred to a thousand feet produces a pleasant climate which has long been praised:

. . . indeed the hill climate of Barbados is truly delightful: there we have warmth without heat; coolness without cold . . . the thermometer by day is commonly below 75°; there even in the hottest season, and the hottest time of the day, its ascent above 80° is of rare occurrence in the shade and within doors; and there in addition, the comfort of the coolness is enhanced by the almost total absence of those troublesome insects which prevail more or less in the lower grounds.[61]

---

[60] *A Report on the Present Condition and Future Outlook of the Sugar Industry of Barbados,* published as a supplement to the *Barbados Official Gazette,* February 27, 1936, p. 13.

[61] Davy, *op. cit.,* p. 50.

The northern black-soil district.—The northern end of the island has shallow black soils, suffers severely from drought, and has difficulty in getting its produce to the market. The plantations are, in general, small, and in poor condition. The poorer areas have been subdivided. The peasant farmers usually have very small holdings on which they raise guinea corn, cotton, and sugar cane.

The southern black-soil district.—Like its smaller northern counterpart, much of this region suffers from drought and shallow soils. Many of the estates have been subdivided, especially in the poorer coastal districts. Little difficulty has been experienced in selling the land because of the nearness of much of it to Bridgetown. Drought has limited cultivation in this area, and cotton and guinea corn are the major peasant crops, especially toward the east.

The leeward district.—This region of relatively poor soils may be subdivided into two sub-regions: the coastal strip and the red-sand strip which adjoins it. The former area has thin, black soils which are usually poorly cultivated. It includes the settlements of Holetown and Speightstown and a number of peasant villages. It has good access to Bridgetown by boat and by bus. On the whole, a relatively sparse population earns a living here by farming, fishing, and picking up odd jobs in the towns. The sandy strip often produces good crops but suffers severely in times of drought. Taking the area as a whole, the cost of sugar production is higher in this district than in any other part of Barbados.[62]

The Scotland district.—This, the most isolated region of Barbados, is an area of apparent contradictions. It contains largely rugged areas of poor, thin soil farmed by Negro and poor-white peasants; yet it also contains some exceptionally fertile strips in the valleys and on the gentler slopes. The shelter offered by its hills allows the growth of fruit trees which grow only with difficulty elsewhere in Barbados; yet the winds are so strong that Barbadians visit its coasts because of the surf bathing and the

[62] *Report of the West India Royal Commission* (London, 1897), Part III, Appendix C, p. 198; also confidential information prepared for the 1930 West Indian Sugar Commission.

bracing breeze. Its people are poor, backward, and almost universally afflicted by hookworm, yet it contains the major handicraft industry of the island—the pottery industry. It is the most scenic part of Barbados, yet it is rarely visited by foreign tourists. The region suffers from isolation and inability to get its produce to the markets, yet the railroad which terminated there has been discontinued. On the whole, the author's impression is that this, the most interesting part of Barbados, has had a smaller part of its resources used than has any other Barbadian region.

CHAPTER III

The Beginnings of the Sugar and
Slave Economy, 1625–51

THE STUDY of environmental variability as it affects the people of Barbados cannot be reduced to the examination of universal and simple relationships. In each period of history, the relationships are, in part, different from those in other periods because of variations in technology, in discovery, and in conditions of trade. (See page 10.) The following chapters present a description of the economic history of Barbados so that the operation of the environmental conditions in various historical settings may be revealed.

HISTORY TO 1638

Barbados was first occupied by Arawak and, later, by Carib Indians.[1] Whether these Indian settlers lived by fishing, hunting, farming, or a combination of these is uncertain. In any case, the Indians had deserted Barbados by 1536 when Pedro a Campos, a Portuguese navigator, visited it and left hogs to breed so that shipwrecked mariners might not be without a meat supply.[2] Schomburgk believed that the island had been discovered by the Spanish early in the sixteenth century, and cited as evidence the instructions of Charles V to Rodrigo de Figeroa which suggested that the Indian population was removed by the Spanish slavers.[3]

However, Spanish visits to Barbados seem to have been rare,

[1] For accounts of Indians in Barbados, see J. Walter Fewkes, "Archeology of Barbados," *Proceedings* of the National Academy of Science, I (1915), 48; Sven Loven, *Origins of the Tainan Culture;* C. N. C. Roach, "Old Barbados," *Journal of the Barbados Museum and Historical Society*, III (1936), 137–48.

[2] Vincent T. Harlow, *A History of Barbados, 1625–1685*, p. 1n.

[3] Sir Robert H. Schomburgk, *The History of Barbados*, p. 255.

for it possessed no gold to attract them and it was off the common route of the Spanish galleons which passed through the Antilles near Dominica.[4] The Portuguese visited the island more frequently, for it was close to their usual sailing course from Brazil to Europe.[5] It was visited by English ships, for Captain John Smith wrote of it as "this fortunate Ile which had been oft frequented by Men of Warre to refresh themselves and set up their Shallops." [6]

Among the visitors to the island was a Dutch captain who was specially licensed by Spain to trade with Brazil. He visited the island, and informed Sir William Courteen, a London merchant of Flemish origin, of its virtues. Soon after, one of Courteen's vessels was blown ashore at Barbados. Its crew landed, hunted for hogs, explored the island, and found it uninhabited. Their report to Courteen verified the earlier Dutch reports, hence Courteen immediately started plans for its settlement.[7]

The European political situation and the progress of American colonization elsewhere were especially favorable for the colonization of Barbados at this time. The Spanish, who might have been expected to interfere with a new colony at the entrance to the Spanish Main, had been weakened by the long struggle with the Dutch, by the expulsion of the Moors and the Jews, and by the disastrous defeat of the Spanish Armada. Moreover, Spain, along with France, was engaged in the Thirty Years' War on the continent and, from 1626 to 1629, in a rather mild war with England. Portugal, because of dynastic difficulties, came under the control of Spain in 1580, but neither the Portuguese nor their Spanish overlords were able to keep the Dutch out of Brazil during the first half of the seventeenth century. The Dutch, flushed with victory in their War of Liberation against Spain, were expanding in the East Indies, South Africa, Brazil, Guiana, and the Hudson Valley.

[4] W. R. Shepherd, *Historical Atlas*, p. 108.   [5] Schomburgk, *op. cit.*, p. 257.
[6] Captain John Smith, "The First Planting of the Barbados," *Works, 1608–1631*, p. 908.
[7] Harlow, *op. cit.*, pp. 3–4; Schomburgk, *op. cit.*, p. 259; John Oldmixon, *The British Empire in America* (London, 1741), II, 3.

Until the middle of the seventeenth century, the Netherlands had been welcomed by the English as an allied Protestant power instead of being considered a hated commercial rival, as it was later. English emigrants, such as the Pilgrims, had been welcomed in the Netherlands, and Dutch and Flemish refugees from the Spanish persecution had been equally welcome in England. Thus were formed many Anglo-Dutch commercial ties which account for much of the rapid development of Barbados.

Late in 1626 Sir William Courteen's ship, the *William and John,* set sail for Barbados from London with fifty settlers. En route they captured an enemy ship and took from her ten slaves; thus from the beginning Barbados was a slave colony. On February 17, 1627, the settlers landed at Holetown on the leeward coast and began to clear the land and build log cabins along the shore.[8] The hunting of wild hogs added some fresh meat to the grain and salted meat which Courteen had supplied them, but the hunting was so intensive that in three years the hogs had all been killed.[9] On the small clearings, the settlers planted tobacco, evidently in imitation of the prosperous colony of Virginia.[10]

Meanwhile, Captain Henry Powell sailed the *William and John* to the Dutch colony of Guiana to learn from his old friend, Governor Groenenwegen, what crops to plant, and to obtain a supply of seed. The visit was a complete success because some forty Arawak Indians offered to come to Barbados as free men and to instruct the settlers in tropical agriculture in exchange for some land.[11] Soon the new colonists were growing cassava, sweet potatoes, cotton, tobacco, maize, and other tropical crops. They were learning, too, to sleep in Indian hammocks, a custom which persisted at least as late as 1732.[12]

The colony was not isolated, for Henry Winthrop sent off a

[8] Harlow, *op. cit.,* pp. 4–5.   [9] *Ibid.,* p. 5.
[10] Henry Winthrop to John Winthrop, *Massachusetts Historical Society Collections,* Fifth Series, VIII, 179.
[11] See *Colonizing Expeditions to the West Indies and Guiana, 1623–1667,* ed. by Vincent T. Harlow, pp. 36–38, for Powell's relations with the Indians as given in his own words.
[12] *Caribbeana,* I, 62.

letter from Barbados to London, August 22, 1627, and to Plymouth Colony (by direct ship) on October 15, 1627.[13] Proprietor Courteen sent frequent ships to the island with supplies and more settlers so that "by 1629 there were between sixteen and eighteen hundred people on the island."[14]

A court intrigue upset the rapid development. In July, 1627, Charles I granted Barbados along with the rest of the Lesser Antilles to the Earl of Carlisle, and in July, 1628, a second settlement was established by Carlisle's representatives on the shores of Carlisle Bay. At first, relations between the rival groups were friendly, but soon a struggle for control began which stopped the progress of the island until after the Carlisle group finally established their supremacy in 1630.[15]

The proprietorship dispute in the English court resulted in a great irregularity in the dispatch of supply ships from England to Barbados. The shortage of supplies was aggravated by a period of drought which started in 1629 and greatly reduced the supplies of home-grown provisions.[16] Barbados consequently had its "Starving Time" which left the island in poor condition. Two years later the droughty period had not yet passed, for Sir Henry Colt, who visited Barbados in July, 1631, notes: "You have seldome any Rayne but 6 moneths in ye year" and "ther corne, it was most part of it Blasted."[17] The farms were in a primitive state, for no man wanted to put great labor on his land until he was sure of his title. Colt further pictures Barbadian life thus:

You are deuourers upp hott waters & such good distillers thereof. . . . Your plantations . . . Behold ye ordre of them; first in 10 days trauayle about them, I neuer saw any man at work. Your grownd & plantations shewes whatt you are, they lye like ye ruines of some village lately burned, heer a great timber tree half burned, in another place a rafter singed all black. Ther stands a stubb of a tree aboue two yeards high, all ye earth couered black with cinders, nothing is cleer. What digged or weeded for beuatye? All are bushes & long grasse.[18]

---

[13] *Massachusetts Historical Society Collections,* Fifth Series, VIII, 79–181.
[14] Harlow, *op. cit.,* p. 6.   [15] *Ibid. et seq.*
[16] For data on this period, see *ibid.,* pp. 7–14, and Schomburgk, *op. cit.,* pp. 259–65.
[17] *Colonizing Expeditions* . . . , pp. 65, 74.   [18] *Ibid.,* pp. 65–66.

But in spite of this dismal picture, Colt notes also the presence of oranges, lemons, figs, pineapples, plantains, cassava, peas, guavas, papaws, cows, hogs, turkeys, hens, and pigeons, and thus shows that the Barbadians had not been slow in introducing many cultivated plants and domesticated animals. Lignum vitae and fustic wood were by-products of the clearing of the land. Colt does not mention tobacco, the first export, but states that "now ye trade of cotton fills them all with hope." [19]

In 1634 another visitor reported that the chief articles of trade were grain and cotton.[20] The principal grain was Indian corn. That Barbados was already of some importance as a way station is suggested by White's statement that it "serves as a granary for all the rest" [21] of the Lesser Antilles, and by the fact that his ship en route to Maryland set its course so as to put in there for provisions. The staple articles of diet were corn bread and sweet potatoes, of which the latter grew "in such Abundance that you can carry off whole wagon loads of it for nothing." [22] The alteration of English customs was not limited to diet, for "the climate is so warm that the inhabitants in the winter months wear linen clothes and bathe frequently." [23]

Compared with earlier descriptions, White's account suggests that the planters were depending less on imported foodstuffs and more on tropical foods. This greater self-sufficiency probably resulted from the uncertainty of foreign supplies and from an Order in Council which in 1631 restricted the planting of tobacco until such time as more foodstuffs were raised.[24] The raising of tobacco was further discouraged by an English tariff of one shilling per pound on Barbadian tobacco, which compared unfavorably with the ninepence per pound levied on Virginia tobacco.[25] Thus legal restrictions combined with the "earthy and worthless" quality of Barbadian tobacco, the need of more food, and the in-

---

[19] *Ibid.*, p. 69.

[20] Father Andrew White, "Narrative of a Voyage to Maryland," *Maryland Historical Society Fund Publication* No. 7, p. 25.

[21] *Ibid.*, p. 23.   [22] *Ibid.*

[23] *Ibid.*, p. 24.   [24] Harlow, *op. cit.*, p. 23.

[25] *Acts of the Privy Council*, Vol. I, Nos. 269, 270, 291, and 380.

creased importance of such crops as cotton, indigo, and ginger led to a greater self-sufficiency and to the decline in tobacco exports shown below:

TABLE 6

Tobacco Imports into London (1,000 Pounds) [a]

FROM	*1628*	*1638*	*1639*
Barbados · · · · · · }	103	204	28
St. Christopher's · · · · }		407	107

[a] Vincent T. Harlow, *A History of Barbados 1625–1685,* p. 21, and *Caribbeana,* III, 197.

Ten years after the first settlement, the 6,000 [26] English settlers had exploited only the leeward coast. Ligon's map suggests that a row of plantations lined the shore from South Point to Harrison's Point, for, as Colt explains: "ther plantations by reason of carriage & shippinge cannott stand commodiously but by ye sea shoar." [27] Somewhat larger plantations followed the shores of the river which enters Carlisle Bay, while the largest plantations were developed on the level lands east of Bridgetown, including the western third of St. George's Valley.[28] Except from this last group of plantations, the produce was transported to the ships in Carlisle and other bays by small boats. The St. George's Valley estates used the crudest of roads [29] to send their produce to Bridgetown by pack animals.

The houses were but primitive log cabins and were rarely close together, except for a small cluster at Bridgetown.[30] Trade was conducted mostly by barter with English and Dutch captains, while taxes and payments made in local business were invariably paid in cotton or tobacco.[31] Thus life in Barbados during this

[26] *Calendar of State Papers, Colonial Series,* 1575–1660, p. 240.

[27] *Colonizing Expeditions . . .* , p. 75.

[28] See Harlow, *op. cit.,* p. 307; John Poyer, *The History of Barbados,* p. 32; Richard Ligon, *A True and Exact History of the Island of Barbados,* p. 86.

[29] As late as 1654, many of the major roads (including that over the Indian Bridge) were not good enough for carts, and the use of carts on them was prohibited. See *Acts and Statutes of Barbados,* p. 171.

[30] *Colonizing Expeditions . . .* , p. 71.   [31] Harlow, *op. cit.,* pp. 16–21.

period included many of the crudities characteristic of pioneer areas.

After the settlement of the proprietorship dispute, settlers had come to Barbados in increasing numbers, mainly to avoid the political disputes in England. It has been recorded that 521 land grants totaling 37,772 acres were given between 1631 and 1637.[32] Although exact figures are not available, it seems probable that there was an increasing number of settlers after 1638, since 37,-300 white settlers were on the island in 1643.[33] Nor does this figure represent the total number of arrivals, for many of the pioneers sold their land at a profit, and settled in other islands less developed than Barbados.[34] Thus the rapidly increasing population had already started a land boom which was accentuated by the development of the sugar industry and by the period of free trade which resulted from the English Civil War between the Roundheads and the Cavaliers.

The introduction of coffee and tea in Europe during the seventeenth century increased greatly the demand for sugar. The early European market for sugar had been supplied by scattered Spanish possessions and by the Portuguese in Brazil. About 1630 the Dutch obtained control of Brazil, and Dutch planters began an expansion of the Brazilian sugar industry. Since Dutch ships returning from Brazil commonly touched at Barbados, it is not surprising that certain enterprising Barbadians learned the secret of sugar-making, and that several even visited Brazil to learn the technique.[35]

Although sugar cane had been grown, and used as a source of

[32] *Memoirs of the First Settlement of the Island of Barbados*, pp. 13–14.
[33] Harlow, *op. cit.*, p. 338.
[34] *Ibid.*, pp. 17n, 43. Also note that Ligon (*op. cit.*, p. 22) found that properties had been combined to form estates as large as 500 acres and that it was considered "far better to purchase a plantation there already furnished than to begin a place where land is to be had for nothing."
[35] Poyer, *op. cit.*, p. 40.

rum from the first days of the colony,[36] the technique of sugar manufacture was not generally known in Barbados until after 1639. Three factors gave an impetus about this time to the investigation of the new product. First, Barbadian planters were looking for a substitute for tobacco since the price of their tobacco had fallen to three farthings a pound (1646).[37] Second, a crop was needed to supplement cotton, which would not grow well in the moister interior of the island then being settled. Third, about 1644 the Portuguese began to regain their possessions in Brazil, and certain Dutch merchants and planters moved their sugar trade to Barbados to avoid the struggle.

The Dutch furnished "Negroes, Coppers, Stills and all other things . . . for the making of sugar. . . . The Hollanders . . . did at the first attempt of making sugar give great Credit to the most sober Inhabitants."[38] In 1647, when Ligon arrived in Barbados, the sugar industry was still in the experimental stage, but the industry had developed a technique for making a good product by 1650.[39]

The increased productivity of the land resulting from the success of the sugar industry, combined with the rapidly growing population, increased land prices greatly. An estate which had sold for sixteen shillings an acre before the boom was sold for twenty-eight pounds an acre in 1648.[40]

BARBADOS ABOUT 1650

Let us examine Barbados at the height of its first boom period! Ligon's fascinating account of Barbados which includes many homely details, enables us to reconstruct a good picture of Barbadian life almost at the height of the sugar boom. He found the whole leeward coast occupied, not only along the shore, but also on the terraces so that "the Plantations appeared to us one above

[36] Harlow, *op. cit.*, p. 40; *Colonizing Expeditions* . . . , p. 65.

[37] Harlow, *op. cit.*, p. 39.

[38] Quoted from Sloane MSS 3662, fol. 59a, in Harlow, *op. cit.*, p. 42. Accounts of the introduction of sugar are given in Ligon, Poyer, Schomburgk, and Oldmixon, and are summarized in Harlow, *op. cit.*, pp. 40–43.

[39] Ligon, *op. cit.*, pp. 85–86.   [40] *Ibid.*, pp. 86–88.

the other like several stories in stately Buildings." [41] The land had been cleared from Speightstown to the windward coast, and a road was used for shipping goods from Scotland via Speights Bay, since the waves and deep water made anchorage difficult off the Scotland coast.[42] Other local roads connected plantations with the shore at Conset's Bay, the Crane, and along the leeward coast.[43]

The roads were so poor and so full of ruts that asses were used instead of horses, and camels were being tried by the more distant plantations. One-third of the island was still uncleared, including eastern St. Philip and St. Lucy and the highest part where "passage was stopped by gullies." [44] But the clearing was proceeding rapidly, and, at the edge of the highlands, Ligon found recently cleared lands where "both Maies and bonavists were planted between the boughs." [45]

The houses were of local timber

. . . with low roofs, so low for the most part of them I could hardly stand upright with my hat on, and no cellars at all, besides another course they took . . . which was stopping or barring out the wind.[46]

The houses opened to the leeward and were closed to the windward. This puzzled Ligon, since it made the houses hot and stuffy. The settlers explained that they had no window glass or shutters to prevent the rain from being blown into the house by the trades.

The houses on the larger estates were fortified, and were located at strategic positions such as on knolls or at the edges of terraces so that they could be easily defended in case of slave revolts.[47] Close to the planter's house were the huts of the indentured servants and the Negroes

. . . which makes every Plantation look like a little African City, and the planter's House like the Sovereign's in the midst of it.[48]

These huts were built of mud, sticks, branches, and plantain leaves, and were usually designed and built by the Negroes.[49]

[41] *Ibid.*, p. 21.   [42] *Ibid.*, p. 58.   [43] *Ibid.*, Frontispiece.
[44] *Ibid.*, pp. 58, 94, and map.   [45] *Ibid.*, p. 24.   [46] *Ibid.*, p. 40.
[47] *Ibid.* A slave revolt was attempted in 1649.   [48] Oldmixon, *op. cit.*, II, 131.
[49] *Ibid.*; Frank W. Pitman, "Slavery on the British West India Plantations," *Journal of Negro History*, XI (October, 1926), 606–608.

Life in both the planter's house and in the outlying huts had many inconveniences. The Negroes and the cattle used the shallow, muddy ponds for drinking water; the planters depended either on shallow wells or on rain water which drained from the roofs into cisterns.[50] Both the planters' houses and the huts were stuffy, while the air outside was more humid and oppressive than it is today because of the undrained swamps and the wooded areas which stopped much of the breeze.[51] Mosquitoes, flies, ants, and cockroaches were prevalent pests. Furniture was set in water-filled containers to keep crawling insects off the beds and tables; shelves were hung by tarred ropes; sugar was put on one side of the room or table to attract ants and flies from the occupied portions.[52]

Sugar cultivation had been tried first on the larger plantations east of Bridgetown, but by the time of Ligon's arrival, it had spread over most of the island. However, only the wealthier planters could afford the necessary capital for slaves and sugar works. The sugar factories, as fully described by Ligon, consisted of a cattle mill for grinding the cane, a boiling house, a curing house, and a distillery. They were located on small hills that had "within the compass of eighty foot, twelve foot descent." [53] This enabled the sugar to be carried by gravity through each successive stage of manufacture. The product was a dark sugar which, though not so good as Brazilian sugar for immediate consumption, was sweeter, and was therefore preferred by English refiners.[54]

Although the plantations emphasized sugar, only two-fifths of the land, at most, was in cane (Table 7). A few acres were kept in melons and fruits for the table.[55] There were no fences, and "Hogs and Cows were tied up to trees for there are few Ranges and Inclosures." [56] The livestock on the 510-acre plantation de-

---

[50] Ligon, *op. cit.*, p. 29. [51] *Ibid.*, p. 94.

[52] *Ibid.*, p. 63. The last practice is still seen occasionally in Barbados.

[53] *Ibid.*, pp. 87–88.

[54] John Davies, *The History of the Caribby Islands* (London, 1666), p. 26.

[55] Ligon, *op. cit.*, p. 22.

[56] *Tracts and Other Papers,* collected by Peter Force, II, No. 7, 5.

TABLE 7

Land Utilization on a Barbadian Plantation, 1650

PRODUCT	ACRES
Sugar	200
Woodland	120
Pasture	80
Ground provisions	70
Tobacco	30
Ginger	5
Cotton	5
Total	510

scribed above included forty-five cattle, eight milk cows, sixteen asses, and twelve horses. The labor supply consisted of twenty-eight Christian servants and ninety-six Negro slaves.[57]

The agricultural methods described by Ligon illustrate the amateurishness of the cane cultivation. No manuring is mentioned, and careful weeding was the principal preparation for the crop. When Ligon arrived, the planters had not yet discovered that the cane required fifteen months for full ripening, and the harvest was commonly a year after planting. Nor had they discovered the advantages of fall planting because Ligon states: "Canes are to be planted at all times that they may come in one field after another."[58] Other crops were planted in May and November.[59] Sugar yields were from two to four thousand pounds per acre,[60] or about one-third the present yield.

The sugar industry required cheap labor, and it was forthcoming from two sources: the Guinea Coast and Great Britain. Slaves were brought in by the Dutch in such large numbers that the 5,680 reported in 1645[61] had risen to 40,000 by 1688.[62] Indentured servants were still arriving from England but in smaller numbers, for in 1647 the Earl of Carlisle stated that there would be no more land available in Barbados for servants at the expiration of their terms but that

[57] Ligon, *op. cit.*, pp. 22–23.
[58] *Ibid.*, p. 85.
[59] *Ibid.*, p. 55.
[60] *Ibid.*, p. 95.
[61] Harlow, *op. cit.*, p. 338.
[62] *Cal. S. P., Col.* 1661–68, No. 1788, p. 586.

. . . each freeman who is unprovided of land and shall therefore desire to go off from the Barbados shall have a proportion of land allotted to him in my islands of Nevis, Antigua or any other island under my command.[63]

Furthermore, Barbados obtained a bad name which discouraged voluntary indentures when, from 1649 to 1655, Cromwell sold prisoners of war, especially from Scotland and Ireland, into slavery in Barbados for terms of from ten years to life. This enslavement of whites made possible another practice, the kidnapping of Englishmen for sale in Barbados, which lasted as late as 1660. Minor criminals were also transported to Barbados during the second half of the seventeenth century.[64]

The importation of prisoners, criminals, and slaves brought certain skills, products, and diseases to Barbados. Especially important were such cultivated plants as the yam and Guinea corn, and such animals as the camel and the Barbados woolless sheep (originally from the West African savannas) which were brought in by the slave ships. Less fortunate were the diseases which were carried by the same ships, and which caused Barbados to lose its former reputation for healthiness. Among these diseases was a plague (apparently yellow fever) which reached the island in 1647 and killed 6,000.[65] Ligon states that the living were hardly able to bury the dead,[66] and the health of the island was not helped by the practice of throwing dead bodies into the swamp which adjoined Bridgetown.[67] This plague was aggravated by a severe drought, and the resulting lack of provisions was so great that "ships which rode there were so short of provisions as if our vessels had not supplied them, they could not have returned home." [68]

Although this was a boom period, it was a boom only for those who were able to adjust themselves to large-scale sugar cultiva-

[63] Quoted from *Thomason Tracts,* British Museum, 669, 11(115), quoted in Harlow, *op. cit.,* pp. 307–308n.

[64] For details of this white slavery see Harlow's chapter on the "Labour Problem," especially pp. 295–302. Barbados was so infamous in this trade that a verb "to barbadoes" was used somewhat the same as "to shanghai" was used later. See *Oxford Dictionary.*

[65] *Winthrop's Journal,* 1630–49, II, 329.   [66] Ligon, *op. cit.,* p. 21.

[67] Schomburgk, *op. cit.,* p. 80.   [68] *Winthrop's Journal,* 1630–49, II, 328.

tion. The shift to sugar was often disadvantageous to the small planters who could not afford the slaves, the machinery, the purchase of imported provisions for slaves, or the year and a half or longer wait from the cane planting to the sale of the sugar. But it was drought, disease, and other crises which finally weakened the position of the small landholders. When they were ill, their slaves and servants escaped so that there were "many hundred Rebell Negro slaves in the woods." [69] The small planters soon came under the control of the merchants and the wealthier planters who, "by giving Credit to their profuse and sometimes Necessitious neighbors on severe Termes, insensibly in few years wormed out the greatest part of ye small proprietors." [70] Two successive catastrophes (the drought of 1650–51 followed soon after that of 1647) [71] enabled the wealthy to foreclose on the small holdings, and many were forced to leave the island to escape burdensome debts. This exodus which continued until 1740 (and, more slowly, to the present day) reduced the number of landholders from 11,200 in 1645 to 745 in 1667. [72]

The change to a slave-sugar economy was reflected in the nature of the foreign trade. Barbados had always depended in part on an imported food supply, but the growing slave population multiplied the deficit. New England was the chief supplier and shipped beef, meal, peas, and fish in quantity. Cattle and horses for the sugar mills were imported extensively along with barrel staves and, later, lumber. In return, the New Englanders took sugar, molasses, rum, cotton, tobacco, and indigo, partly for home consumption and partly for transshipment to England, the Azores, and Mediterranean ports. This trade was encouraged by the common practice of sending ships from England to the North American colonies via Barbados. [73] Often the trade was triangular, or perhaps even more complicated, in nature: a sugar cargo from

[69] *Tracts and Other Papers, loc. cit.*

[70] *Thomason Tracts,* British Museum, 669, 11(115), quoted in Harlow, *op. cit.,* p. 43*n.*

[71] *Colonizing Expeditions . . .* , p. 52.

[72] Major John Scott, *Sloane MSS,* 3662, fol. 54a, quoted in Harlow, *op. cit.,* p. 310.

[73] Charles M. Andrews, *The Colonial Period,* p. 35.

Barbados to New England, for example, was partly replaced at Boston by salted fish; the rest of the sugar and the best of the fish were sold at the Azores or Madeira, where wine or manufactures were taken on board and, later, exchanged with the leftover fish for more sugar products at Barbados. Other northern colonies also participated in this trade, although on a smaller scale.

The importance of sugar to Barbados was reflected by its common use in commercial transactions. Sugar, cotton, indigo, and tobacco were legal tender in 1652, and legal machinery was provided to settle disputes arising from offers of poor-quality staples in payment.[74] Taxes, fines, and Government fees were levied in terms of sugar beginning in 1652, and a currency equivalent was not even mentioned until 1670. Before 1652, taxes were levied in cotton or tobacco.[75]

The Dutch also engaged in the Barbadian sugar trade, but they sold most of their sugar in Europe and brought, in return, wines from France and Spain, manufactures, salted meats, and flour from Russia,[76] and, of greatest importance, slaves from West Africa.

Trade with England continued, but was diminished because of the Civil War. Barbados tried to keep neutral during this struggle, for neutrality was almost a necessity since the food supply came from abroad. But neutrality was difficult. Many of the recent settlers were Royalists; and the easiest way to keep out of trouble was to reduce intercourse with England to a minimum.[77]

This method was successful until 1650. In 1647, Lord Willoughby leased Barbados from the Earl of Carlisle and, at the same time, obtained an appointment as royal governor. When the new governor arrived in Barbados in 1650, his authority was at once recognized by the great majority of Barbadians. As a result, Parliament in October, 1650, prohibited trade with Barbados and

[74] *Acts and Statutes of Barbados*, pp. 83–84.

[75] *Acts of Assembly Passed in the Island of Barbados, 1648–1718*, pp. 4, 5, 7, 12, 77.

[76] Ligon, *op. cit.*, p. 37.

[77] For political details of this period, see N. Darnell Davis, *Cavaliers and Roundheads in Barbados*.

other rebellious colonies,[78] and sent Sir George Ayscue with a fleet to conquer Barbados. Ayscue reached Barbados in October, 1651, seized fifteen Dutch vessels in the harbor, and blockaded the island. The blockade was serious, for the island was just recovering from a drought, and provisions were none too plentiful. After several futile attacks, Ayscue won over some of the moderate Cavaliers by an offer of generous terms, and on January 11, 1652, an agreement was signed by the leaders of all parties. This treaty guaranteed certain rights to Barbados, including a representative government, and has since been considered as the Constitution of Barbados.[79]

Thus Barbados about 1650 was an island where sudden changes were taking place, where prosperity was the lot of the more competent and the wealthy, but where bankruptcy was the lot of the slothful, the inefficient, and of those who lacked credit to tide them over short-lived crises. By 1650 there was little doubt that the island was committed to a sugar and slave economy, and to dependence on extensive imports, including even foodstuffs.

[78] *Commons Journals,* VI (1650), 478.

[79] This account is based on Davis, *op. cit.;* also see Harlow, *op. cit.,* pp. 56–82. For a copy of the agreement of 1652, see Schomburgk, *op. cit.,* pp. 280–83.

CHAPTER IV

The Development of the Sugar and Slave Economy, 1652–1748

By 1652 the pattern of the Barbadian economy was well established; a period of readjustments and increasing efficiency in sugar production followed. The principal trends of this period may be summed up as: declining prices for Barbadian exports; decreasing white and growing slave population; increasing dependence on Empire trade; and changes in land utilization. These changes were accompanied by and, in part, hastened by a series of natural catastrophes which, fortunately, have not since been repeated. Political crises combined with nature to keep Barbados in a political, economic, and social ferment throughout the period 1652–1748.

GENERAL TRENDS

Declining prices.—An increasing world supply of tropical products led to a decline in the prices received for Barbadian exports. These price declines were by no means minor fluctuations. The sharp decline in Barbadian tobacco prices has already been noted on page 58. The price of cotton, which had been valued at two to four times as much as tobacco during the early 1630s,[1] had fallen to two pence per pound [2] by 1694. Equally striking were the declines in sugar and ginger prices shown in Table 8.

Sugar prices in Barbados fluctuated even more sharply owing to changes in freights and insurance and in the shipping available. The custom of quoting Barbadian prices in terms of sugar rather

---

[1] Vincent T. Harlow, *A History of Barbados, 1625–1685*, pp. 16–17.

[2] Elizabeth Donnan, *Documents Illustrative of the History of the Slave Trade to America*, I, 410.

TABLE 8

SUGAR AND GINGER PRICES AT LONDON, 1630–94 [a]

YEAR	GINGER PRICE PER CWT.	SUGAR WHOLESALE PRICE PER CWT.	SUGAR RETAIL PRICE PER LB.
1630–41	100s.[b]	80s.[e]	1s. 2d.[h]
1650	25s.[c]		1s. 6d.[i]
1656			10d.[j]
1661		21s.[f]	
1690			6d.[k]
1692–97		As high as 60s.[g] then much lower	
1694	8s.[d]		

[a] For other and later sugar prices, see Figure 2.
[b] Harlow, *A History of Barbados, 1625–1685*, p. 93.   [c] *Ibid.*
[d] Elizabeth Donnan, *Documents Illustrative of the History of the Slave Trade to America*, I, 410.
[e] Harlow, *op. cit.*, p. 170. Part of this drop was attributed to the Navigation acts: "sugars being fallen 20 p. cent since the said Act was put in Execucon amongst us." (Petition of the President, Council and Assembly of Barbados, May 11, 1661.)
[f] *Ibid.*
[g] John Oldmixon, *The British Empire in America* (London, 1741), II, 163.
[h] Ellen D. Ellis, *An Introduction to the History of Sugar as a Commodity*, p. 87n.
[i] *Ibid.*   [j] *Ibid.*   [k] *Ibid.*

than currency was perhaps a way of stabilizing the local financial economy. Only a few Barbadian prices for sugar in terms of currency are available (Table 9).

TABLE 9

SUGAR PRICES IN BARBADOS, 1652–94

YEAR	PER HUNDREDWEIGHT
1652	20s.[a]
1661	15s.[b]
1673–84	12s. 6d.[c]
1687	6s. 5d.[d]
1694	9–10s.[e]

[a] Vincent T. Harlow, *A History of Barbados, 1625–1685*, p. 313n.
[b] *Ibid.*, p. 312n.   [c] *Ibid.*, p. 317n.
[d] Frank W. Pitman, *The Development of the British West Indies, 1700–1763*, p. 129.
[e] Elizabeth Donnan, *Documents Illustrative of the History of the Slave Trade to America*, I, 410.

Thereafter, and during the first half of the eighteenth century, Barbadian prices seem to have been about ten to twelve shillings per hundredweight less than London prices except during periods of naval warfare, when the difference was much greater.

The significance of these prices is in their relation to the cost of production. Although costs must have varied with the season and the prices of slaves and supplies, the cost of production was generally estimated at a minimum of ten to twelve shillings per hundredweight at Barbados (or the equivalent of twenty to twenty-four shillings per hundredweight delivered at London). These figures are based on well-managed plantations of 100 acres [3] and are probably less than the cost of production on less efficient small holdings. Thus it appears that, after 1661, the margin of profit in average years was small or nonexistent, and for the small holders, profits must have been rare indeed.

Decreasing white and growing slave population.—The unprofitableness of the small plantations is clearly demonstrated by the readiness with which the small planters left the island at every opportunity, especially after a drought or hurricane. This tendency was encouraged by the fact that most of the small holdings were the older holdings which were located in the most exposed positions and in those regions most subject to drought, the leeward coast, St. Lucy, and the southeastern part of the island.[4]

The total white population decreased from 37,200 in 1643 to 23,624 in 1684 [5] and 15,252 in 1748.[6] Some of this loss was due to epidemics (as in 1647, 1671, and 1692), but, on the whole, the white birth rate seems to have been in excess of the death rate

[3] Edward Lyttleton, *The Groans of the Plantations* (London, 1688), p. 3; Sir Dalby Thomas, *An Historical Account of the Rise and Growth of the West-India Colonies* (London, 1690), reprinted in *Harleian Miscellany*, IX, 416; John Oldmixon, *The British Empire in America* (London, 1741), II, 163–71.

[4] In 1668 it was reported that 2,017 acres of land were cultivated by poor Catholics in the northwest portion of the island (products: tobacco and provisions), and 23,040 acres were in cotton in the south-southeastern part (N. D. Davis, *Cavaliers and Roundheads in Barbados,* p. 70). Cotton was commonly raised by the small planters.

[5] Harlow, *op. cit.,* p. 338.

[6] Frank W. Pitman, *The Development of the British West Indies, 1700–1763,* p. 372.

in the majority of years up to 1761.[7] Thus emigration, either for settlement or on military expeditions, must account for much of the decrease.

Evidences of emigration are common in the records of the period, and only a few examples need be given here. There

. . . departed between 1646 and 1658 to Virginia and Surinam 2400, between 1650 and 1652 to Guadeloupe, Martinique, Mariegalante, Grenada, Tobago and Curaçoa, 1600 [and in 1655] with Colonel Venables to Hispaniola and since to Jamaica 3300.[8]

A large part of the coastal region of South Carolina was settled by Barbadian emigrants about 1666–69.[9] Other Barbadians left on various expeditions during the wars with the Dutch and French, and many of these were killed in action or lost in hurricanes. Similar accounts could be given for the entire period.[10] Three significant points stand out about this emigration: (1) Many who left were in debt and often attempted to escape heavy obligations which they could not hope to pay; (2) many settled in areas which became serious competitors of Barbados, notably Jamaica, Guiana, and the Leeward Islands; and (3) the emigration was especially great at times of stress.[11]

Although the decline of the white population was largely due to the elimination of the small planter and the declining supply of indentured servants, a small part of it was due to the development of absentee landlordism. In 1669, an act of the assembly noted that the owners of "several of the most eminent plantations . . . have removed themselves to England." [12] Similar references to absentee landlordism are common thereafter. The importance of these absentees was not in their numbers (probably

[7] Pitman (*ibid.*, p. 385) gives the available data from 1683 to 1803. For forty-two years for which statistics are available, there were 22,650 baptisms and 23,192 burials. Twenty-one years had an excess of burials, but twelve of these excesses were after 1761; before that year seven years are recorded with an excess of burials and seventeen with an excess of births.

[8] *Calendar of State Papers, Colonial Series,* 1661–68, No. 1657, p. 529.

[9] *Ibid.*, pp. 153, 161, 162, 267–68.

[10] Pitman, *op. cit.*, pp. 91–98; balance of this chapter, *passim.*

[11] Pitman, *op. cit.*, p. 91; also this chapter, pp. 77, 88.

[12] Richard Hall, *Acts of Barbados,* No. 49; for other examples, see Pitman, *op. cit.*, pp. 31–33.

but a few hundred and perhaps less), but in the fact that the wealthiest planters considered Barbados as a source of income and considered England as their eventual and permanent home.[13] Thus, during the boom period of the colony, houses were poor, and more substantial dwellings came only after a large group realized that they could only hope to make a good living in Barbados, and that retirement in England was unlikely.

While the white population declined, the slave population, after a rapid rise to 1668, increased slowly and fitfully. The figures in Table 10 may not be altogether reliable,[14] but they are the best available.

TABLE 10

NUMBER OF SLAVES IN BARBADOS, 1683–1753

YEAR	NUMBER OF SLAVES
1683	46,602 [a]
1710	52,337 [b]
1724	55,206 [c]
1734	46,462 [d]
1748	47,025 [e]
1753	69,870 [f]

[a] Sir Robert H. Schomburgk, *The History of Barbados*, p. 82.
[b] Frank W. Pitman, *The Development of the British West Indies, 1700–1763*, p. 372.
[c] *Ibid.*   [d] *Ibid.*   [e] *Ibid.*   [f] *Ibid.*, p. 373.

The slow rate of increase was rarely due to lack of supply since Barbados usually received first choice of slaves because of its position.[15] Rather hard treatment, poor rations, overwork, and sexual irregularities kept down the slave birth rate and increased the slave death rate.[16] The excess of males in the slave imports

[13] "Nothing but England can we relish or fancy. . . . If we get a little money, we remit it to England. They that are able breed up their children in England." (Lyttleton, *op. cit.*, p. 34.) Compare this with the earlier spirit: "To gain a livelihood rather than make a fortune seems to have been the leading idea." (Davis, *op. cit.*, p. 80.)

[14] As slaves were sometimes a basis for taxation, the returns may have been below the true figures.

[15] Donnan, *op. cit.*, I, 204, 329*n*, 409; II, xli, L, 176.

[16] See Frank W. Pitman, "Slavery on the British West India Plantations," *Journal of Negro History*, XI (1926), especially 629–49, for a full discussion.

also must have had an important affect on the birth rate. Planters considered that it was cheaper to buy new slaves than to maintain the stock by careful breeding, and not until the abolition of the slave trade did the Creole slave population increase.

The occasional decreases in the slave population may be attributed to three causes (other than possible inaccuracy in the statistics). First, in poor years the planters did not purchase the necessary three thousand or more slaves needed annually to keep up the stock.[17] This was partly due to lack of cash or credit and partly due to less intensive cultivation when prices were low. Thoroughly manuring the land required much labor which was not worth while in poor years.[18] Second, slaves died in large numbers, due to epidemics, droughts, or hurricanes.[19] Since such unfavorable elements reduced the planter's crops, they also decreased the planter's ability to buy replacements. Third, slaves were exported from Barbados to other markets. Although the data is not very conclusive, the evidence suggests that slaves were, in small numbers at least, broken in or trained at Barbados and then exported at higher prices.[20] Slaves were also sold by creditors to visiting ships, and were taken away by debtors who fled from the island.[21]

Increasing dependence on Empire trade.—This trend was not the wish of the Barbadians, whose Golden Age had been during that period of British political disturbance when Barbadian free trade was a fact, whatever may have been its legality. Barbados was subjected to most of those acts which ultimately led the Thirteen Colonies to revolt, and smuggling was as common in the Indies as in the northern colonies. The first Navigation Act

[17] Governor Crowe estimated the number needed at 3,458 (Donnan, *op. cit.*, II, p. 28*n*); in 1750, 2,000 was thought sufficient (*ibid.*, p. li).

[18] ". . . if it was not for this dunging, a third part of the Negroes would do." John Oldmixon, *The British Empire in America*, II, 147.

[19] *Cal. S. P., Col.*, 1700, p. 716.

[20] See Donnan, *op. cit.*, II, xli, 1, 48, 65. A newspaper notice appeared in Boston, November 10, 1712: "A young negro girl born in Barbados that speaks good English to be sold." (Donnan, *ibid.*, III, 25.) Similar items in *ibid.*, 2, 33.

[21] Harlow, *op. cit.*, p. 315; Frank W. Pitman, *The Development of the British West Indies, 1700–1763*, p. 93.

(1651) prohibited almost all foreign trade with Barbados, except in English ships, and required that certain enumerated commodities, including sugar, cotton, and tobacco, be shipped direct to England before being sent to foreign ports. The act was hardly enforced in Barbados except when a visiting English warship touched there. This act was renewed after the Restoration, and made even stricter in 1663. The 1663 Navigation Act prohibited the carriage of European manufactures by colonial ships and thus upset one of the common forms of triangular trade engaged in by New England vessels. Not that the trade stopped, for smuggling was common, but when more legal and equally profitable trade was available elsewhere, the Yankee ships were attracted away from Barbados.

A trend to Empire trade occurred also in the slave trade. Originally, it had been in the hands of the Dutch, Spanish, and Portuguese. In 1660 the Royal African Company was established, and thereafter this British company and private British traders (including small Barbadian vessels) handled the British West Indian slave trade.[22] At the beginning of the seventeenth century, British slavers even supplied the Spanish colonies.[23]

Changes in land utilization, and crisis and prosperity.—The general trends outlined above oversimplify the picture and give but a poor idea of the many major and minor crises that faced the islanders. Therefore, with this chronological study will be combined those changes in land utilization which were the fourth of the trends noted for the period 1652–1748 on page 66.

1652–61, A DECADE OF CHANGE

Although lower prices, droughts, and the need for capital were forcing the small planter out, the period from 1652 to 1661 was the height of Barbadian prosperity. Wealthy planters were improving their methods as well as increasing their estates at the expense of the small holders.[24] Indentured servants and

---

[22] Donnan, *op. cit.,* I, 85.   [23] *Ibid.,* II, xxxv.

[24] "Captain Waterman's estate, comprising 800 acres, which at one time had been split up among no less than forty proprietors." (Harlow, *op. cit.,* p. 43.)

slaves were plentiful, and the soil was still naturally fertile.[25] Crops ranged from 7,500 hogsheads (7,500,000 pounds) of sugar [26] following the drought of 1650–51, to 30,000 hogsheads.[27] No record of a poor crop occurs from 1653 to 1662.

This Golden Age did not last long. As early as 1652, Colonel Modyford predicted: "Barbados cannot last in an height of trade three years longer especially for sugar, the wood being almost spent." [28] Thus not only building lumber and firewood, but also the fuel for the sugar factories was running short. The dried trash from the sugar mill was substituted as fuel, but it was not considered so good as wood.[29] As late as 1850 the trash was often inadequate in quantity, and coal, mineral tar (from the Scotland district), and cornstalks were used to supplement it.[30] The scarcity of local timber is demonstrated by the appearance of boards as well as barrel staves among the major imports from New England.[31]

At the same time, the planters realized that their methods were inefficient. In 1652, the assembly passed

An Act for the Encouragement of such Persons as shall first invent and publish the grinding of sugar cane with half the strength that is now commonly used.[32]

Windmills were being tried in 1655, "for the mills they now use destroy so many horses that it begors the planters." [33] Cattle were also substituted for horses (although not entirely), for most later references are to "cattle mills." However, the windmill won. On

[25] "It is a most riche soile, all wayes Grone and baring frutes." "Henry Whistler's Journal, March, 1654/55," *Narrative of General Venables,* ed. C. H. Firth, p. 145.

[26] These figures are calculated from the statement: "Lord Willoughby had 4 percent on all goods exported, which last year amounted to 300m. [lbs.] of sugar." *Cal. S. P., Col.,* 1574–1660, p. 388.

[27] Oldmixon, *op. cit.,* II, 166.

[28] *Cal. S. P., Col.,* 1574–1660, p. 374. The wood was reported "made use of and destroyed" in 1671. *Cal. S. P., Col.* 1669–1674, No. 674, p. 284.

[29] Oldmixon, *op. cit.,* II, 148.

[30] John Davy, *The West Indies Before and Since Slave Emancipation* (London, 1854), p. 120.

[31] One Salem firm shipped 37,512 feet of boards to Barbados during the first quarter of 1659. (Harlow, *op. cit.,* pp. 278–79.)

[32] *Acts and Statutes of Barbados,* p. 140.

[33] *Narrative of General Venables,* p. 146.

a map dated 1690,[34] windmills and cattle mills appear in equal numbers, often side by side on the larger plantations. The larger plantations have two or three windmills which, much more commonly than the cattle mills, are located on exposed ridges and uplands.[35]

Another important change seems to have occurred about this time, although it cannot be definitely dated. In contrast to Ligon's description of land utilization (pages 58–61), diversification of agriculture seems to have lost favor until, by 1685, eighty acres of each 100 acres were being used for sugar, and only twenty acres were left for pasture, provisions, and a nursery for canes.[36] This trend, which may have been due to the difficulty of teaching the slaves to raise a variety of crops, is reflected in an increasing emphasis on food imports and in agonizing protests when food ships were not sent.[37]

Life in Barbados, at least among the planter and merchant aristocracy, was losing some of the pioneer plainness described by Ligon. Fontabelle, the oldest building still standing in Barbados, was erected in 1648, and is a substantial stone mansion of pleasing proportions. In 1656, Du Tertre described Barbados as boasting of

. . . two regular cities, in each of which more than a hundred taverns may be reckoned as well furnished as in Europe.

and de Rochefort in 1658 described Barbados as having

. . . a great number of fine houses . . . many were built in English fashion; the shops and storehouses were filled with all kinds of merchandize; fairs and markets were held here; and the whole island was divided into parishes, each of which had a handsome church.[38]

Regular highways were being built which, according to an act of 1661, were to be sixty feet wide in woods and twenty-four feet wide in open ground and along which hedges and bushes were to

---

[34] "A New Map of the Island of Barbados" (London, 1690).

[35] Oldmixon, *op. cit.*, II, 148.

[36] *Cal. S. P., Col.*, 1681–85, No. 3671 (September 14, 1685), p. 416.

[37] *Ibid.*, 1661–68, p. lix and numerous later references.

[38] Quoted by Sir Robert H. Schomburgk, *The History of Barbados*, p. 241.

be trimmed "so that wind and sun may dry the highways." [39] These highways were no longer short stretches connecting with landing places, since definite provision was made for the inland and windward parishes to contribute toward the building of trunk highways to Bridgetown and Speightstown.[40]

1661–76, A PERIOD OF HARDSHIP

The following decade, 1661–71, brought one trouble after another. The clearing of the woods caused the indigenous monkeys and raccoons to attack the fields, and a bounty was offered for each animal killed.[41] Rats, which had been brought by English ships, became troublesome, for they nibbled the canes and came into the houses toward the end of the rainy season.[42] A common method of combating the rats was to burn the cane field they inhabited by lighting fires on all sides and thus driving the rats toward the center. Unfortunately, the strong winds often caused the fire to spread out of control so that losses as high as £10,000 were reported.[43] Since the worst fires occurred during the dry season when the water supply was low, it was almost impossible to stop them. Several acts to prevent cane fires were passed, each increasingly severe, until in 1666 smoking or carrying a fire in a cane field (except on one's property) was punishable by twenty lashes or a fine of 500 pounds of sugar.[44] Nevertheless, the use of the cane fire has continued until the present day. Planters have used fires to destroy rats, diseased cane, or canes that came up unevenly.[45] The Negroes set fires to revenge themselves against cruel masters and, after Emancipation, when they needed money, to hurry up the date of harvest. Fires have also been caused by smoking, cooking fires, sparks from chimneys, and the like.

[39] *Acts of Assembly Passed in the Island of Barbados from 1648–1718,* p. 31.
[40] *Ibid.,* p. 35.
[41] *Laws of Barbados* (London, 1764), p. 106; this act was revived in 1684 (*Acts of Assembly Passed in the Island of Barbados,* p. 115).
[42] Richard Ligon, *A True and Exact History of the Island of Barbados,* pp. 88–89.
[43] Oldmixon, *op. cit.,* II, 131.
[44] *Acts of Assembly Passed in the Island of Barbados from 1648–1718,* p. 47.
[45] Oldmixon, *op. cit.,* II, 147. Burnt cane will grow up again as a ratoon crop. If ripe, it must be crushed soon after burning.

About 1661, soil exhaustion was first noted. Probably because of this, many small planters left the island with their slaves and thus defrauded their creditors. Subsequently, an act was passed making slaves real estate and allowing creditors to have them sold for debts.[46] In March, 1662, £100,000 worth of slaves, probably taken from debtors, were sold to the Spaniards.[47] Other signs of Barbadian decline appear at the same time. Thus on July 10, 1661, a report from Barbados stated:

The land is much poorer and makes much less sugar than heretofore . . . all people are so generally indebted to the merchants that they have but a small portion in their own estates.[48]

Also a letter from Surinam, dated August 15, 1662, notes:

. . . we shall see this colony wonderfully prosper by reason of the decline of Barbados whence we daily expect sixty passengers and planters.[49]

This decreased yield and the decline of prices resulting from the Navigation Act of 1660 brought the income of Barbados to "so low a rate that the merchants send no goods to Barbados, but only empty ships to take away the sugar." [50]

A series of natural catastrophes added to the bankruptcy of the island. In 1663

. . . strange and unusual caterpillars which like the locusts of Egypt came upon the land and devoured all things so that the poorer sort of people who were very numerous were very hard put to it.[51]

This pest was followed by a fire in 1666 which destroyed Bridgetown, and, in 1667, by a hurricane of moderate violence which destroyed some of the buildings.[52] A drought followed in 1668, and the crops were "so burnt up that the inhabitants are ready to desert their plantations." [53] In 1669, "excessive rains and want of winds have caused the crops to fall out one-third less than formerly," [54] and in March, 1670, it was reported that

---

[46] John Poyer, *The History of Barbados,* p. 332; also *Acts of Assembly,* No. 178.
[47] Harlow, *op. cit.,* p. 141.   [48] *Cal. S. P., Col.,* 1661–68, July 10, 1661.
[49] Historical Manuscript Commission, *Tenth Report,* Appendix, Part VI, p. 96.
[50] *Cal. S. P., Col.,* 1661–68, July 10, 1661.
[51] *Ibid.,* p. lix.   [52] Oldmixon, *op. cit.,* II, 29.
[53] *Cal. S. P., Col.,* 1661–68, p. 586.   [54] *Cal. S. P., Col.,* 1669–74, p. 43.

. . . incessant rains they had for seven months, have had since upwards of three months of very dry weather so that the ground gapes as if it would devour its inhabitants; this is accompanied with a great dearth even to famine of corn and potatoes their bread provisions for that plague of the caterpillar has passed over the island two or three times eating away most of the slips of potatoes.[55]

This drought was accompanied by an epidemic, as has been so often the case in Barbados, which lasted until 1671.[56]

A new tax, which burdened the trade of the island until 1837, was the final blow at the prosperity of the island. In return for the abolition of the proprietorship and for the guaranteeing of land titles, the Barbadian Assembly agreed to the levying of a 4½ percent export duty on all the dead produce of the island.[57] Contrary to Barbadian expectations, this 4½ percent duty was not used to pay the expenses of British officials in Barbados nor was it used for the defense of Barbados. Instead, most of the funds collected went to the King. Thus the duty became an additional expense in the production of local goods for export. It was estimated that the duty amounted to 10 percent of the profits.[58]

The natural, economic, and political troubles of Barbados during this decade explain why the white and slave populations alike declined at the end of the decade.[59] It is no wonder that

. . . emigration to New England, Virginia, Surinam, Carolina and Jamaica was very considerable in the earlier years of Charles II reign, the number being computed at upwards of 12,000.[60]

and that it was later reported that "4000 inhabitants within the last three years [1669–71] . . . deserted the island." [61]

Barbados had just about returned to normal crops and a fair amount of prosperity when the renewal of the Dutch War

[55] *Ibid.*, March 23, 1670, p. 60.   [56] *Ibid.*, May 17, 1671, p. 219.

[57] The Courteen-Carlisle dispute had never really been settled, and now that Barbadian land was highly valued, the planters feared that they might lose their estates through court intrigues.

[58] For details of the 4½ percent dispute, see Harlow, *op. cit.*, pp. 135–36, 146–47. During the proprietorship, duties of from 2 to 4 percent had been collected on exports, partly to pay the expenses of government.

[59] Harlow, *op. cit.*, p. 339.   [60] *Cal. S. P., Col.*, 1661–68, p. lix.

[61] *Ibid.*, 1669–74, p. 284.

(1672–74) led to the capture of the Barbadian sugar fleet by the enemy.[62] A more lasting result of the war was the levying of the "enumeration dues" on all intercolonial trade beginning in 1673. These amounted to 1*s.* 6*d.* per hundredweight on brown sugar and did much to discourage trade with New England, which thereafter began to purchase steadily increasing amounts of sugar from the foreign West Indies.[63] The reduction in the New England trade endangered the food supply and gave rise to profiteering in provisions. Thus the island was in poor condition to withstand its first recorded severe hurricane.

A moderately severe hurricane passed over Barbados on August 10, 1674; it was followed about a year later (August 31, 1675) by one of the three major hurricanes in Barbadian history.

The Leeward Part of the Country suffered most; for the Sugar-Works, and Dwelling-Houses were all thrown down; very few Wind-mills except Stone-mills, stood out the Storm. The Houses and Sugar-Works to the Windward were very much shattered; the Canes were blown down flat, and some up by the Roots. All Ships in the Road were brought ashore; the Pots in the Curing-Houses were all broken. Windward the Storm was not so violent. From thence Leeward, and all over *Scotland,* there was neither Dwelling-house, Out-work or Wind-mill standing, except a few Stone mills. All the Houses in the Bay were blown down, as were most of the Churches; and almost all the Corn in the Country was destroy'd. . . .

. . . Besides that their Canes in the Ground were all ruined, the Planters were forced to take off so many of their Hands, to employ them about re-building their Houses, that there was no Likelihood of their having a Crop the next Year. At the same Time they suffered also by Want; for the Supplies of Provisions that used to be sent from *New-England,* were in a great Measure stop'd. . . .

. . . The Houses being levelled with the Ground by the Hurricane, the best Planters in the Island lived in Huts; and when they built again, were afraid to run up their Houses to any Height for a long Time. The Terror of this Tempest stuck so upon the Inhabitants, that few people cared to meddle with Estates.[64]

Governor Atkin's report of the same hurricane states that

. . . 200,000*l.* will not repay the damage caused by the hurricane of last August, churches, houses and mills being destroyed and the sugar canes

---

[62] *Cal. S. P., Col.,* 1669–74, pp. 431–32, 452, 455.   [63] Pitman, *op. cit.,* pp. 167, 175.
[64] Oldmixon, *op. cit.,* II, 33–34.

twisted and spoiled. . . . Bridgetown was "being" rebuilt with very fair houses, some of brick but most of stone. . . .[65]

1677–84, A PROSPEROUS INTERLUDE

Those planters who survived the storm entered a period of prosperity (1677–1684) beginning with the "fair crop" predicted by Governor Atkins for 1677. The governor also reported that

. . . there is not a foot of land in Barbados that is not employed even to the very seaside . . . so that whoever will have land . . . must pay for it dearer than for land in England.[66]

In February, 1680, the next governor, Sir Richard Dutton, found the island in a flourishing condition,[67] and by 1683 the number of ships trading with Barbados had increased to 338 annually compared with 150 in 1676.[68]

1685–89, A PERIOD OF DEPRESSION

Then came another period of depression (1685–89). Sugar prices dropped, reaching a low of 6s. 5d. at Barbados in 1687.[69] In 1685, the island was

. . . under great affliction by the loss of this year's crop through ill weather, and by the mortality among negroes and servants through smallpox.[70]

About the same time a decline in the slave population was noted due to disease, accidents, suicide, and probably malnutrition (since the slaves were poorly fed when there was a shortage of supplies).[71] Adding to these troubles, King James levied a new tax of 2s. 4d. per hundredweight on brown sugar to raise funds to put down the Monmouth Rebellion.[72]

The troubles of the sugar planters were dramatically summed up in several pamphlets, from one of which the following is quoted:

[65] *Cal. S. P., Col.*, 1675–76, pp. 347–49. [66] *Ibid.*, p. 421.
[67] Oldmixon, *op. cit.*, II, 37. [68] Schomburgk, *op. cit.*, p. 147.
[69] Pitman, *op. cit.*, p. 129. [70] *Cal. S. P., Col.*, 1681–85, No. 419, p. 109.
[71] Pitman, "Slavery on the British West India Plantations," *Journal of Negro History*, XI (1926), 642.
[72] Oldmixon, *op. cit.*, II, 40–41.

. . . the plants in the ground are very often subject to be devoured, wounded, and torn by ants, or undermined and destroyed at the roots by mugworms. Too much rain, or too much drought, in either season, is a certain diminution of the crop, if not a total destruction of the plants; nay, if the rains come too late, which often happens, a whole year's planting is lost. When all these mischiefs are escaped, and the canes of a considerable heighth, then are they liable to be twisted, broke, and totally spoiled by the furious hurricanes, that once in three or four years, like a fit of an ague, shake the whole island, not only do the crops an injury, but sometimes tumble down and level their mills, work-houses, and strongest buildings; but, escaping all these, as the canes ripen, they grow more and more combustible, and are thereby subject to the malice and drunken rages of angry and desperate run-away negroes, as well as so many other accidents of fire; the fury whereof, when once got into a field of canes, is extremely quick, terrible, and scarcely to be resisted before it has destroyed the whole parcel; but when they are brought to full perfection for cutting, and the planter's expectation as ripe as they, if unseasonable rains happen, or that no winds blow, then do they all rot and perish in the ground. . . . Not to mention . . . all those accidents, or storms and pirates in bringing their commodity to market, nor which is worst of all, their loss by breaking customers, who not only run away with all their produce, but with the freight, factoridge, and customs, which have been paid for those sugars they were trusted with, thereby subjecting the industrious planter to new and unforeseen debts and interest for them, from whence he expected the reward of all his labour. Nay, besides all has been said, sometimes diseases amongst slaves and cattle will in a very short time sweep away a whole year's profit, besides the constant charge of recruiting the natural decay of all living creatures.[73]

Thomas also gives a complete description of the technique of sugar cultivation and manufacture.[74] According to Thomas, the average yield of sugar was the same as in Ligon's day, i.e., 2,000 pounds per acre. A careful system of cultivation was worked out so that canes were planted during the six wet months and harvested and manufactured during the six dry months. The canes were planted in holes as they are today in Barbados, and hoes were used rather than plows. Plant canes were raised rather than ratoon crops, for Thomas notes that

[73] Thomas, *op. cit.*, IX, 420.   [74] *Ibid.*, pp. 415–21.

. . . when the soil was first broke up, the same canes would yield two, three, or more cuttings, before they were replanted, to the wonderful ease and advantage of the first planters.[75]

Thus by 1689 the diversified agriculture described by Ligon, with its careless, uncertain methods of cultivation, had been replaced by a one-crop system of sugar cultivation adjusted to the vicissitudes of nature. The planters, as a group, now consisted of men familiar with this one-crop sugar system who, in addition, had the necessary capital and credit to withstand considerable spells of misfortune. The largest elimination of the inefficient planters had occurred by 1689; the half century of crises and prosperity which followed resulted in further elimination of the unfit.

1689–1713, AN ERA OF WAR AND UNCERTAINTY

The next quarter century (1689–1713) was a period of war with its concomitant uncertainties of markets and supplies. It was for Barbados also a period of further decline in white population due to war and disease. Economically, it was a period of opportunism, of occasional large profits interspersed with economic makeshifts.

The war with France from 1689 to 1697 improved sugar prices,[76] but drought, hurricane, and epidemics offset this advantage for many of the planters. Thus a letter dated July 2, 1691, states:

Our crops this year have been very small; in all probability next year will be smaller, we not having had the usual seasons to plant.[77]

The next year was no better:

In the Year 1692, there was very unseasonable Weather, and such Rains, that the Planters could not send their Sugars to the Ports. Most of the Masters of Ships who came to this Island at this Time were buried here; and the Condition of the People was truly deplorable.[78]

---

[75] *Ibid.*, p. 416.
[76] Oldmixon, *op. cit.*, II, 46.
[77] Quoted in Oldmixon, *op. cit.*, II, 47.
[78] *Ibid.*, p. 52.

The last sentence refers to the epidemics which raged in the island from 1691 to 1698 and which have been attributed to the influx of soldiers as well as of slaves.[79] As a result,

. . . the Island which before was reckoned to be the healthiest of all the Isles thereabouts, has ever since been very sickly, vast Numbers of Merchants, Captains of Ships, Planters, Labourers, and Negroes have been swept away by this Disease; and 'tis to be wished, they may have such Supplies of Men sent them, as they want for their Defence.[80]

The epidemics were especially severe about Bridgetown. This was attributed to "beds wet with sweat," bad provisions, "nastiness of houses," and to the filling up of the canal that drained the swamp east of Bridgetown.[81]

It is not certain what diseases were introduced about this time. Smallpox and yellow fever can be identified in earlier accounts; it seems probable that dysentery, typhoid, elephantiasis (Barbados leg), and leprosy arrived at this period or soon after, since these were reported as common and established diseases a half century later.[82]

War and disease rapidly reduced the white population; the number of white men decreased from 7,235 in 1683 to 2,330 in 1698.[83] The slaves were also decreased by disease, but heavy imports prevented any such decline as in the white population. Anxiety over the large proportion of Negroes was increased by a slave revolt in 1693 which was described as "the most General the Slaves ever hatched and brought nearest to Execution." [84]

Among the attempts to increase the white population were "An Act to encourage the bringing of Christian Servants to the Island" passed by the assembly, June 20, 1696, and in 1697, "An Act for the Settlement of the Militia of this Island." [85] These acts

[79] Donnan, *op. cit.*, I, 409; Oldmixon, *op. cit.*, II, 117.

[80] Oldmixon, *op. cit.*, II, 49–50.

[81] *Cal. S. P., Col.*, 1700, pp. 228–29. A molehead was erected by the assembly in 1694 "which was destroyed by a hurricane the same year. By barring the bar, this mole is one of the greatest causes of infection of the air."

[82] William Hillary, M.D., *Observations of the Changes of the Air and the Concomitant Epidemical Diseases in the Island of Barbados* (London, 1759), *passim*.

[83] Schomburgk, *op. cit.*, p. 144.   [84] Oldmixon, *op. cit.*, II, 53.

[85] *Laws of Barbados* (London, 1764), p. 489.

required estate owners to maintain a certain number of white servants (based on acreage and number of slaves), and from these servants the militia was organized.

Many of these white servants were given ten-acre plots by their masters,[86] and their descendants formed the "red-legs" or poor whites who still survive in several of the more isolated parts of Barbados. New planters could not be attracted to Barbados, for a capital investment of £5,000 was needed to operate even a 100-acre estate.[87] For those who had money there were better investments for

. . . 100 l. carried to the Indies are worth 120 l. and 100 l. carried to Barbados will bring but 80 l. by reason of the hurricanes.[88]

Undoubtedly, another reason for the poor rating of Barbadian investments was the tremendous shipping losses; in 1695 the losses of ships in the Barbados trade were reported to be £387,-100.[89] Yet profits were high with sugar selling at sixty shillings per hundredweight in London; everything depended on the luck of the planter in getting his produce to market despite hurricanes, pirates, and privateers. The high rates were "occasioned by bad Crops, Storms or Captures";[90] but Barbados managed to get 19,377 hogsheads to the London market for the year ending June 24, 1699,[91] and several other fairly good years had preceded it. Yet during this period, in spite of the decreasing white population, there was "no room for settlers" for "the little plantations were swallowed up by great ones."[92] It appears that the process of elimination was still operating with a resulting strengthening of the planter aristocracy. Thus may be explained the many signs of wealth noted by Père Labat in 1700:

The houses are well built in the style of those in England with many glazed windows; they are magnificently furnished. In a word the whole

[86] Schomburgk, op. cit., pp. 84–85.   [87] Thomas, loc. cit.
[88] From a letter (1696) in Historical Manuscript Commission, The Manuscripts of the House of Lords, N.S., II, 62.
[89] Ibid., II, 64.   [90] Oldmixon, op. cit., II, 163.
[91] Cal. S. P., Col., 1702, p. 58; Historical Manuscript Commission, The Manuscripts of the House of Lords, N.S., IV, 445.
[92] Cal. S. P., Col., 1697–98, p. 29.

place has an appearance of cleanliness, gentility and wealth which one does not find in the other islands. . . . The shops and merchants' warehouses are filled with all that one could want from every part of the world. One sees a number of goldsmiths, jewellers, clock-makers, and other artificers; . . . the largest trade in America is carried on here.[93]

As has happened so often in Barbados, the peak of prosperity did not last. The exports to England dropped sharply both in value and quantity:

TABLE 11

Exports of Sugar from Barbados, 1699–1702

YEAR	£
1700	350,000 [a]
1701	275,000 [b]
1702	110,000 [c]

YEAR	HOGSHEADS
1699 (year ending June 24)	19,377 [d]
1700	14,411 [e]
1701	11,524 [f]

[a] Frank W. Pitman, *The Development of the British West Indies, 1700–1763*, graph facing p. 98.
[b] *Ibid.*   [c] *Ibid.*
[d] Historical Manuscripts Commission, *The Manuscripts of the House of Lords*, N.S., IV, 445.
[e] *Ibid.*   [f] *Ibid.*

The agents of Barbados in London reported the decline of the island in terms which suggest that such prosperity as Labat found in 1700 was much less than that of a decade earlier:

By their great losses at sea during the war, the very high duties laid on the commodities of the growth of the island exported, by the mortalities of many thousands of their negroes, which reduced them from 70,000 to about 40,000, whereby more than one-third part of their lands which used to be planted for sugar, ginger and cotton lie uncultivated, and by that means not over 220 or 230 ships are yearly employed, whereas there used to be near 400.[94]

---

[93] Quoted in Algernon Aspinall, *The Pocket Guide to the West Indies*, p. 77.
[94] *Cal. S. P., Col.*, 1700, p. 716.

The decline continued. The epidemics, which had abated between 1698 and 1702 (except for a slight recurrence in 1700), returned in 1703, and by the end of the dry season Barbados was "more unhealthy than it was ever yet known to be." [95] This epidemic occurred during the third successive year of low exports and was probably accompanied by and encouraged by a lack of provisions occasioned by drought or by the failure of the necessary supply ships to arrive. Normal trade was again handicapped by war (War of the Spanish Succession, 1702–13), and attacks on Barbadian commerce were so serious that frigates were ordered to cruise around the island "during the winter season." [96] Except for two years (1705, 1706), the exports of Barbados remained low in value until the end of the war.[97]

War conditions caused a shortage of capital and resulted in many changes (some makeshift, a few permanent) in the economy of the island. The shortage of funds was largely owing to a cessation of trade with the Spanish Caribbean which had formerly brought in sufficient quantities of pieces of eight to purchase slaves and provisions. Not only was the currency supply cut off, but the need for it was increased, for New Englanders were insisting on cash payments for their foodstuffs and lumber, instead of the sugar, rum, and molasses which they had formerly accepted. The reason for this change was the cheaper price at which sugar could be purchased in the foreign West Indies.[98]

In 1706, paper money (issued with sugar as security) was resorted to. However, the paper soon depreciated, and slave and trading ships avoided the island while it was legal tender. The act providing for its issuance was disallowed by the home government, and the paper money was retired. The paper money crisis drove many planters into bankruptcy, and some left the island with their slaves to avoid their debts, in spite of the governor's

[95] *Ibid.*, 1702–3, pp. 189, 303.

[96] Historical Manuscript Commission, *The Manuscripts of the House of Lords*, N.S., V, 316.

[97] Pitman, *The Development of the British West Indies, 1700–1763*, graph facing p. 98.

[98] Richard Pares, *War and Trade in the West Indies*, p. 396.

orders forbidding such emigration.[99] The shortage of cash continued until after 1763, and "sugar at market prices was everywhere accepted as Money." [100]

During the depression, Barbadians supplemented their meager incomes by various shifts, legal and illegal. Many of these were possible because "vessels used to arrive there first as the windwardmost and best starting point in their quest for markets down the range of the islands." [101] Routes from Africa, Guiana, Jamaica, the Spanish Main, the Leeward Islands, and the northern colonies converged at Barbados and made it a convenient entrepôt for smuggling as well as for legitimate trade. Thus tobacco was shipped from Virginia to Barbados and successfully smuggled into England because the "officers do not expect tobacco on board Barbados ships." [102] Even during wars, trade with the enemy was carried on:

. . . flags of truce were believed by Admiral Walker and "most people of Barbados" to be only pretexts for collusive trade between Barbados and Martinique. Governor Lowther, the attorney-general, and the Magistrates at Barbados all countenanced the trade with Martinique and hindered the customs collector from obtaining writs to take up offenders.[103]

Foreign sugars were brought into Barbados and reëxported to England as Barbadian produce in such quantities that a tariff of 12*s.* 6*d.* per hundredweight was finally levied on them to protect the Barbadian planters.[104] Hence Barbados "lost that trade entirely, excepting what is carried on clandestinely, which is very common." [105] Another illegal practice was the shipping of "clayed sugar," a semirefined product, as muscovado to avoid the higher import duty on the refined product.[106]

---

[99] Pitman, *op. cit.*, pp. 141–44.   [100] *Ibid.*, p. 145.

[101] Pares, *op. cit.*, p. 291.

[102] Historical Manuscript Commission, *The Manuscripts of the House of Lords*, N.S., IV, 327.

[103] Pitman, *op. cit.*, p. 222.   [104] Hall, *op. cit.*, No. 132.

[105] From a pamphlet quoted in Pitman, *op. cit.*, p. 227.

[106] "The amount of clayed sugar which the statistics of imports show was small, but the real proportion was much higher for the Barbadians cheated the customs by a long-sanctioned abuse." (Pares, *op. cit.*, p. 307.) See Oldmixon, *op. cit.*, II,

Barbados was the only one of the sugar islands which had a good local supply of clay suitable for claying sugar. When convoys were necessary, this fact caused complications, for it took two months longer to produce clayed sugar than muscovado, thus Barbadian sugars that were clayed were not ready to be shipped at the end of the harvest season as were the sugars of Antigua and St. Kitts.

If the last convoy sailed in July, as Antigua desired, many of the Barbados sugars could get no convoy at all, or must wait until the next year; if it was delayed until September, some of the Leeward Islands had to wait into the hurricane season which exposed it [their sugar] not only to danger but to a heavier insurance.[107]

This situation put the Barbadians in a dilemma. They could not very strongly insist on delaying the sailing of the convoy, for they did not admit that they exported much clayed sugar, hence most Barbadian sugar was shipped late without convoy and with correspondingly heavy insurance and losses. Some governors delayed the convoys and were popular at Barbados; others encouraged early departures and became popular in the Leeward Islands.[108]

The smaller importations of slaves increased the proportion of Creole slaves. This was important in a colony with such a small proportion of whites, for the Creole slaves often felt more sympathetic toward their masters than toward untutored, raw slaves imported from Africa. Thus added responsibilities and privileges could be given to the Creole Negroes. In 1707 provision was made for their part in supplementing the white militia, and freedom was offered to any slave who killed an enemy.[109] Creole slaves were given positions as assistant overseers, head drivers, head cattle and mule men; others learned trades and were even allowed to practice them off the estate and pay their master a weekly sum from their earnings for the privilege. The neater and better-looking slaves became skilled cooks and domestics. All in all, the

---

152, for a typical Barbadian argument: that Barbadian muscovados were so pure that they looked like clayed sugar.

[107] Pares, *op. cit.*, p. 307. The insurance rates changed on July 26.

[108] *Ibid.*   [109] *Laws of Barbados* (London 1764), p. 175.

increasing proportion of Creole slaves meant better treatment for the Negro population.[110]

1713–23, A BRIEF BOOM FOLLOWED BY HARD TIMES

After a quarter of a century of uncertain trade, it is not surprising that Barbados welcomed the Peace of Utrecht (1713) and started a short-lived boom (1713–18) which seemed to be favored by the rapidly increasing consumption of sugar in England. There was some immigration and

. . . many planters, who began in a small way with fifteen or twenty slaves for the production of provisions, cotton and ginger, which were inexpensive to raise, soon became ambitious to engage in sugar culture.[111]

The slave population increased from 41,970 in 1712 to 55,205 in 1724, and the exports to England in 1714 and 1716 exceeded those in 1699 and from 1714 to 1718 were much above the average for 1707–13.[112] A severe drought early in 1715 caused "a great scarcity of Corne and all ground provisions" [113] and probably aggravated "the contagious distemper that hath raged for some time among cattle, sheep and horses," [114] but the exports to England that year, although reduced, were still fairly high.

Again the prosperity ended abruptly, and from 1719 to 1723 hard times again beset Barbados. The exports to England in 1719 were but half the average of the preceding five years; 1720 showed a partial recovery, but 1721 and 1722 established new lows.[115] Again nature and the world situation combined to bring on another crisis so that "many hundred families have gone from Barbados to Carolina and Pennsylvania," [116] while others were considering settlement in St. Lucia with its virgin soil and plentiful lumber which could be sold profitably in Barbados.[117] The pri-

[110] Pitman, "Slavery on the British West India Plantations," *Journal of Negro History*, XI (1926), 595–99.

[111] Pitman, *The Development of the British West Indies, 1700–1763*, pp. 132–33.

[112] *Ibid.*, p. 372, and graph facing p. 98.

[113] *Cal. S. P., Col.*, 1714–15, p. 186, Governor Lowther to the Council of Trade and Plantations, May 20, 1715.

[114] *Ibid.*   [115] Pitman, *op. cit.*, graph facing p. 98.

[116] *Cal. S. P., Col.*, 1720–21, p. 66.   [117] *Ibid.*, 1719–20, p. 229.

mary cause of this movement seems to have been an expansion of the world sugar supply which exceeded by far the increase in demand. The French were expanding the industry in Guadeloupe, Martinique, and Haiti; and the Barbadian Assembly in a petition pointed out that the French:

. . . have the advantage of a newer soil and consequently can sell their sugar far cheaper than the planters of Barbados can, who have a soil almost worn out, for a plantation of 200 acres in any of the French colonies may be cultivated with 30 or 40 negroes and few cattle and horses because their land is fresh and rich, which in Barbados would require 150 negroes with 50 or 60 head of cattle and a dozen horses.[118]

Other new sources of competition arose from expansion in the Dutch colonies, Jamaica, and Antigua. Especially striking was the rise of the St. Kitts's sugar industry which doubled its exports from 1715 to 1725 and redoubled them in the following decade.[119]

The distemper among the animals, mentioned on page 88, was but the first of the natural catastrophes and was probably in part the cause of some of the others. In 1718 an act of the Barbadian Assembly stated that:

. . . the Expence of Land-carriage of the Produce here to be very great, but in wet Weather impraticable by reason of the great Mortality that has happened amongst the Cattle and Horses, through a malignant Distemper which has raged amongst them for three years Past.[120]

The shortage of animals must have reduced the manure supply and probably explains the frequent references to declining soil fertility. Likewise, the final blow to the cattle mill probably came about this time, for on Mayo's map, published about 1722, only windmills are shown. An epidemic was brought to Barbados by ship and reached its height in 1723 when both men and animals were reported infected.[121] Added to these troubles was "the unseasonable weather with which Providence has of late years visited

[118] *Ibid.,* 1717-18, p. 38; Pitman, *op. cit.,* pp. 70-71.

[119] Pitman, *op. cit.,* graph facing p. 244.

[120] *Acts of Assembly Passed in the Island of Barbados, 1648-1718,* pp. 322-24. Because of the shortage of draft animals, it was enacted that "no roads to the seashore shall be closed to the public" so that sugar could be shipped by coastwise boats.

[121] *Ibid.,* p. 356; *Cal. S. P., Col.,* 1722-23, p. 308.

this island." [122] It is no wonder that the exports from 1718 to 1723 were declining!

1724-39, A REVIVAL FOLLOWED BY HARDER TIMES

In 1724, Barbadian trade again revived, and a series of good to indifferent years followed which were succeeded by a ten-year period of depression lasting from 1730 to 1739. A slump in prices, caused by French competition, was again the cause,[123] again unfavorable seasons added to the seriousness of the economic distress; and again there was the hasty departure of debtors from the island. The shortage of labor which had accompanied the crises at the beginning of the century was lacking, for since 1712 the annual importation of slaves exceeded 2,500 except in the depression years, 1720-23, and in 1730 Barbados was reported to be the only British sugar island adequately stocked with slaves.[124] Nor was the sugar production low, for the sugar exports to England were variously reported as 22,769 hogsheads [125] and 250,075 hundredweight [126] in 1730. Thus the price decline from 1728-33 was the primary cause of the distress, and the natural catastrophes from 1731 to 1739 made worse a bad situation.

The first of the natural catastrophes was the hurricane of August 13, 1731. This has been vividly described in a Representation of Barbadoes to the Board of Trade, August 27, 1731: [127]

... the inhabitants ... have had not only a great number of their Corn Fields, Plantain Walks, Fruit and Timber Trees blown down, broken or torn up by the Roots, and their Canes damaged, but their dwelling Houses, Wind mills, Boyling houses and other ... Substantial buildings, some of them wholly demolisht, and others overset, rent, uncovered or otherwise greatly demnified; ... The Consequences are still more grievous, for that there is not in this Island (nor has there been for some Years since that pernicious Trade between the Northern British

---

[122] *Cal. S. P., Col.*, 1722-23, pp. 188-89. The unseasonable weather included a hurricane of minor proportions (Oldmixon, *op. cit.*, II, 74).

[123] Pitman, *op. cit.*, p. 234.   [124] *Ibid.*, pp. 72-73.

[125] Schomburgk, *op. cit.*, p. 148.

[126] Pitman, *op. cit.*, p. 244. If it be assumed that the average hogshead contained eleven hundredweight at this time, the two figures are almost the same.

[127] Quoted in *ibid.*, p. 247*n*.

Colonies and the Foreign Sugar Colonies began) Lumber sufficient to
repair a tenth part of the Buildings damaged by this tempest . . . great
is the Number of poor Inhabitants who now have no place to lay their
heads in, and ly exposed to all the Injuries of the approaching rainy
Season for want of those Northern Supplies which our Neighbors the
French are plentifully furnished with . . . many of the poorer Inhabitants will be driven to quit the Island.

A drought followed in 1733–34, which was especially severe in
the south of the island, where some of the inhabitants were said
to have perished from famine.[128] The emigration which had started
after the hurricane, continued, even "the principal Planters daily
declining and deserting it." [129]

Meanwhile, the troubles of the sugar colonies were receiving
the attention of Parliament. After a bitter war of pamphlets between the northern colonies and the sugar colonies,[130] the Molasses Act of 1733 was passed. It levied a duty on foreign sugar
products imported into British colonies and provided for a draw-
back of the entire import duty of British sugar reëxported from
Great Britain. Unfortunately for the sugar islands, the Molasses
Act was never thoroughly enforced, and soon the colonies began
agitation for direct trade in sugar with European markets.

Meanwhile, Barbadians were doing what they could at home to
offset the reduced value of their exports.[131] Numerous patents
were granted for improvements in sugar cultivation and manufacture; [132] in 1738 an "Act to Encourage the Raising of Cattle and
Other Livestock" was passed, and soon after, the export of all
livestock and "Provisions planted and reaped here" was for-
bidden.[133]

[128] Schomburgk, *op. cit.*, p. 322.
[129] See authorities quoted in *ibid.*, p. 322; Pitman, *op. cit.*, pp. 92–93, 98, 247, 248, 372.
[130] See Pitman, *op. cit.*, pp. 246–63, 266–70.
[131] According to Pitman's graph of exports to England (*ibid.*, facing p. 98), the exports during this period never rose above £250,000 and averaged about half those of the preceding periods of prosperity (1713–17, 1723–27).
[132] *Acts of the Assembly Passed in the Island of Barbados, 1648–1718*, pp. 365, 403, 426, 427–28; also *Laws of Barbados* (London, 1764), pp. 357, 359, 373, 376, 377, 400, 504.
[133] *Ibid.*, pp. 407, 408.

The neighboring islands were evidently importing Barbadian clay and exporting clayed sugar, for in 1736 the assembly, after noting that Barbadian soils were "for the most part worn out" and could not compete with their more recently settled neighbors, placed an export duty of five shillings per pound on clay for claying sugar.[134]

While the agitation for direct trade was going on, no very good or very bad crops were noted until 1739 when the crops were "rather small." [135] The sugar crop declined to 13,948 hogsheads (average 1740–48) of fifteen hundredweight (209,220 hundredweight) [136] which may be attributed to further soil exhaustion, insufficient manuring (due to cattle shortage), or increased attention to provision crops, or possibly to all three.

In 1739, a new Sugar Act permitted direct trade with continental Europe; sugar prices recovered sharply, and a gradual upward trend in prices followed.[137] The War of the Austrian Succession (1739–48), may have discouraged the development of direct trade with the continent. The privileges of the Sugar Act were rarely used, only five vessels taking advantage of it from 1739 to 1753, but its potentialities kept up prices in British markets.[138]

1740–48, ANOTHER PERIOD OF WARFARE

The period 1740–48 greatly resembled the period during the War of the Spanish Succession: there were the same difficulties in trade, the same prevalence of smuggling, the same emigration of planters, and the same irregular crops, due not to the war, but to "the weather which caused yearly fluctuations in the size of the crops." [139]

Freights from Barbados to London jumped at the outbreak of the war from about 3s. 6d. per hundredweight to 7s. 6d. or 8s., and insurance jumped from 7 percent to 25 percent.[140] Similar increases applied to trade with New England, which found it

134 *Ibid.*, p. 396.
135 Pares, *op. cit.*, p. 513.
136 Schomburgk, *op. cit.*, p. 149.
137 Pitman, *op. cit.*, pp. 182, 134, 186.
138 *Ibid.*, pp. 184–86.
139 Pares, *op. cit.*, p. 473.
140 *Ibid.*, pp. 495, 498, 500.

easier to trade with its supposed enemy, the French West Indies, than with Barbados.[141]

Uncertain crops and uncertain connections with British markets combined to bring about the last *large* elimination of the less efficient and less wealthy planters. Oldmixon notes that the insurance was so high that many planters "run their own Risk and some of them have lost ten thousand Pound in a Year too by the Venture." [142] Uneven prices and crops also contributed to the elimination: 1741 produced a large crop, but prices were declining; [143] in 1744 there was a very small crop, prices were only fair, the exports were the lowest in value for nearly a half century,[144] and considerable emigration was noted.[145] Prices improved in 1745; but lower prices combined with a "rather small" crop brought further emigration in 1746.[146] Altogether, the white population declined 2,551 during the war [147] and reached a figure of about fifteen thousand which, with but small gains and losses, was maintained without much immigration or emigration until about 1891. The planter aristocracy was now established, although not on so haughty a scale as in Jamaica.[148] There were also the poor whites and the slaves. The number of Negro slaves was increased by heavy importations until it reached 68,548 in 1773 and then was maintained at around 60,000 until a natural increase began with the abolition of the slave trade.[149]

[141] Pitman, *op. cit.*, pp. 285–86.   [142] Oldmixon, *op. cit.*, II, 166.
[143] Pares, *op. cit.*, p. 513; Pitman, *op. cit.*, pp. 134, 186, graph facing p. 98.
[144] *Ibid.*   [145] Pitman, *op. cit.*, pp. 94–96.
[146] Pares, *op. cit.*, p. 476.   [147] *Ibid.*, p. 513.
[148] "Barbados . . . escaped to a marked degree the evils of capitalistic exploitation. Thus, in 1765, there were nearly 4,000 proprietors in the island while at the same time St. James Parish, Jamaica, of almost the same size, was divided among but 132." Lowell Joseph Ragatz, *The Fall of the Planter Class in the British Caribbean, 1763–1833*, p. 4n.
[149] Schomburgk, *op. cit.*, p. 86; Pitman, *op. cit.*, p. 372.

CHAPTER V

Barbados under the Planter Aristocracy, 1748–1833

THE RECURRING crises which have been so conspicuous in our account did not cease with the elimination of the small planter. They were, however, less serious in their effects, partly because the large planter could better withstand the crises and partly because sugar prices remained high until after the Napoleonic Wars. Before proceeding with the historical account, it seems advisable to describe Barbados and its planter aristocracy as they were about 1750.[1]

BARBADOS ABOUT 1750

By this time, the island was almost fully occupied. The primeval forest remained only in a few places—most of them inaccessible. The bulk of the arable land was in sugar or in catch crops. However, the drier parts of the island, especially northern St. Lucy and eastern St. Philip, were "entirely planted with Coren." [2] Some cotton and ginger were planted in the drier areas. It was also reported that:

The whole island is cultivated by the Inhabitants in some manner or other, except such parts as are worn out and Improverished, that the Labour of Manuring the same would not be recompensed, of wch sort there are several thousand Acres, part whereof the Owners of the Sugar Work Plantations use as Pasture for the large Quantities of Cattle they

---

[1] It is fairly easy to get a picture of life in Barbados at this time because of the full contemporary accounts, especially: John Oldmixon, *The British Empire in America*, II, 97–171; Griffith Hughes, *Natural History of Barbados; Caribbeana*, mostly reprints from Barbadian newspapers and letters of the preceding decade; William Mayo, *A New and Exact Map of the Island of Barbados;* William Hillary, *Observations of the Changes of the Air and the Concomitant Epidemical Diseases in the Island of Barbados.*

[2] Oldmixon, *op. cit.*, II, 116.

are obliged to keep for the Manure even of their best Lands and for carrying their Effects to Markett.[3]

Cattle mills apparently were obsolete; the main use of cattle seems to have been for pen manure. The system of cultivation was that described by Edwards,[4] which did not differ much from that described by Thomas in 1689 (pages 79–81) and which was followed with but minor changes until Emancipation. Orchards and gardens were rare and

. . . they are at very little Labour to cultivate any Thing besides Sugar-Canes, and the Commodities that are fit for a home Market.[5]

Some ground provisions were grown, but they were mostly for the slaves. The planters seemed to depend on England and the northern colonies for a large proportion of their food. Local supplies of fresh meat, fish, poultry, fresh fruits, and milk were used by the planters at their tables, while flour and breadstuffs, smoked and salted meat and fish, pickles, malt liquors, and the like were imported. The wealthier planters even used imported French brandy instead of rum in their punches.

The highway system was fairly complete, and the main roads were the same as today except for certain roads which cross the gullies. Most of the roads were paved with broken coral stones and were passable for carts and carriages (instead of only for the horses and pack animals used earlier). Coastwise boats carried some of the produce to market, especially when wet roads or lack of cattle made overland transport difficult.

The island was well defended by forts, lines, and parapets along the leeward coast, and elsewhere for the most part by natural barriers. Guns were mounted at the few landing places along the windward coast, and laws prohibited the making of new landing places by the removal of rocks along the shore.

Bridgetown was a city of "1200 Houses, built of Stone, the

[3] Governor Thomas Robinson to the Board of Trade, February 20, 1747, Colonial Office 28: *Barbadoes, Original Correspondence with the Board of Trade*, 27, BG 57.

[4] Bryan Edwards, *The History, Civil and Commercial, of the British Colonies in the West Indies*, III, 17–68.

[5] Oldmixon, *op. cit.*, II, 117.

Windows glazed, many of them sashed; the Streets broad, the Houses high and the Rents dear." [6] It was equipped with wharfs and quays and defended by several forts. The swamp, which had made the city so unhealthy at the end of the seventeenth century, had been drained, but the river, which in the early days of the colony permitted sloops to go about a mile into the country, was choked by mud brought down by the freshets which occasionally flooded the town.

The private Buildings are not so stately as one would expect from the Riches of the Planters. There are many high Houses, and some low ones; for such as built immediately after the Great Storm of 1676 were so apprehensive of another, that they lowered their Buildings; but those who have built since them, not having those Apprehensions, have raised their Houses to three and four Stories high, and the Rooms are as lofty as in England. Hung Rooms are very scarce here; for the Walls are so damp, occasioned by the Moistness of the Air that the Hangings would soon rot. The Planters study Convenience more than Magnificence in their Buildings, which are generally neat, and fit for the Habitations of Gentlemen. . . . Every Dwelling-house, and other Outhousing, looks like a handsome Town, most being new built with Stone, and covered with Pantile or Slate, brought hither in the Ballasts of Ships, as is also Sea-Coal for Forges; and the Freight being by that Means made cheap, there is plenty enough of those Necessaries. [7]

The Master Merchants, and Planters, live each like little Sovereigns in their Plantations; they have their Servants of their Household, and those of the Field; their Tables are spread every Day with Variety of nice Dishes, and their Attendants are more numerous than many of the Nobility's in *England;* their Equipages are rich, their Liveries fine, their Coaches and Horses answerable; their Chairs, Chaises, and all the Conveniences for their travelling, magnificent.

The most wealthy of them, besides this Land-train, have their Pleasure-Boats, to make the *Tour* of the Island in, and Sloops to convey their Goods to and from the *Bridge*.

Their Dress, and that of their Ladies, is fashionable and courtly; and being generally bred at *London*, their Behaviour is genteel and polite; in which they have the Advantage of most of our Country Gentlemen, who living at great Distances from London, frequent the World very little; and from conversing always with their Dogs; Horses, and rude Peasants, acquire an Air suitable to their Society. The Gentlemen of

---

[6] John Oldmixon, *The British Empire in America,* II, 98.   [7] Ibid. pp. 105, 128.

Barbados are civil, generous, hospitable, and very sociable. . . . But this Hospitality is now almost lost there, the Gentlemen learning in *England* to keep their good Things to themselves, and to part with them very sparingly; Yet some there are, whose Houses are still free to Strangers, and who receive all with a cheerful Look, and open Heart.[8]

The tendency to ape England had its undesirable aspects; Dr. Hillary noted that the clothes were much too heavy for the climate, and that English amusements were unsuitable. He remarked that dancing was "much too violent an Exercise in this hot climate and many do greatly injure their Health by it, and I have known it fatal to some." [9] Better suited to the climate were games of cards which, as was perhaps natural among men whose business was such a gamble, were accompanied by gambling for very high stakes. This gambling so upset business and social life that several laws were passed to regulate it.[10] There was considerable pretense at culture, as is reflected in the verse and essays printed in the *Barbadoes Gazette*,[11] but much of it seems a very poor imitation of English models.

Life in the tropics in the eighteenth century had made serious inroads on the constitution and character of English people in Barbados.[12]

concludes Pitman. An observant traveler at the end of the eighteenth century agrees with this estimate:

. . . from the meagre and sunken appearance of the native yeomanry and citizens, their sunken eyes, relaxed countenances, and languid motions, I felt always on beholding them that the climate was irreconcilable with the constitution of their race. I am afraid also from the mean and disingenuous behavior of some of the inferior white inhabitants of the town, that the climate, and perhaps their association with the blacks have not a little relaxed in them the strength and integrity of the British Moral character.[13]

---

[8] *Ibid.*, p. 127.   [9] Hillary, *op. cit.*, p. xi.

[10] Richard Hall, *Acts of Barbados* (London, 1764), No. 160 (1729), No. 186 (1744).

[11] *Caribbeana* (London, 1741). These volumes of reprints were published to convince the English people of the English culture in Barbados and thus evoke sympathy for favorable legislation.

[12] Frank W. Pitman, *The Development of the British West Indies, 1700–1763*, p. 13.

[13] Daniel McKinnen, *A Tour through the British West Indies in the Years 1802 and 1803*, pp. 30–31.

Although "Britons are usually seized by fever," Dr. Hillary considered the island healthy, for "some have died here lately who were above a hundred years old." [14] Unhealthy spells were seasonal, and Hillary observed that they varied with the weather.[15] Dr. Hillary also noted that yellow fever occurred at all seasons but was "somewhat aggravated by the hot season." [16] As to dysentery, he noted:

If the months of May, June, July, and August were very hot and dry and the following months of September, October, November were accompanied with much rain and if the intermediate days between the rainy days were very hot, dysenteries were very frequent.[17]

The life of the Negroes was in a transition period.

John Braithwaite, proprietor of estates in Barbados and agent for the island, stated that prior to about 1768 the treatment of slaves was marked by much more cruelty than since that date. The wanton killing of a slave in Barbados remained nevertheless, by law of August 8, 1788, punishable by a fine of £15 only. It was not uncommon, he said, for slaves to suffer for food when corn [breadstuff] was high or a sugar crop failed. Industrious Negroes, of course, raised some provisions, hogs, and poultry about their own huts or on allotments. Even so, he thought a slave was as well off as a free Negro and better than an English laborer with a family. The usual allowance of a waistcoat, Osnaburg breeches, and a cotton or woolen vest left the slave underclothed. The annual expense of supporting a slave was computed by some at £4, or two day's labor out of six. Many slaves were let out to hire. The only instance of task work that Braithwaite was aware of was where hired slaves were paid by the acre for holing; for this their owners were paid £3 or £3 10s. currency per acre; they were fed by the person who hired them; working tools were supplied by the slave's owner. The Negroes had to themselves Sundays, holidays, the day after Christmas or "boxing day" in England, and Good Friday; other authorities included Saturday afternoon. Slaves usually worked "from sun to sun," allowing for breakfast and two hours at noon. After six o'clock they were at liberty. In sickness they were given great care.[18]

The slaves lived in small huts of which the older ones were made of sticks, mud, and thatch; the newer, of boards with shin-

---

[14] Hillary, *op. cit.*, p. ii.   [15] *Ibid.*, pp. 15–48, *passim.*
[16] *Ibid.*, p. 108.   [17] *Ibid.*, p. 146.
[18] Frank W. Pitman, *Journal of Negro History*, XI (1926), 624–25.

gled roofs. Usually they were separated at least a short distance from each other (to prevent fires from spreading), and the land around the hut was the personal garden of the hut-dweller. Often the slaves raised surplus provisions and livestock on this land and sold them through their masters for extra clothing and luxuries.

Thus by 1750 Barbadian life, both among the planters and the slaves, had lost most of that pioneer plainness which characterized it a century earlier.

GENERAL TRENDS

The preceding period (1652-1748) was characterized by the elimination of the inefficient, by waves of emigration, and by the crystallization of the pattern of Barbadian society. The period now to be considered (1749-1833) is characterized by increasing efficiency in agricultural techniques, by a trend toward greater self-sufficiency, by a humanization of the sugar-slave economy, and by a decrease in the political power of the planter aristocracy. As in the preceding period, these changes were hastened by, and, in part, resulted from a series of crises, caused by natural, political, and economic forces. Among these forces were wars, the agitation against slavery, changing duties on sugar prices, hurricanes, droughts, and pests. As the influence of these forces on Barbadian society was exerted largely in combinations, we shall proceed to a chronological consideration of their combined effects without separate consideration of each.

1748-65, A PERIOD OF MODERATE PROSPERITY

From 1748 to 1765 were years of moderate prosperity with the usual fluctuations due to favorable or droughty years.[19] The trade with Spanish America was resumed, and the money received from it was drained away by payments for provisions from New Eng-

[19] Dr. Hillary kept a careful record of the weather in Barbados from June, 1752, through 1757. The first rainfall statistics for Barbados are among his data and show that 1752 was wet, 1753 droughty (38 inches), 1754 wet (87 inches), 1755 average (57 inches), 1756 droughty (41 inches), and 1757 dry.

land.[20] The Seven Years' War was, at first, unfavorable to Barbados because of the increased freights and insurance on Barbadian sugars, and because of the increased illegal and traitorous trade of the northern colonies with the French West Indies.[21] Expeditions against the French West Indies, and French military and naval defeats, removed these troubles; but these favorable factors were partly offset by taxation to pay for the expedition and by reduced sugar prices due to sugar from captured colonies entering the British market. However, heavy crops from 1761 to 1765 resulted in extensive exports during these years, and Barbados was generally prosperous.

At the end of the Seven Years' War, a dispute arose between the sugar colonies and the rest of the Empire as to the disposition of the conquered French colonies. Since 1740 the price of sugar had been relatively high; thus the acquisition of more sugar lands seemed to the British consumer to be an easy way of increasing the sugar supply and reducing sugar prices. On the other hand, the British planters felt that they could not compete with the newer soils of the French islands. They were supported by Franklin and other northern colonists who felt that Canada was a logical place for British expansion. The sugar interests were successful in the Peace of Paris, and "through it the planting interest became triumphant." [22] The power of the planters was reflected by the number of seats held by absentee landlords in the House of Commons. This control enabled them to secure the passage of the Sugar Act of 1764 which strengthened the provisions of the Molasses Act of 1733.

1765–88, A PERIOD OF STRESS

The influence of the planter class was unable to prevent the American Revolution or to cope with a series of natural calamities which coincided with it; hence the following period (1765–88) is

[20] Frank W. Pitman, *The Development of the British West Indies, 1700–1763*, p. 152.

[21] *Ibid.*, pp. 318–33.

[22] *Ibid.*, p. 360. For a discussion of the whole argument preceding the Peace of Paris, see pp. 334–60.

one of declining trade accompanied by attempts at greater self-sufficiency to offset the loss of supplies from the northern colonies. The calamities started with an increase of the rat pest as early as 1748.[23] Much more serious was the plague of sugar ants which occurred about 1760, and which has been attributed to several causes. The most probable explanation is that the ants came in with loads of earth brought from Guiana or Tobago to fertilize the exhausted soil of Barbados.[24]

In 1766, a law was passed permitting creditors to seize the slaves of debtors and to sell these slaves or export them. This law was bitterly attacked by Poyer, who lived in Barbados through this period. He summed up the troubles of the island thus:

> During the American War, when, added to the evils incident to a state of hostility, the hopes of the industrious planter were frequently frustrated by a series of natural calamities, the fairest portions of the island were desolated and sacrificed to an unwise and iniquitous policy. Afflicted by continued drought, and visited by tribes of vermin, more destructive than the locusts and caterpillars of old, Barbados was then reduced to a state of comparative poverty; her soil and her negroes had sunk fifty per cent below their original value. A total failure of crops, instead of exciting commiseration, sharpened the avidity of the rapacious; and the wretched slaves of the unfortunate debtor were dragged in crowds to market, and thence transported to cultivate and enrich by their labor those colonies which, at the conclusion of the war, passed into the hands of our enemies.[25]

Fortunately, at this point a chart (Figure 10) can be offered which gives a clearer idea of the ups-and-downs of the Barbadian planter than has hitherto been possible. The steady decline in the

[23] "Whereas great damage having been done by the increase of rats in this land, . . ." (*Laws of Barbados*, Act of April 26, 1748.)

[24] Sir Robert H. Schomburgk, *The History of Barbados*, p. 643, states "this insect had been brought to Barbados from Tobago in some mould"; on p. 166, Schomburgk states that rich soil was imported from Guiana, but that "ants committed such ravages in the vessel that the attempt was never repeated." According to *Sugar, a Handbook for Planters and Refiners*, pp. 86–87, this type of ant was introduced into Jamaica from Cuba by Thomas Raffles in 1762. The ant attacked the rats as its sponsor had expected but also attacked domestic animals as well (as it did in Barbados—see Schomburgk, p. 642). It seems not unlikely that the ant may have been carried from Jamaica to Barbados, since Jamaica ships commonly called at Barbados.

[25] John Poyer, *The History of Barbados* (London, 1808), pp. 334–35.

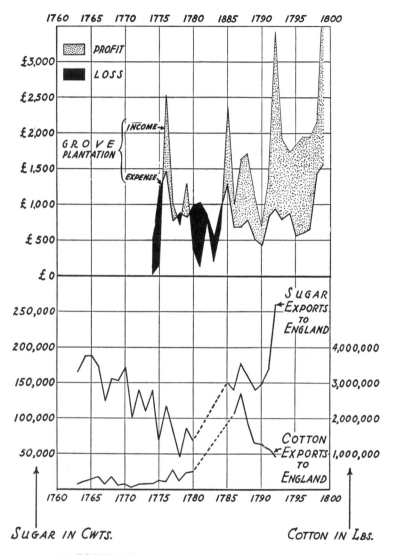

10. ECONOMIC CONDITIONS IN BARBADOS, 1763–98

Sources: The profit and loss statistics for Grove plantation in the highlands of
St. George, an area of moderate rainfall, are from the *Journal of the Barbados
Museum and Historical Society*, III (1936), 90. The sugar and cotton exports
are from Lowell Joseph Ragatz, *Statistics for the Study of British Caribbean
History, 1763–1833* (London, 1927), p. 14; and from Bryan Edwards, *The
History, Civil and Commercial, of the British Colonies in the West Indies*
(Philadelphia, 1806), Vol. I, Appendix, *passim*.

sugar export from 1763 to 1780, probably largely due to the sugar ant, is evident. During the latter part of this period, the great increase in cotton production suggests that cotton was displacing sugar in some of the drier areas, probably in response to the increased demand for cotton in England. The effects of drought, the hurricane of 1780, and fluctuating prices both of sugar and supplies are obvious.

The importance of the Barbados-New England trade has been often stressed throughout the preceding chapters. At first the consequences of its discontinuance were small, for both the drought of 1774 and the expectation of trouble in the northern colonies had led to an unusual stocking-up of the Barbadian warehouses. By the end of 1776 the surplus was exhausted; flour prices rose from 15s. to 30s. 6d. per hundredweight; Indian corn, from 3s. to 10 to 13s. per bushel; and other supplies went up in similar proportions. Impending famine, due in part to drought, was reported by Barbadian planters toward the end of 1777, and eight supply ships were sent from England to Barbados in 1778. Sugar prices had increased 50 percent in 1776 and 1777, but the planters could not take full advantage of them; they raised less sugar and more provisions. The restrictions on direct trade with Ireland were removed in 1778 in an attempt to remedy the situation, but Yankee privateers, venturing even into Speight's Bay, made external trade hazardous. The trade hazard was further increased by the proximity of the French fleet, which captured St. Vincent in June and Grenada in July, 1779.[26]

The uncertainties brought by the war were at their height when the hurricane of October 10, 1780, nearly destroyed the island. This horrible disaster had one virtue: it completely destroyed the sugar ants. Its effects can be plainly seen in the profit-and-loss account of the Grove estate, which was unable to show a profit until five years later. The damage to this estate was estimated at £2,448, which included an almost total loss of the crop, £1,430

[26] Based on Lowell Joseph Ragatz, *The Fall of the Planter Class in the British Caribbean, 1763–1833*, pp. 142–58; see also Schomburgk, *op. cit.*, pp. 334–38; and Poyer, *op. cit.*, pp. 363–404.

damage to the buildings, and the death of six slaves, two horses, twenty-nine cattle, and nineteen sheep. For the entire island the loss was estimated at £1,350,564, including the value of 2,033 slaves, 211 horses, and 6,606 cattle which were killed.[27] The number of free persons killed is uncertain and has been estimated at from 700 to 2,300.

The work of reconstruction was slow, and it must have been more than a decade before the damage was repaired. Most of the buildings, except near Speightstown had been leveled to the ground; and in 1786 it was reported that "the greater number of buildings were still lying in ruins, and none of the churches were rebuilt." [28] When the reconstruction finally began, tall steeples were omitted from the churches, and one- and two-story buildings became the rule on the plantations and, for a while, in Bridgetown. Mr. Senkhouse, the owner of the Grove estate, started the practice of building the Negro yard away from his house rather than on "the ground immediately surrounding it, which usually in Barbados was appropriated for the use of the Negroes, their houses forming a nuisance." [29] The new Negro yard was laid out in regular streets, and the plantation was further beautified by the planting of rows of trees. Mr. Senkhouse's innovations were at first scorned, but, later, copied.

Private citizens in Great Britain and Ireland raised funds for the relief of the hurricane-struck islands. Parliament appropriated £80,000 for the relief of Barbados, which was not received until 1782 and then was distributed only in part to the sufferers from the hurricane.[30] The generosity of the British Government was somewhat offset by an increase on the custom duties on sugar from 6s. 7 13/20 d. per hundredweight in 1779 to 12s. 3 2/5d., effective July 25, 1782.[31]

High prices for sugar, caused by the war and increased taxation, decreased the British demand for sugar and resulted in a sharp decline of prices at the end of the war to the prewar level.

[27] *Journal of the Barbados Museum and Historical Society*, II (1935), 206. For full accounts of the hurricane, see Schomburgk, *op. cit.*, pp. 47–50.

[28] Schomburgk, *op. cit.*, pp. 47, 50.   [29] *Journal B.M.H.S.*, III, 14, 96.

[30] Poyer, *op. cit.*, pp. 522–25.   [31] Ragatz, *op. cit.*, p. 164.

Even more serious was the decreased demand for molasses and rum, for satisfactory and cheaper substitutes had been devised during the period of high prices.[32]

The economic position of Barbados at the end of the war (1783) was poor, and a number of the planters left the island rather than undertake to repair the damage done by the hurricane. A contributing factor was the high price of building materials: lumber, in 1784, sold for double or triple the prewar prices because of the cessation of legal trade with New England. British North America could not supply sufficient cattle, lumber, staves, or foodstuffs to cope with the West Indian demand.[33] Consequently, the West Indian prices remained high, while the planters argued for free trade with the United States, and secured partial relief through smuggling.

A small but significant shift in population occurred at the end of the American Revolution. Among the Barbadians who left the island was a General Payer who introduced Sea Island cotton (*Gossypium barbadense*) into Georgia and who is said to have been responsible for the growth of cotton planting in the United States.[34] On the other hand, Loyalist refugees from the United States emigrated to the West Indies, and "the healthy, leavening influence of this new element in planter society was felt throughout the British Caribbean."[35]

Meanwhile, other difficulties arose. The health of the island was poor, and the burials exceeded the births in every year reported from 1776 to 1803.[36] The slave population declined from 68,548 in 1773 to 57,434[37] in 1783. Only part of this decline can be attributed to the hurricane; the bulk of the decline was due to smallpox, yellow fever, and failure to "keep up the stock" through slave importations.[38] Even more striking was the mortality of the white regiments stationed at Barbados, which averaged 185 per 1,000

[32] *Ibid.*, pp. 168–72.   [33] *Ibid.*, pp. 186–87.
[34] Massachusetts Historical Society, Proceedings, III (1857), 228.
[35] Ragatz, *op. cit.*, p. 199.   [36] Pitman, *op. cit.*, p. 385.
[37] Schomburgk, *op. cit.*, p. 86; Pitman, *op. cit.*, p. 373.
[38] *Journal B.M.H.S.*, III, 4; Schomburgk, *op. cit.*, pp. 77–78; Sir Rupert W. Boyce, *Health Progress and Administration in the West Indies*, pp. 11–15.

from 1796–1805, including a maximum rate of 413 per 1,000 in 1796. The failure of the British army to change its regulations to suit tropical conditions combined with tropical fevers and excessive use of cheap rum brought about this frightful mortality.[39] On several occasions, the British Government urged the organization of slave regiments to replace the bulk of the white troops, but the planters, fearing that Barbados might become a second Santo Domingo, steadily and successfully opposed such plans.[40]

A transient development was the shift to cotton cultivation which started about 1775 and which apparently was greatest while the island was recovering from the hurricane of 1780. Although the only certain reason for the shift was the demand of the British textile industry for more raw materials,[41] local evidence suggests that upset conditions following the hurricane of 1780 (prolonged by the mild hurricane of September 2, 1786,[42] favored the increased emphasis on cotton. Cotton had a number of advantages over sugar for planters who were sorely in need of capital: it yielded a return much sooner after planting; it did not require expensive machinery to prepare it for market; it was not so perishable; and it made possible the raising of ground provisions on all the arable land during some part of the year. Barbadians after 1780 could take advantage of each of these points, for most of the sugar factories had been destroyed, a quick cash crop was needed to get supplies to rebuild them, provisions from abroad were costly, and transportation was difficult because of the almost impassable condition of the Barbadian roads and the uncertainties of sailings for England. Among the signs of increased interest in cotton were two patents: one issued in 1779 on a windmill for

[39] Ragatz, *op. cit.*, pp. 13, 31–32. The scarlet woollen uniforms, poorly ventilated quarters, and rations consisting mostly of salt meat and biscuit are examples of the failure of the army to adjust its regime to the tropics.

[40] Schomburgk, *op. cit.*, pp. 353–55.

[41] Ragatz, *op. cit.*, p. 201. Ragatz's assertion on the same page that Barbados did not increase its cotton production, is contrary to the statistics from Edwards used in Figure 10 (p. 102).

[42] Schomburgk, *op. cit.*, p. 50. Schomburgk states that "every vessel in the Bay was driven on shore, great damage was done to the houses and crops, and several persons were killed."

ginning cotton; another, in 1786, on a device for removing seeds.[43]

The heavy rains which accompany most Barbadian hurricanes had wrought havoc with the roads of Barbados. The coral roads, although quite satisfactory under normal conditions, form a slippery mud when there is excessive rain. In the Scotland district, landslips occurred culminating in a great slip, extending over a mile, which on October 11, 1785, destroyed the Walcott plantation and the neighboring roads. This and other results of the weather made the roads "almost impassable" and "a subject of general complaint." [44] A bill was enacted in 1787 for the establishment of turnpikes. Poyer notes that "turnpikes were established and the roads were effectually repaired." [45] Meanwhile, the poor roads were decentralizing the trade which had become almost the monopoly of Bridgetown. In 1789, provision was made for exports of cotton through Speightstown, Holetown, Bridgetown, and Oistin's Town,[46] and in 1792 further provision was made for export from the Crane, St. Philip.[47] As Poyer notes, the "spirit which animated the measure [the turnpike act] soon evaporated; it was neglected and forgotten." [48] The roads declined further during the heavy rains of November, 1795, which flooded Bridgetown and several plantations, destroyed the bridges, and washed out the roads so that they were "entirely broken up and became impassable." [49] Although the roads were then repaired by the parish authorities, until 1845 "certain parts of the public roads remained in a state which rendered them scarcely passable, and the communication with the distant parishes was in consequence sometimes entirely checked." [50]

1789-1815, A QUARTER CENTURY OF WARS AND UNCERTAIN TRADE

The period 1789 to 1815 was influenced largely by political and military events in Europe. The price of sugar started upward with

[43] Ragatz, *op. cit.*, p. 65.
[44] Schomburgk, *op. cit.*, pp. 67–68, 184; Poyer, *op. cit.*, pp. 569–71.
[45] Poyer, *op. cit.*, p. 574.
[46] *The Public Acts in Force Passed by the Legislature of Barbados, 1762–1800,* pp. 283, 315.
[47] *Ibid.*, pp. 283, 315.   [48] Poyer, *op. cit.*, p. 574.   [49] Schomburgk, *op. cit.*, p. 50.
[50] *Ibid.*, p. 184; *The Public Acts in Force . . .* (1799), p. 360.

the outbreak of the French Revolution and the revolts in the French sugar colony of Santo Domingo.[51] At the same time, Barbadian planters decreased their cotton production and increased their cane plantings.[52] Continuous profits are shown by the Grove estate until 1800, and West Indian sugar prices were described as "improving" from 1789 to 1793 and "high" from 1794 to 1799.[53] Prosperity was helped by considerable free trade with the United States during the wars with France. This trade was not fully opened (except in British vessels) until 1806, but West Indian governors were authorized to allow trade with American vessels in times of emergency. These emergencies seemed to occur with great regularity throughout the war—probably every time an American ship had some cargo that the islands wanted.[54]

A large part of the profits of the sugar industry during the period may have been due to the new and better varieties of cane which replaced the Creole cane sometime between 1790 and 1803. Two principal varieties were introduced: the Otaheite (from Tahiti) and a closely related cane, the Bourbon, from the French island of Bourbon (Indian Ocean). The two canes were so much alike that many could not distinguish them. Their advantages were:

> They are much larger than the Brazilian, the joints of some measuring eight or nine inches long, and six in circumference. They are ripe enough to grind at the age of 10 months; they appear to stand the dry weather better, and are not so liable to be attacked by that destructive insect, the borer. Indeed, these are considered so much superior to the old canes, that their adoption has nearly banished the original Brazilian plant from our Islands.[55]

The new canes had a few disadvantages; they exhausted the soil more rapidly and did not ratoon so well as the Creole canes.

[51] For prices, see Ragatz, *op. cit.*, pp. 167, 350 (charts).

[52] Figure 10, p. 102. Note that it takes two years to replace cotton with cane and get a sugar crop.

[53] *Report from the Committee on the Commercial State of the West India Colonies,* p. 66.

[54] For an interesting and full discussion, see Ragatz, *op. cit.*, pp. 229–36, also 298–304.

[55] George R. Porter, *The Nature and Properties of the Sugar Cane,* pp. 23–24.

They also produced bumper crops which reduced the prices in London markets. Ragatz considers that "in the long run, then, the introduction of the new canes proved catastrophic." [56] This statement does not seem economically or geographically justified, for if the new canes had not been introduced into Barbados, their sugars from the East Indies would have competed with Barbadian sugar in any case. However, it seems probable that the increased production in the West Indies did increase the severity of the price decline at the end of the century.

The new canes were but part of the widespread introduction of new plants into the West Indies which occurred during the eighteenth century, especially in its last decade. Aside from the canes, the breadfruit, introduced by Captain Bligh of *Bounty* fame, was the only plant of great importance to the Barbadian economy. Its importance lay in the possibility (only partially realized) that it would replace imported breadstuffs in the West Indian diet.[57]

The prosperous period terminated with a financial panic in Hamburg during the summer of 1799. Within six months, wholesale prices in London dropped from 68s. per hundredweight to 41s. Bumper crops in the West Indies and increasing imports of East Indian sugar kept the price down. A brief period of recovery in 1801 brought prices with limits of 58s. and 33s.; a brief boom at the end of the Napoleonic Wars brought quotations of 80 and 90s.; then prices sagged steadily to a low of 22s. at the end of 1831.[58]

The detailed reasons for the fluctuations in prices do not concern this study; the factors involved were interruptions in trade due to war, speculation, fluctuating sugar supplies from the East Indies, the West Indies, and captured French and Spanish possessions elsewhere. The uncertainties of market and nature were increased by the precariousness of political relations with the United States and France. Thus it is not surprising that the victory of

[56] Ragatz, *op. cit.*, p. 80, also p. 79.
[57] *Ibid.*, pp. 71–79. For a complete statement of the available information on the date of introduction of various exotic plants into Barbados, see F. Hardy, "Some Aspects of the Flora of Barbados," *Agricultural Journal*, II, 33–54.
[58] Ragatz, *op. cit.*, pp. 340–41.

Nelson at Trafalgar was hailed by Barbadians, for it made certain that their goods would reach the European market..No such certainty was attained in relations with the United States; at first the American trade was interfered with by British orders to enforce the Navigation Acts; next, by the American Embargo and Nonintercourse Acts; and finally by the outbreak of the War of 1812, which exposed Barbadian commerce to frequent and effective attacks by American privateers.[59]

These trade uncertainties started a trend toward self-sufficiency which was accentuated by the growing strength of the English Abolition Movement. The abolition of the slave trade (May, 1807) forced the island to breed its own labor supply. This, and the desire to avoid any mistreatment which would strengthen the Abolition Movement, improved the living conditions of the slave population. In 1805, the killing of a slave was reclassified as murder by an act of the Barbadian Legislature, and the first indictment for slave murder occurred in the same year.[60] This legislation was but a part of the tendency in Barbados to improve the conditions of the slaves which had been noticeable for a half century.[61] From Ligon down to the Emancipation, accounts of kind treatment of slaves occur, as well as occasional accounts of cruelties inflicted by planters who were either sadistic or fearful of slave revolts. The increasing difficulty in getting new slaves after about 1775 made it profitable as well as charitable to look after the welfare of the Negroes. The increase in the Negro population throughout the nineteenth century proved what had long been argued: that with good treatment Barbados could maintain its labor supply without importations.

The trend toward greater self-sufficiency is shown indirectly by the downward trend of Barbadian sugar and cotton production

[59] An interesting account of this period from the Barbadian point of view is in Schomburgk, *op. cit.*, pp. 357–92. For more detailed evidence from a broader viewpoint, see Ragatz, *op. cit.*, pp. 286–330.

[60] Schomburgk, *op. cit.*, p. 370. The story of the Abolition Movement as it affects the West Indies is given in detail in Ragatz, *op. cit.*, pp. 239–85, 384–457.

[61] See quotation on p. 98; also Oldmixon, *op. cit.*, II, 131, for an opinion on the treatment of slaves in the first half of the eighteenth century.

from 1805 to the end of the Napoleonic Wars. In 1806 a great scarcity of provisions was reported, and bounties were offered to increase the amount of provisions brought to the island.[62] In August, 1807, the president of the council urged "the prudence of increasing the cultivation of provisions." [63] In 1808 the legislature, after noting the increased cultivation of provisions, stated (in reply to the president's address of November 1, 1808):

The industrious precautions of our planters, through the blessing of divine Providence, has set at defiance the vain attempt of America by her impolitic embargo to wound through our sides that parent state which we trust will ever be able to withstand all attacks made upon her.[64]

The need for greater self-sufficiency aroused an interest in better methods of cultivation. The first agricultural society was formed in 1812,[65] and devoted much of its attention to crop rotation and land utilization on various estates. One of the first estates examined had ninety-six acres in canes, sixty-eight acres in Guinea corn, twenty-five acres in pasture and forage, and eighteen acres (aside from catch crops) in provisions. The society was of the opinion that there was "too large a proportion of canes." [66] Fifty years earlier or later, such a proportion of canes would have been thought very small. All this demonstrates "the increased cultivation of provisions . . . a measure that is of great advantage" which Governor Leith remarked in 1815.[67]

The end of the Napoleonic Wars resulted in an increased production of sugar (Figure 2). It seems probable from Davy's account of the agricultural societies that some of this increase was the result of better methods rather than of any great decrease in the acreage in provisions. The plow, which had been tried without favorable results about 1785,[68] was tried again along with the harrow.

---

[62] Schomburgk, *op. cit.,* p. 150.   [63] *Ibid.,* pp. 367, 370.
[64] *Ibid.,* p. 373.
[65] John Davy, *The West Indies before and since Slave Emancipation,* p. 136n. On p. 130, Davy quotes a report of the society dated August 3, 1811.
[66] *Ibid.,* pp. 130–31.   [67] From a speech quoted in Schomburgk, *op. cit.,* p. 392.
[68] Ragatz, *op. cit.,* p. 58.

The success was marked and encouraging till the arrival of unpropitious seasons . . . commencing 1819–20. Then the plough fell into disuse, and the exclusive hoe was resumed . . . on the belief that it,—the plough—as much as the peculiarity of the weather was to blame for the short comings and scanty produce. . . . The use of the plough was not resumed till 1839–40, and that only very partially,—gradually increasing.[69]

The use of imported guano, careful spacing, and trashing are other techniques which are first mentioned about this period.

1815–34, THE DIFFICULT PRELUDE TO EMANCIPATION

The period from 1815 to 1834 was an unpleasant one for Barbadian planters, as was shown by evidence presented before a House of Commons committee.[70] Witnesses pointed out that the average price of sugar for 1831 (23s. 8d. per hundredweight) was 6d. below the average cost of production including freight. They attributed the decline in price to the competition of the East Indies, Cuba, Brazil, and new colonies brought into the British colonial system as the result of the Napoleonic Wars. The decrease in the tariff preference given the West Indian colonies and the exclusion of molasses from British distilleries were additional reasons for the planters' difficulties. It was further pointed out that to avoid high prices for imported provisions, two-thirds of the land of each estate were used for corn and other necessary articles for the Negroes. Partly as the result of provision crops and partly because of the heavy manuring, the sugar crop in Barbados was only four hundredweight per slave compared with eleven hundredweight in the newer colonies of Trinidad, St. Vincent, and Grenada. Finally, to show that the planters' position was becoming worse and that the 4½ per cent duty should be removed, the planters offered Table 12 as an exhibit.

While the "fall of the planter class" was in progress, the Negro was advancing in privileges, health, and numbers. The report of the Codrington estates for 1822 notes that

[69] Davy, *op. cit.*, pp. 413–14.
[70] *Sessional Papers, 1831–32*, XX, 4, 5, 6, 110, 179.

. . . there are now fifty-three more slaves on the estate than there were in the year 1815, though three mulattoes have purchased their liberty and no purchases been made.[71]

The working and living conditions on the better-managed estates seem to have been very pleasant.[72]

TABLE 12 [a]

CROP, PROFIT, AND TAXATION FOR A BARBADIAN ESTATE OF 453 ACRES
WITH 200 NEGROES AND 90 CATTLE

YEAR	CROP IN HOGSHEADS	NET PROFIT	4½ PERCENT DUTY	TAX PERCENTAGE
1827	60	£787	£61	8.00
1828	105	1,090	78	7.25
1829	81	298	45	15.00
1830	83	210	42	20.00

[a] *Sessional Papers, 1831–32,* XX, 180.

The events immediately preceding Emancipation were generally unfavorable to the Barbadian planters. The principal exception was the renewal of legal trade relations with the United States which took effect in October, 1830. Offsetting this important commercial advantage, were the declining credit of the West Indian planters due to the certainty of Emancipation, further declines in the prices of sugar and cotton, and, finally, the hurricane of 1831, commonly known as the Great Hurricane. The losses from this catastrophe were estimated at a minimum of £1,602,800 and 1,591 killed.

Perhaps the benefits of peace and normal trade relations are demonstrated by the rapidity of the Barbadian recovery. Although the hurricane was commonly agreed to have been more destructive than that of 1780, no period of low production followed. "Favoured by highly seasonable weather; the sugar-crops of 1832 to 1833 had surpassed their expectations." [73] Davy states a belief common in Barbados during the following decades:

[71] Quoted in Frederic Bayley, *Four Years' Residence in the West Indies, during the Years 1826, 7, 8, and 9,* p. 107.
[72] *Ibid.,* pp. 89–91.
[73] Schomburgk, *op. cit.,* p. 441.

Hurricanes are not purely evil in their consequences; there is reason to believe that they have often been beneficial. After some of them, especially the last which occurred in Barbados, the seasons were more favorable, vegetation more active; there was improvement in the health of the people, certain diseases even disappeared, benefits in the opinion of many, more than compensating for the instant losses sustained. . . .

. . . Since the last great hurricane there has been a decided improvement in the public health, and especially in that of the planters and their families, attributable it may be in the first instance to an immediate purifying effect, . . . but chiefly, afterwards, to an altered manner of living, more simple and less luxurious; to having better dwellings—the successors of the old ones swept away by the storm,—to extended cultivation, and to the increased use of carriages, with an extension and improvement of the roads, now in most parts of the island (excepting the Scotland district) good carriage roads, many of which before were little more than bridle paths or cart tracks.[74]

Many of these improvements were aided by hurricane-relief contributions of £50,000 from the British Government and of £14,210 from private citizens. Further help was given by the temporary lifting of custom duties after the hurricane and by the final abolition of the 4½ percent duty in 1838. Much more important was the compensation of £1,721,345 awarded by Parliament to the slaveholders for the loss of their property in slaves.[75]

A psychical change may also have contributed to the progress after the "twin disasters" of the hurricane and Emancipation.

What the hurricane did for the physical atmosphere of Barbados, emancipation effected for its moral and domestic atmosphere, it purified that in a remarkable manner, and to the matron ladies and their daughters, always exemplarily correct, was an incalculable comfort. Licentiousness, whatever it might have been before, was almost entirely banished from society: young men no longer exposed to the same temptations as before, acquired new ideas of correctness and purer tastes and habits, all of an elevating kind and favoring the development of the higher energies.[76]

Thus, contrary to the gloomy predictions of the opponents of Emancipation, Barbados was ready to enter a period of progress. The cost of raising sugar did not increase 19¾s. per hundred-

[74] Davy, *op. cit.*, pp. 63, 73–74.
[75] Schomburgk, *op. cit.*, pp. 438–42, 459–61.　　　[76] Davy, *op. cit.*, p. 74.

weight as was prophesied by experts; [77] the island was not de-populated of its white population; the sugar estates did not go out of cultivation; and the sugar production and trade of Barbados increased rather than declined. In Barbados, "the fall of the planter class" seems to have stopped soon after Emancipation. Contrary to the general conclusion of Ragatz that "Emancipation, bringing to an end the old order, completed the downfall of the planter class," [78] Emancipation seems to have been a spur which awoke Barbados to a new period of activity.

[77] *Sessional Papers, 1831–32,* Vol. XX. Also see the voluminous pamphlet litera-ture of the preceding decade.

[78] Ragatz, *op. cit.,* p. 457. The general conclusion of Ragatz is probably correct for Jamaica and some of the other islands which had different demographic and geographic conditions than Barbados.

CHAPTER VI

Barbados since Emancipation

ON AUGUST 1, 1834, slavery was ended in Barbados, and the slaves became the apprentices of their former masters. At first, the results were as favorable as the most enthusiastic abolitionists could have wished: crops were large; good feeling existed between apprentices and masters. The almost universal testimony of Barbadians was that abolition was a success from every point of view.[1]

However, after the first enthusiasm for freedom had subsided, dissatisfaction arose among both the masters and their apprentices. The latter

. . . had no right to dispose of their own labour or to select their own masters. Nor did the system prove satisfactory to the masters of the former slaves: it entailed a great expense upon the planter, without giving him a full return for his outlay, and never failed to produce strife and discontent between the master and labourer. The special magistrates appointed for hearing and adjusting complaints seldom decided to the satisfaction of either the labourer or his employer. . . . It was generally acknowledged . . . that the whole system was a signal failure.[2]

The disappointing results of the apprenticeship led to the granting of complete freedom on August 1, 1838, or two years earlier than originally provided. A fortnight later the 4½ percent duty was abolished and customs duties were instituted to provide revenue in its place. Thus a tax on the exports of the planters was replaced by a duty on imports of lumber, food, cloth, and the like which were purchased by both the planters and the former slaves. Meanwhile, the labor situation of the island was in a state of fer-

---

[1] See James A. Thome and J. H. Kimball, *Emancipation in the West Indies,* pp. 211–342; Joseph Sturge and Thomas Harvey, *The West Indies in 1837, passim.*
[2] Sir Robert H. Schomburgk, *The History of Barbados,* p. 477.

ment; many laborers moved to other estates either because of higher wages or to escape unpopular employers. Others were induced to emigrate to the less populous sugar colonies such as Trinidad and British Guiana.[3]

1838–43, A PERIOD OF READJUSTMENT

The unsettled conditions (1838–43), both of labor and of weather resulted in but half the usual output of sugar and also, probably, in a reduced crop of provisions. Schomburgk was of the opinion that although the drought

> . . . contributed greatly to this fearful decrease, . . . the chief cause of the deficiency was the relaxed labour of the peasantry, and the great injury which the cultivation and manufacture of sugar suffers by a want of continuous and regular labour.[4]

The emigrating laborers included the younger and more ambitious ones; those who remained behind were, for the most part, the very young, the very old, and the lazier element. Many of these were not able to care for themselves as well as their former masters had cared for them. The Archdeacon of Barbados collected statistics from the clergy and estimated that 541 laboring-class children died during the summer months of 1841, compared with an average of 185 for the same months during the three preceding years. The poor health of the children was attributed to nonsupport by fathers who had emigrated, and poor care of the children by their mothers. It seems probable that a shortage of ground provisions, and inability to purchase imported necessities may also have been important factors.[5]

The unstable conditions just described led to the development of the located-laborer system [6] which lasted until 1937 when it lost

---

[3] *Ibid.*, pp. 463–91.   [4] *Ibid.*, p. 151.   [5] *Ibid.* pp. 75, 491.

[6] In a debate on the abolition of the located-laborer system, Sir George Walton described it thus: "The plantation sets aside a couple of fields and the labourers are each allotted an acre or half an acre of land. They put their houses on it and the understanding is that they will give their labour to the plantation on which they reside when required. They also occupy this land at a lesser rent than the market value of the land—something like 30% less. . . . When their crop is ripe, they are assisted with the plantation carts to bring the canes to the mill. The plantation helps them with chemical manure; the plantation also helps them to re-

its legal status because many Barbadians thought it smacked of serfdom and slavery. The system had evolved naturally from the apprenticeship, for many of the apprentices were willing to stay on the estates if they could be given some sort of security, while the planters were glad to enter into a paternal, almost feudal, relationship with the laborers to get a monopoly on the labor supply.

The fall of the planter class and the concomitant decline in sugar production did not occur in Barbados as in Jamaica and most of the other islands. Undoubtedly, the dense population and the lack of free land made it easier for the planters to secure labor after the threat of emigration was met. Then again, the Negroes tended to raise sugar cane on their "spots," not only because it was a good cash crop, but also because it seemed a step toward becoming members of the planting class. Some bought land and built huts around Bridgetown, far enough from the crowded district to include some farm land but near enough to be able to obtain any transient jobs around the port.[7] The desire of the Negroes to buy land, to raise sugar, and to be near the Barbadian metropolis has persisted steadily ever since Emancipation.

Another important factor prevented the decline of sugar cultivation in Barbados, namely, the presence of a permanent, white population interested in sugar cultivation. Although many Barbadian estates were owned by residents of England, absentee landlordism was not so common as in Jamaica, and those Barbadian "attorneys"[8] who managed English-owned estates were competent planters who usually had estates of their own. These attorneys and the more progressive Barbadian planters formed a small but closely knit group organized into agricultural societies. Their leaders published the only periodical in the West Indies, *The Agricul-*

---

pair their houses and gives them very easy terms of payment. . . . The labourer has many kindnesses extended to him during the course of his work. He also has the first choice of the work offered on the plantation. In the slack season when very few labourers are employed on the plantation as at the present time, the crops being finished . . . , these located labourers have the great advantage of getting what little work there is." (*Barbados Official Gazette*, July 26, 1937, pp. 101–102.)

[7] W. L. Mathieson, *British Slave Emancipation*, p. 56.

[8] An "attorney" in Barbados is the agent of an absentee proprietor.

tural Reporter,[9] and, in general, tried experiments and new methods so far as the limited capital available permitted.

1844–53, A PERIOD OF INCREASING PRODUCTION

Sugar production was not only maintained, but was considerably increased. The previous record crop of about 27,600 large hogsheads was exceeded in 1837 and 1838, and new records were established in 1847 (33,111 hogsheads), in 1850 (35,302 hogsheads), in 1851 (38,731 hogsheads), in 1852 (48,611 hogsheads), and in 1858 (50,778 hogsheads).[10] Undoubtedly part of this increase was due to a greater acreage in canes,[11] but better cultivation was probably more important.

The details of cultivation are well described by Davy;[12] only the improvements introduced after Emancipation need be noted

[9] John Davy, *The West Indies before and since Slave Emancipation,* p. 532*n.* Davy notes that only 300 copies of this periodical were printed, of which only 235 were regularly sold: 183 in Barbados, forty-three elsewhere in the West Indies, and nine in England. The copies of the paper that I have examined are evidence that the limited circulation was not due to lack of merit. There were about five hundred sugar factories on the island (*Barbados Blue Book* [1850]), so that about one-third of the sugar estates were interested enough to pay $1.00 per year for the paper. As to the small number of subscribers in the other islands, as Davy remarks it "needs no comment to the reflecting mind."

[10] Schomburgk, *op. cit.,* p. 150; Botanic Station, Barbados, *Occasional Bulletin,* No. 8.

[11] The following statistics for the Claybury Estate, a 309-acre estate in the highlands of St. John, are probably typical of the better estates a few years after the abolition of the apprenticeship:
45 acres of plant canes to be reaped in 1842
47 acres of first ratoons to be reaped in 1842
40 acres of plant canes to be reaped in 1843
32 acres of Negro allotments
35 acres of Guinea corn for fodder
42 acres of sour grass pastures
10 acres of potatoes
58 acres of ravines, roads, buildings, Negro yards, and pasturage
Stock: 10 horses, 4 mules, 85 cattle, and 11 pigs
Labor: 82 field laborers, 4 superintendents, 2 watchmen, 13 grooms and storekeepers, 9 artificers, and 4 domestics
Other Negroes: 67 children too young to work and 14 old and infirm
Crop: Average in 1833–39, 140 hhds.; average in 1840 and 1841, 90 hhds.; expected in 1842, 110 hhds.
Source: Evidence of Mr. W. Sharpe, *Report from the Select Committee on the West Indian Colonies* (London, 1843), pp. 125–26.

[12] Davy, *op. cit.,* pp. 108–54.

here. These include the use of chemical and green manures, better weeding, better spacing, increased mulching, more careful timing of operations to fit the season, and better methods of manufacturing. Davy mentions one planter who

. . . obtained from 50 acres, 180 hogsheads of sugar, 112 more than he had previously procured from 100 acres cultivated with less care, the yield from them not exceeding 68 hogsheads. There was no marked difference in seasons.[13]

No better explanation of these increased yields can be given than the statement in *The Agricultural Reporter:* [14]

What then, and how great are our improvements? To begin with the field; ten years ago the system of farming, or jobbing out fields to the labourers to weed by the week was unknown; now it is universally practiced; ten years ago the first ploughing match had not come off; now there is scarcely an estate that will admit of their use, in which the plough, grubber, and horse hoe are not daily at work; and to these two improvements conjointly we owe the comparative steadiness of our labour market, the destruction of devil's grass, the beautiful thyme-bed appearance of our fields, and under providence the unprecedently large crops which have crowned our efforts. Let us pass to the mill; ten years ago there were not a dozen horizontal mills in the whole island, now it is hardly too much to say that there are as many in every parish, and more to follow every day. Next, look in at the boiling house; ten years ago there was scarcely a planter in Barbados who knew what a vacuum pan was, or had any idea of the possibility of evaporating cane juice at a lower temperature than that produced by a roaring fire under an open taiche; now there are four vacuum pans, besides the plant at the Refinery; Gadesden-pans innumerable, and other means and appliances which have been more partially adopted; above all, ten years ago we were unacquainted with those valuable adjuncts to the production of good sugar, Precipitators, and Centrifugal Dessicators; now they are coming so rapidly into fashion, that we shall not be surprised if the man who is unprovided with them next crop is accounted a very slow coach indeed.

As has been noted, Emancipation and the great hurricane were important impulses in starting these improvements; extra-insular conditions made it necessary that they be continued. Sugar and cotton had long been staple Barbadian products. The rise of the

13 Davy, *op. cit.*, p. 145.   14 *The Agricultural Reporter,* April, 1853.

American cotton belt had forced an abandonment of cotton. After Emancipation, increasing production of slave-grown, East Indian, and beet sugars was taking away from Barbados the sugar markets of Europe. The Barbadian situation became especially critical because the population had been increasing steadily since 1805; [15] thus it was becoming more and more difficult to get along without extensive food imports. Two things saved Barbados from bankruptcy: the rapid growth of the demand for sugar which generally kept pace with the increasing supply; and the ability of the Barbadian planter to improve his methods.

The danger to Barbados increased because the growing British industrial population was winning its fight for the removal of protective tariffs on foodstuffs. The Sugar Act of 1846 provided for a gradual reduction of the protective duties on colonial sugar. The rate on muscovado sugar, raised by free or slave labor, was reduced to twenty-one shillings per hundredweight and was to be reduced further by gradual stages until it reached the colonial rate of fourteen shillings on July 5, 1851.[16] A loud outcry resulted in Barbados,[17] but aside from temporary financial stress and a trend toward the more sparing use of labor, no harm seems to have resulted from the resulting decline in sugar prices. The Negroes probably suffered the greatest loss, for means of cutting down the labor bill during the slack season were discovered.

Meanwhile, the crisis pushed forward other improvements, for example, the substitution of steam engines for windmills. There was only one steam factory on the island in 1841, and there were "not over a dozen" in 1859.[18] The first record in the *Barbados Blue Book* (1890) shows that the number had increased to ninety-five. Since steam factories were estimated to produce 10 to 15 percent more sugar than the windmills,[19] this change must have been

[15] Total population: 1805, 77,130; 1812, 85,494; 1829, 103,007; 1844, 122,198; 1851, 135,939; and 1861, 152,275.

[16] W. P. Morrell, *British Colonial Policy in the Age of Peel and Russell*, p. 232.

[17] See Schomburgk, *op. cit.*, pp. 520-28; Davy, *op. cit.*, pp. 19-24, 543-50.

[18] W. G. Sewell, *The Ordeal of Free Labor in the British West Indies*, p. 59.

[19] *Ibid.*, p. 59; according to *Sugar, a Handbook for Planters and Refiners*, p. 163, windmills extracted from 50 to 56.4 percent of the sugar compared with 61.8 percent obtained by steam power.

very beneficial to those planters who could raise the capital for
the new factories.

The decades from 1854 to 1884 were, on the whole, an uneventful era, compared with the preceding periods. The outstanding
event was the cholera epidemic in 1854 which resulted in 20,727
deaths, "chiefly colored, black, and Scotland district whites"; [20]
but the upward surge of black population was so great that the
population increased from 135,939 in 1851 to 152,275 in 1861 in
spite of the plague. This increase continued until 1891 (or possibly later; no census was taken between 1891 and 1911), but at a
slower rate.

Some emigration had been noted since the end of the apprenticeship (see page 117), but large-scale colored and Negro emigration was first noted by Governor Rawson, who estimated that 20,-
408 Barbadians had emigrated during 1861–71.[21] This emigration
and the disproportion of the sexes caused by it, along with poor
health conditions caused by crowding and unemployment, probably account for the lessened increase in the population. Governor
Rawson noted that:

Pestilence or emigration is, apparently, the alternative as an escape
from starvation, in the event of one or two unfavorable seasons occurring.[22]

Fortunately, no hurricanes or unusually bad seasons occurred during the period, and only once (1869) did the sugar crop fall below
35,000 hogsheads.

The population was growing throughout the island, but the
greatest growth was around Bridgetown where there were the
best opportunities both for emigration and for obtaining casual
employment. Some of the "red-legs" emigrated or obtained positions in Bridgetown; in either case, small farms were put on the
market for sale to colored owners. A few of the sugar estates were

[20] Governor R. W. Rawson, *Report upon the Population of Barbados, 1851–71*,
p. 8.

[21] *Ibid.*, p. 2.   [22] *Ibid.*, p. 3.

broken up (there were sixteen estates less in 1871 than in 1850) and sold for peasant holdings.[23]

Compared with the previous period, the sugar industry was stagnant. The trend of production was slowly upward, probably because of more plentiful labor, the substitution of steam factories for windmills, and increasing applications of manure. According to the reports in the travel books of the time, the planters seemed to be well satisfied with their methods. Most of them were making a comfortable living, and some were able to retire to England. One Barbadian may be quoted to illustrate this point: "My father brought up his eight children and sent me to Oxford on an estate of only 100 acres." [24] On the other hand, especially at the beginning of the period, many planters got into difficulty; thus more than four thousand acres of estates went into chancery each year in 1856, 1857, and 1859. Other estates were mortgaged to merchants in Barbados and England.[25] From 1860 to 1887, the number and acreage of estates sold were small, and the average price per acre stayed above £50 in most years.[26]

The trade of Barbados was remarkably steady from 1864 to 1884. The upward trend in sugar production offset the decreases in price so that the export trade did not depart greatly from the average of about £1,000,000 per year (see graph, page 166). The most notable change was the increase in exports to the United States. In 1845 the exports to the United States were only £1,750, compared with imports from the United States of £188,686. Almost no sugar was included in this small export since the planters sold their sugar through English merchants to whom they were indebted.[27] The increasing importation of East Indian and, later, beet sugar into the English market suggested the disposal of Barbadian sugar in the North American market. In 1855 the export of Barbadian sugar to the United States started on a moderate scale (£8,865), and by 1858 it had increased to £60,000. The increase

[23] *Ibid.,* pp. 4, 8, 17; *Barbados Official Gazette,* November 26, 1891; Report on the Census of Barbados (1881–91), p. 1739.
[24] Quoted in *Colonial Reports: Barbados* (1897), p. 17.
[25] *Report of the West India Royal Commission* (1897), p. 207.
[26] *Ibid.*   [27] Schomburgk, *op. cit.,* pp. 155, 164.

continued until by 1893 the exports to the United States were £755,465 (mostly sugar and molasses), or 60 percent of the total export trade. Thus, after a period of political disturbance which upset the complementary trade between Barbados and New England, this trade was reëstablished and remained important until Cuban competition and an American protective tariff (1902) diverted much of it to Canada.

1884–94, A PERIOD OF INSTABILITY

Beginning with 1884, the Barbadian economy entered another period of instability (1884–1902). The primary cause was a sharp drop in sugar prices [28] which resulted from the bounties and the consequent increased sugar-beet production in Europe. Irregular weather and the sudden exhaustion of the Bourbon cane aggravated the bad economic situation. The exports of 1886 were only half the value of those of 1884; sugar estates were sold at £65 per acre in 1884, at £63 in 1886, and at £26 in 1887.[29] Retrenchment measures were undertaken in 1887, but unusually favorable weather from 1887 to 1890 produced record crops, and the economy measures were abandoned.[30] Thus Barbados was in poor condition when the crisis reached its most critical point during the 1890s.

A rapid decline began in 1891 when the fungoid disease (caused by *tricho-sphaeria saccharis*) attacked the canes. The Bourbon canes seemed to be especially susceptible to this disease, and it became necessary to use other varieties of canes.[31] The deterioration of the Bourbon canes is shown by the decrease in the amount of sugar produced for each inch of rainfall (Table 13).

A drought in 1894 injured the canes further. The local canes, weakened by severe drought, were:

. . . vigorously attacked by the "moth," "weevil," and "shot-borer" . . . while the fungus disease which attacks the roots and stems of the canes made rapid and fatal progress.[32]

---

[28] The price dropped from $3.85 (1883) to $1.85 (1885) per hundredweight at Barbados. *Report of the West India Royal Commission* (1897), Appendix C, p. 199.
[29] *Ibid.*, p. 207.   [30] *Ibid.*, pp. 185–86.   [31] *Ibid.*, p. 212.
[32] *Colonial Reports: Barbados* (1894), p. 29.

TABLE 13

NUMBER OF HOGSHEADS OF SUGAR PRODUCED IN BARBADOS PER INCH
OF RAINFALL IN THE PRECEDING YEAR, 1882–99 [a]

YEAR	HOGSHEADS	YEAR	HOGSHEADS
1882	780	1891	962
1883	1,056	1892	892
1884	984	1893	774
1885	1,170	1894	854
1886	1,038	1895	781
1887	832	1896	617
1888	1,058	1897	654
1889	945	1898	733
1890	1,108	1899	666

[a] Dodds Botanic Station *Bulletin* No. 8.

The planters, almost bankrupted by poor harvests and falling prices, found it difficult to maintain their former high standards of cultivation: less labor was used; less manure was applied; and fewer chemical fertilizers were imported.[33] The results of these troubles are reflected in the decline in the value of property to £20 per acre by 1896, and in the inability of the planters to raise new credits.[34]

Meanwhile, certain experiments had been progressing in Barbados. "In 1859, Parris, in a letter to the *Barbados Advocate*, announced that he had seen self-sown seedlings." [35] No use was made of this discovery; in fact, many sugar authorities thought it a hoax. However, after John Bovell, superintendent of the boys' reformatory at Dodds, was shown a self-sown seedling by one of the overseers, he began experiments with the raising and cultivation of sugar cane. Bovell coöperated with J. B. Harrison, Island Professor of Chemistry, in studies of:

(1) the effect of manures;
(2) the comparative value of already existing varieties of sugar cane;

[33] *Report of the West India Royal Commission* (1897), Appendix C, Part III, *passim.*
[34] *Ibid.,* p. 229 and Part III, *passim.*
[35] Noel Deerr, *Sugar and the Sugar Cane*, p. 23.

(3) the raising of new varieties of sugar cane from seed . . . ;
(4) . . . cane diseases in Barbados.[36]

The manurial experiments produced the most immediate results. The planters, to offset the low prices, welcomed an opportunity to increase their crop by applying superphosphates and sulphate of ammonia as suggested by Bovell and Harrison. The value of artificial manures used in 1888 was double the figure for 1887. Even more manures were utilized in 1889, and the bumper crop of 1890 was probably the result of this increased fertilization.

The collapse of the Bourbon cane turned Bovell's attention to a more intensive study of new varieties. His seedling canes were showing promise; but, meanwhile, an immediate substitute for the Bourbon variety was needed. For this purpose, the White Transparent variety was adopted because it seemed to be most resistant to the diseases and insects which were destroying the Bourbon.

Sugar prices in London had dropped to 12.53s. per hundredweight in 1887; then prices recovered slightly until 1894, when a new decline started which brought cane sugar prices down to nine shillings.[37] This new low price created a crisis throughout the West Indies; consequently, in 1896, a Royal Commission was appointed to investigate the situation. Its report touched on many aspects of Barbadian life. Among other things, it pointed out that the situation of Barbados was more critical than that of the other islands. For Barbados, it recommended the construction of central sugar factories, the encouragement of peasant agriculture, retrenchment in the colonial government, and financial aid from the Imperial Government to support the sugar industry while readjustments were being made. In addition to these special recommendations, the report urged that the British Government take action to stop the practice of paying export bounties on beet sugar.[38]

Nearly five years passed before any action resulted from the report of the 1897 Royal Commission. In 1902, the British Government contributed £80,000 to Barbados to tide over the sugar industry until action could be taken on the bounties. This money

[36] *Report of the West India Royal Commission* (1897), p. 202.
[37] *Ibid.*, p. 4.   [38] *Ibid.*, pp. 31–34; 69–70.

was used as the capital of the Sugar Industry Agricultural Bank, a government institution which advances money to finance current crops or improvements in machinery. The following year, the Brussels Convention removed the bounties on beet sugar exports.

While Barbados was awaiting this action, the sugar market was temporarily improved by the removal of much of the Cuban and Puerto Rican sugar supply from the world market in the disturbed period before and during the Spanish-American War. This resulted in higher prices which, together with somewhat better crops from the new canes, kept the value of sugar exports increasing slowly from 1898 to 1901.

Meanwhile, several factors affected the public health of Barbados. Most notable of these was the development of the public water supply system. Water had been piped to Bridgetown since 1859, but until near the end of the century most of the rural sections depended on water from ponds, cisterns, and private wells. Widespread epidemics of dysentery and other water-borne diseases were common, and were probably due to impure water. The drought of 1894 was accompanied by epidemics of typhoid and dysentery which were probably caused by malnutrition as well as by impure water. The colonial secretary thought the cause was the impure condition of the surface water which formed the drinking water of many of the peasants. He noted that:

. . . the rains, when they did come, were insufficient to either carry into the sea the vegetable matter washed down from the higher to lower lands, or to drive the disease-producing germ sufficiently deep into the ground to render it innocuous. The topographical analysis of the death-rate during this period is instructive. From the highlands of St. John and St. Andrew it rose from 16.7 and 19.6 per 1000 respectively to 33.1 and 45.5 per 1000 in the low flat districts of Christ Church and St. Philip.[39]

The belief that the poor water supply caused the increased death rate "materially hastened 'the water question' to its final culmination."[40] Consequently, the legislature, in spite of the depressed condition of the island, appropriated the money for the

[39] *Colonial Reports: Barbados* (1894), p. 10. For another explanation see page 19.
[40] *Ibid.*, p. 11.

systems of mains and standpipes (Queen Victoria's Pumps) which extends over most of the island.[41] In 1896, it was reported that

. . . there was decided immunity from bowel complaints and typhoid fevers . . . the ample supply of pure water has had a marvelous effect in stopping our annual outbreak of dysentery and untractable diarrhoea and typhoid.[42]

September 10, 1898, is remembered by most Barbadians as the date of the last hurricane to visit the island. So far as can be determined, it was much less severe than the storms of 1780 and 1831. Eighty-five persons were killed and 18,000 laborers' huts were blown down. Most of the more substantial buildings suffered only minor damage, and the crops seem to have been only slightly injured. The death rate among the laborers, however, was increased, due to new outbreaks of typhoid and dysentery.[43] Contributions totaling £65,000 were received from the British Government, the British people, and from neighboring colonies. These funds paid for the rebuilding of the laborers' huts and a considerable part of the other damage.

In 1902 an epidemic of smallpox occurred which demonstrated what damage can be done to an island when it is attacked by a foreign disease. Smallpox had at one time been very common in Barbados, and inoculation had been used to prevent its spread. At the beginning of 1902, the disease had been gone for so long that very few, if any, Barbadians had been vaccinated. In February, 1902, several cases occurred, all of which were traced to a person arriving from Canada.[44] The epidemic lasted until April, 1903, and, altogether, 1,466 cases (118 deaths) were reported. Neighboring colonies quarantined Barbados, and the transit trade had to be temporarily discontinued. The loss in trade was estimated at £60,000; government revenues decreased £21,690, while at the same time government expenditures were increased £17,804 by the epidemic.[45] An epidemic of yellow fever in 1908 (the first since 1881)

---

[41] *Colonial Reports: Barbados* (1894), p. 11.   [42] *Ibid.,* (1896), p. 22.
[43] *Ibid.* (1899), pp. 10, 15, 22, 23, 26, 27.   [44] *Ibid.* (1902), p. 45.
[45] *Ibid.* (1902–3), pp. 1–15.

resulted in similar losses of trade and government revenues.[46]

Returning to the history of the Barbadian sugar trade, we find that the Brussels Conference and its restrictions on export bounties on beet sugar did not bring the relief to the British West Indian sugar industry which had been anticipated. This was due largely to the recovery and increased growth of the Cuban and Puerto Rican sugar industries. The products of these industries displaced Barbadian products in the American market so that Barbadian exports to the United States dropped sharply from £554,825 in 1901 to £292,137 in 1902 and then slumped until they amounted to only £51,502 in 1909.[47] In part, these decreases were compensated for by increased exports to the United Kingdom and Canada, but, on the whole, these markets were not so advantageous as the United States from which Barbados was accustomed to import a large part of its foodstuffs.

1903–13, THE SEARCH FOR NEW SOURCES OF INCOME

As a result of this trade disturbance, the following decade (1903–13) was largely occupied by a search for new sources of income. The resemblance of this decade to several earlier decades (especially 1660–70, 1702–12, and 1803–13) is remarkable: all were characterized by emigration, makeshift ways of making a living, better agricultural methods, and shifts in crops and products. But whereas the earlier periods were, on the whole, periods of hardship for the middle and lower classes, the decade 1903–13 was one of relative prosperity. The explanation lies in the nature of the emigration, which was largely colored and black rather than white as in the earlier periods. Furthermore, the emigrants did not sever their connections with Barbados but, instead sent to their Barbadian relatives large sums from their earnings.

The source of this prosperity is often referred to as "Panama money." The earnings of Barbadians in building the Panama Canal

[46] *Ibid.* (1908–9), p. 9; Sir R. W. Boyce, *Health Progress and Administration in the West Indies,* pp. 76–87.

[47] *Statistical Abstract for the Several British Overseas Dominions,* No. 54 (1903–17), pp. 278–79; No. 44 (1892–1906), pp. 222–23.

were not the only source of these remittances, but for many years they were the chief source. In general, it may be said that Barbadian emigrants went wherever work was obtainable along the shipping routes touching at Barbados. Barbadians worked as sailors on Caribbean vessels, as servants in the cities of eastern United States, as laborers along the shores of the Caribbean, and as agricultural laborers in Cuba, Haiti, Jamaica, Trinidad, British Guiana, and Central America. The total of the remittances must be estimated, since the only data available shows merely the amounts handled through the post office (Table 14). Other large amounts are known to have been sent in as cash, merchandise, and bank drafts. The total amounts must have been large, and they sufficed to pay for one-tenth to one-fifth (at least) of the Barbadian imports.

TABLE 14

REMITTANCES RECEIVED THROUGH THE BARBADOS POST OFFICE
1900–10 [a]

YEAR	Canal Zone	United States	British Colonies	Total	ESTIMATED TO BE IN REGISTERED LETTERS
		MONEY ORDERS			
1900	. . .	£2,954	£21,222	£27,208	. . .
1901	. . .	4,010	23,702	31,347	£9,722
1906	£7,508	16,665	13,745	41,870	28,251
1907	46,160	19,323	14,758	89,924	30,189
1909	66,272	14,006	10,962	96,907	32,389
1910	62,102	15,078	12,518	93,361	34,766

[a] *Annual Reports of the Barbados Post Office.*

A second source of additional income was from the increased sale of molasses, especially to Canada. This increase, which made up in part for the loss of sugar sales to the United States, was due largely to the development of the sirup business which was started about 1902–1903. Sirup (fancy molasses) is manufactured by boiling down the juice of the sugar cane without removing any of the

sugar content. Unlike ordinary molasses, which is a residual product, the production of sirup reduces the production of raw sugar.
The production of sirup in 1904 was the equivalent of 151 tons
of sugar; by 1907 this production had increased to the equivalent
of 12,462 tons, or one-quarter of the Barbadian sugar extractable
from the juice.[48] Molasses exports which were valued at £136,548
in 1903 rose to £232,920 in 1907.[49]

A third source of additional income was obtained by reviving
the Sea Island cotton industry. Cotton was an especially good crop
for the drier parts of the island which were marginal or submar-
ginal for sugar production. Furthermore, cotton was thought to
be a good rotation crop for areas of moderate, uncertain rainfall,
since it was believed that poor sugar weather would produce a
bumper cotton crop. Consequently, with the encouragement of the
Government, cotton was planted in 1903. The industry remained
important until the war boom in sugar prices made it more profitable to devote much of the cotton land to sugar. Cotton occupied,
at most, 7,000 acres or about one-fifth the cane fields harvested
annually.

Other crops were attempted as substitutes for sugar, but they
were, in general, unsuccessful. Among the most promising of those
tried were bananas and winter vegetables. In both cases, because
of lack of adequate refrigerated transportation facilities, difficulty
was experienced in getting the produce to the Canadian and British markets in good condition. The small quantities shipped were
a further handicap to the development of this trade.

The last of the new developments to add to the Barbadian income was the tourist trade. Two types of visitors were attracted to
Barbados: tourists from North America and the United Kingdom
who stayed at the principal hotels during the winter months; and
visitors from South America, who rented houses near the sea and
who stayed for considerable periods.[50] The second group came

[48] H. C. Prinsen Geerligs, *The World's Cane Sugar Industry, Past and Present,*
p. 215.
[49] *Statistical Abstract for the Several British Overseas Dominions* (1903–17),
No. 54, pp. 192–93.
[50] *Colonial Reports: Barbados* (1910–11), p. 20; *ibid.* (1911–12), p. 20.

largely from Brazil and was able to reach Barbados easily since the New York–Brazil boats commonly stopped at Barbados for coal, water, and supplies. The exact value of the tourist trade to Barbados is not known, but the colonial secretary considered that "the colony owes much of its increasing prosperity to the visitors who stay in the island." [51]

The decade under consideration ended with a period of severe drought which lasted from December, 1911, to the end of March, 1912. The drought was especially disastrous to the peasantry, who suffered from the failure of the ground provisions. Another drought lasted through the first nine months of 1914.

The planters were not so seriously affected by the drought. The sugar crop was better than expected, partly due to the introduction of new varieties such as the drought resistant variety, B. 6450, and partly due to the surprising recovery of the canes when the rain came.[52] In addition, the planters were in good financial condition because of the successful sirup sales and the good crops in 1910, 1911, 1912, and 1914.

1914–1920, THE WORLD WAR BOOM AND COLLAPSE

The World War of 1914–18 (with its destruction of many of the world's sugar-beet fields) brought an era of unparalleled prosperity to Barbados which ended abruptly with the crash in sugar prices in 1921. The estate owners prospered more than the laborers, for prices of imported foodstuffs soared more rapidly than wages. However, ideal rainfall conditions and more intensive cultivation brought in bumper crops, and there was adequate work for all.

Thus Barbados enjoyed the combination, unusual in her history, of a large sugar crop and continued high prices. Records were established in revenue and trade, and money was subscribed for local loans. Estates have, for the most part, been cleared of debt, and profits are being largely applied by the estate-owner to the erection of improved machinery and general estate improvement.[53]

---

[51] *Colonial Reports: Barbados* (1911–12), p. 20.   [52] *Ibid.* (1912–13), pp. 20–22.
[53] *Ibid.* (1916–17), p. 11.

The high sugar prices led to a partial abandonment of the system of crop rotation. Ratoon crops became more common, and ground provisions were neglected to such an extent that

. . . the planting of ground provisions during the War was enforced by statute, the area to be planted, and the control of reaping and sale being left to a committee appointed under the Vegetable Produce Act.[54]

Laborers often had difficulty in getting adequate food, and the death rates from 1916 to 1920 (32.2; 28.8; 25.9; 38.2; and 32.9) were high for a period of prosperity. On the other hand, the estate owners engaged in land speculation which culminated with an average price of £146 per acre for the estates sold in 1920.[55] Bank loans were granted on both the crops and the estates, and indebtedness among the planters was common.

Then came the crash! In May, 1920, raw sugar had sold in London as high as 146s. per hundredweight; by the following December, sugar sold for 25s. per hundredweight in London, and the average price for 1921 was almost seven shillings lower.[56] To make matters even worse for Barbados, the crop for 1920 was below average, while that for 1921 was much poorer. Drought had injured not only the sugar crop, but also the provision crops. No wonder that the Colonial Secretary reported that:

The year 1921–22 can be described . . . as probably one of the most difficult which the colony has experienced in recent times.[57]

The most serious results of the crash were financial. Many estates, purchased at boom prices, were "subsequently abandoned with the loss of large installments of the purchase price." [58] Owners who managed to hold their estates were heavily indebted to the Sugar Industry Agricultural Bank, to the commercial banks, and to the merchants. Of the £538,302 which the Sugar Industry Agricultural Bank had loaned against the 1921 harvest, £462,107 was outstanding at the end of the crop year, and £221,311 was still

---

[54] *Ibid.* (1917–18), p. 10.
[55] *Report of Proceedings, Imperial Sugar Cane Research Conference, London, 1931,* pp. 26–27.
[56] *Ibid.*   [57] *Colonial Reports: Barbados* (1921–22), p. 4.
[58] *Ibid.,* p. 6.

outstanding at the end of the crop year of 1922.[59] Government revenues decreased sharply with declining imports, and an income tax was imposed to collect the necessary funds.[60] Likewise, remittances from Barbadians abroad declined, wages in Barbados were cut, and work on the estates was minimized; thus even the poorer classes felt the financial depression.

As we have noted many a time in Barbadian history, the coincidence of drought and low prices leads to disease. The usual concomitant of Barbadian depressions, emigration, was lacking in 1921, for there was no more prosperous place to which Barbadians could emigrate. But disease, encouraged by low water supplies and low food supplies, both the result of the drought, produced the record-breaking death rate of 43.4 per 1,000. The infantile death rate was also high, 401 per 1,000. Typhoid and dysentery were especially important in contributing to the high death rates.[61]

1922–25, A RAPID RECOVERY

Rapid recovery after such crises is also a characteristic phenomenon in Barbadian history. This was illustrated again in 1922 and 1923. Normal rainfall brought an average crop in 1922, followed by a bumper crop in 1923. Sugar prices rose to 25*s.* per hundredweight in 1923. Of the Barbadians who had returned home during the world depression of 1921, some two thousand were able to emigrate to New York in 1923.[62] Remittances from Barbadians abroad nearly doubled. The "year 1923 was indeed one of exceptional prosperity." [63]

The financial situation improved along with the crops. All but £45,099 of the remaining 1921 debt to the Sugar Industry Agricultural Bank was paid. The income tax, which had yielded but £18,244 from the year 1921, yielded £31,869 from 1922 and £121,314 from 1923. The Government surplus became so large that the

---

[59] *Colonial Reports: Barbados* (1922–23), p. 5.   [60] *Ibid.* (1921–22), p. 5.
[61] Statistics from *Barbados Blue Books;* other data from *Colonial Reports: Barbados* (1921–22).
[62] *Colonial Reports: Barbados* (1923–24), p. 5.   [63] *Ibid.*

Barbadian Legislature established a reserve of £100,000 to be used only in case of a public calamity such as a hurricane.[64]

1925–38, INCREASING PRODUCTION TO OFFSET PRICE DECLINES

In 1925 began the decline in sugar prices which has continued almost to the present time. From that date, the history of Barbados has been a steady fight to increase sugar production more rapidly than its price was falling. This has been accomplished with remarkable success, due very largely to the efforts of the Department of Science and Agriculture. The experiments started by Bovell and Harrison have brought forth almost miraculous results. New seedlings, better manuring, better cultivation, and better extraction have doubled and even tripled the sugar yields of three decades ago. The details of these changes will be considered in the next chapter; here it need only be noted that without these scientific improvements it is difficult to understand how Barbados could have survived.

The poor prospects for sugar caused a renewed interest in alternative crops. The cotton industry grew again after 1920 but was restricted by pests which finally necessitated long closed seasons. Many of the marginal sugar estates were broken up into small farms and sold to Barbadians returning from abroad. Usually these peasant farmers raised some sugar cane, but many raised ground provisions in sufficient quantities so that a considerable quantity was exported to British Guiana. As a result of these changes, Barbados became somewhat more self-sufficient.

The weak economic condition of the sugar industry caused the appointment of another Royal Commission under the chairmanship of Lord Olivier. This Commission reported [65] that the sugar situation was especially serious in Barbados and found that alternative crops and emigration offered few possibilities for relief for Barbados. Two specific recommendations of the Commission were

[64] *Ibid.* (1924–25), p. 4.
[65] *Report of the West Indian Sugar Commission* (London, 1930), pp. 123–24 and *passim.*

put into effect: (1) the maintenance of the price of West Indian sugar by adding to the imperial preference; (2) the establishment of a West Indian Cane Breeding Station at Barbados.

After the Olivier Commission's report, the price of sugar in the free world market continued to drop as plans such as the Chadbourne Plan collapsed. The price of sugar in 1935 was less than half that in 1928. For Barbados, this decline in price was partially offset by an increase in the preference granted colonial sugars imported into the United Kingdom. This preference, which had been £3 15s. per ton in 1931 was increased to £4 15s. per ton during 1932 and 1933. To this preference was added a special, or certificate, preference which was limited in amount, and therefore varied per ton with the quantity of sugar produced. The net result of these preferences has been to enable Barbadian producers to receive, since 1932, approximately twice the open-market price for sugar.

In 1935 the Barbados Legislature appointed a committee to "report on the present condition and future outlook of the sugar industry of Barbados." It was feared that sugar prices might decline further and that the British preferences might be reduced or abolished. The report, dated August, 1935, was pessimistic and pointed out that "Barbados producers in the black soil areas have been marketing their sugar at a loss for the past five years, even although no allowance has been made for depreciation or interest on capital." [66]

As has been so often the case in Barbadian history, the forebodings of the planters were not subsequently justified. The following note was added to the report when it was published six months later:

We were faced at that time with what was generally estimated to be a very short crop, the price of sugar was deplorably low and the outlook for the syrup industry was confused and chaotic. The crop yield has since proved very much better than was anticipated, especially in the higher rainfall districts owing to late rains in December and January; in addition more syrup was marketed than in any previous year and this was sold at a price above the parity of sugar (even including the certificated

---

[66] *Barbados Official Gazette,* supplement, February 27, 1936, p. 16.

preference). Owing to these circumstances, there was much less sugar made, and in consequence, the certificated preference when divided amongst this sugar amounted to more per cwt. than ever before.

The result of these various factors is that the black soil estates, even with a low yield of cane, were on the average, almost able to balance revenue and expenditure. In the red soil districts, where the yield was much the same as last year, the estates did better than the previous year. It can, therefore, be stated that the financial results were much better than seemed possible when the address was sent.[67]

The world-wide depression of 1929 apparently reversed the Barbadian population trend which had been downward since nearly the beginning of the century. Many of the former destinations of Barbadian emigrants—such as, especially, the United States, Brazil, and Venezuela—had been closed to them. Other places where work had been obtained—such as Cuba, Santo Domingo, Trinidad, and British Guiana—now had no work to offer because of the depression. Furthermore, many Barbadians who had become unemployed in foreign lands returned home. Hence all recent government estimates indicate an increasing population.

This increasing population suggests that Barbados is approaching another crisis in its economic history. Will an enforced wholesale migration to new tropical lands (as British Guiana) become necessary? Will some unexpected turn in world sugar prices enable Barbados to support more people? Will technological improvements make the sugar industry profitable at present price levels?

Still another threat looms. May not the British Government remove the protective tariffs again as it did after 1846? If this occurs, what will happen to Barbados? The writer's belief is that the marginal black-soil estates will be subdivided into subsistence farms, while the more profitable estates will increase their efficiency, as they did after 1846, and make a reasonable profit at the lower prices. Larger factories, better cane varieties, mechanized tillage, more efficient business management, and better marketing still offer possibilities for more economical production. Whether under sufficient economic pressure, such increases in efficiency will result

[67] *Ibid.,* p. 6.

(as they have so often in the past), the writer does not claim to know. At this point, he wishes only to emphasize that overcrowded Barbados is worth watching because it represents on a small scale what may happen in other agricultural regions with growing populations and subject to frequent crises.

CHAPTER VII

The Recent Barbadian Economy: Production

BARBADIAN history has been a series of economic booms and collapses. The preceding chapters have shown that many of these economic fluctuations have received their initial impulse from economic and political disturbances in Europe and America. Often the seriousness of the Barbadian repercussions has been influenced by the presence or absence of favorable environmental conditions in Barbados; for example, the bumper crops in recent years have kept Barbados solvent in spite of the lowest sugar prices and worst market conditions in Barbadian history. Likewise, the seriousness of a drought, a hurricane, or pests, is greatly influenced by the exchange value of Barbadian exports; hence Barbados recovered from the hurricane of 1831 in one-third the time needed to recover from the equally severe hurricane of 1780 because relations with the British and American markets were more favorable at the later date. A coincidence of unfavorable economic and physical conditions, as in 1895 and 1921, has almost bankrupted the island.

But even when such bankruptcy seemed inevitable, Barbados has made remarkable recoveries. Perhaps its one-crop economy has been its great strength as well as its great weakness. Since there was no other major industry to which they could turn, Barbadians have been forced either to succeed with sugar or to migrate. Emigrations under such circumstances have been mentioned frequently in the preceding chapters. The success of those who remained, in increasing the sugar crop, although less well known, has often been more striking than the emigrations. Barbados today produces more sugar in a drought year than it produced in such unusually favorable years as 1890; the bumper crop of 1935, for instance, was nearly ten times the bumper crop reported at the height of the sugar boom. Throughout Barbadian history, it has appeared that the periods of great progress have occurred after the periods of great catastrophe.

The historical evidence presented so far is broken by serious gaps. However, sufficient data are available to show that similar relationships have existed between the variability of the environment, the conditions of the world markets, and Barbadian prosperity and progress throughout the island's history. Here it is proposed to analyze these relationships of the last three-quarters of a century, for which fairly complete and comparable statistics are available. In this way, some of the inferences drawn from the historical data will be tested by more exact methods.

The importance of environmental variability to Barbados has been nowhere better summed up than in the following:

> The drought of 1912 . . . caused a decrease in the revenue and a decrease in the trade of the colony, as well as a practical failure of the provision crops, with resulting high prices for imported foodstuffs, increasing the cost of living for all classes. It diminished the wage earnings of the people and swelled the ranks of the recipients of poor relief. It increased the number of criminals, brought many to the verge of starvation and most serious of all it was the undoubted cause of the very high increase in the deathrate.[1]

As this quotation implies, the drought with its effects on crops and income, is through those effects, the basic cause of many other consequences. It is, however, not to be expected that every fluctuation in environmental conditions will bear a direct relationship to those economic and social conditions which ultimately depend upon the environment. Every additional link between the environment and the ultimate human response lessens the chance of a close correlation. For example, the relationship which exists between the amount of rainfall and the death rate must be considered not as a simple, direct relationship, but rather as an indirect relationship resulting from the series of simpler relationships shown in Figure 11.

A complete graphic presentation of this situation would, of

[1] *Colonial Reports: Barbados* (1912–13), pp. 24–25.

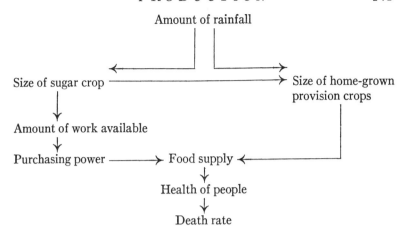

11. THE RELATIONSHIPS BETWEEN THE AMOUNT OF RAINFALL AND
THE DEATH RATE IN BARBADOS

course, necessitate the addition of so many other factors to the above diagram that it would become very complicated. For instance, many factors other than rainfall, such as manuring and pests, influence the size of the crops. Moreover, the amount of work available is influenced by other factors than the sugar crop, for example, the ability of the planters to make repairs and improvements. Purchasing power is influenced not only by the amount of work, but also by the wage rate and by the prices of supplies. Finally, the health of the people is influenced by the presence or absence of epidemics, by the quality and amount of medical service available, by the water supply, and by a multitude of other factors. Hence the following analyses must be made by considering, as much as possible, the links in the chains of relationships as well as the relationships between the ends of the series.

AGRICULTURE

Climate.—The influence of climatic fluctuations, especially in the amount of rainfall, stands out more persistently in Barbadian history than any other environmental factor influencing Barbadian production (Figure 2). Temperature fluctuations have been

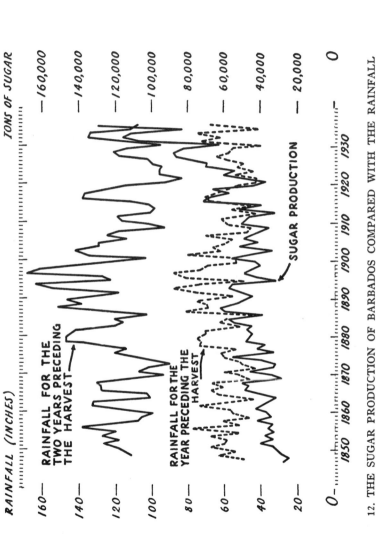

12. THE SUGAR PRODUCTION OF BARBADOS COMPARED WITH THE RAINFALL

1847–1935

Sources: "World Weather Records," *Smithsonian Miscellaneous Collections,* LXXIX (Washington, 1929), 1014–15; *Ibid.,* XC (1934), 376; records of the Department of Science and Agriculture.

minor and have had no perceptible effect. The fluctuations in winds have been dominant only in rare years through the destructive effects of hurricanes. But the fluctuations in rainfall have been more closely related than any other factor to the annual variations in Barbadian productivity.

1. Rainfall.—Figure 12 shows that in general the production of sugar fluctuates with the annual rainfall of the year preceding the harvest (broken line). This generalization clearly applies to sixty-nine of the eighty-nine years for which both sugar and rainfall statistics are available. A year of moderate drought following a series of good years does not always have a marked effect on the crop. Thus the decreases in rainfall in 1849, 1851, 1854, 1863, 1871, 1882, and 1899 are not followed by corresponding decreases in sugar production in the following year. This may be explained by the great water-absorbing capacity of both the soils and the underlying rocks of Barbados.[2]

The upper line (total of the preceding two years' rainfall) in Figure 12 also is closely related to the sugar production; in fifty-eight out of eighty-eight years, the two lines trend together. That the storage of water in Barbadian soils is important is demonstrated by the fact that the upper curve in Figure 12 often follows the production more closely than the lower curve, for example, in 1850, 1852, and 1855. A very sharp decrease in rainfall, as from 1868 to 1869 or from 1933 to 1934, apparently exhausts the moisture reserve in the subsoil, for the production curve drops more rapidly than the two-year rainfall curve.

In seventy-six out of eighty-nine years, fluctuations in the sugar production are largely accounted for by either the rainfall of the preceding year or that of the two preceding years. Some of the fluctuations in the remaining thirteen years are accounted

[2] "In fact the chief feature to lay stress on in connexion with the effect of the structure and topography of the coralline region of Barbados on the vegetation of the Island is this ability of the coral rock to absorb and retain water. The apparently remarkable character which the cane plant is locally credited with possessing, being able to live through severe drought, is really in great part due, not to any special features of the structure of the plant itself, but rather to the peculiarity in the water supply with which it is provided." (F. Hardy, "Some Aspects of the Flora of Barbados," *Agricultural Journal,* January, 1932, p. 61.)

for by pests, plant diseases, changes in manuring practices, and changes in acreage (see Figure 13); many are explained in part by freak distributions of rainfall.[3] Thus the excellent crop of 1861 was better than the annual rainfall would lead one to expect, due to unusually good distribution of the rainfall. The 1862 crop was smaller despite a higher annual rainfall because of less even distribution (including a rainless month during the harvest). The bumper crop of 1875 may probably be attributed to good rains just preceding the harvest. A somewhat heavier annual rainfall resulted in a much reduced crop in 1876 because the rain was excessive in several months; for example, in September, 1875, the rainfall was three times the normal amount.

Similar comparisons were made between the yield of cotton per acre (Table 15) and the amount of annual rainfall (Figure 11), but only in a few years of exceptional drought, such as 1912 and 1921, does there seem to be any significant correlation between cotton yields and rainfall. Nor do better correlations exist between cotton yields and the rainfall considered by growing seasons and by other fractions of the year. Insect pests, changes in seed, and changes in the acreage involving the use of a larger or smaller proportion of good land almost mask any relationship which may exist.

No statistics are available to show the relationship between ground provisions and rainfall. However, since these crops are in the ground for only two or three months (compared with from fifteen to eighteen months for sugar cane), it is to be expected that a drought of several months' duration would have more serious effects on ground provisions than on the cane. The opinions of

[3] "It was shown on theoretical grounds at the meeting of the Agricultural Society that a 28-ton crop of cane would have to actually take from the soil and transpire through its leaves the equivalent of 21 inches of rainfall. This rainfall was termed the 'effective' rainfall since it measures the water actually used by the plant to make its growth. In order to double the crop the 'effective' rainfall would have to be doubled. It is obvious that only a part of the annual rainfall can be 'effective.' It is well known that a smaller but well distributed rainfall gives a bigger crop than a larger but badly distributed rainfall." (S. J. Saint, *Pamphlet No. 8, Agricultural Notes, July–December, 1930,* p. 23.)

TABLE 15

Yield of Cotton per Acre in Barbados, 1905–35 [a]

YEAR	YIELD PER ACRE IN POUNDS	FACTORS INFLUENCING THE YIELD
1905	116	
1906	172	
1907	83	Less intensive cultivation because of lower price
1908	142	Better prices
1909	146	
1910	156	
1911	153	
1912	97	Drought, disease, and pests
1913	107	
1914	96	Drought, disease, and pests
1915	127	
1916	123	
1917	77	Better land given to sugar
1918	144	Doubling of cotton prices
1919	89	Drought
1920	85	Drought
1921	57	Drought
1922	183	Better seed imported by Department of Agriculture
1923	148	
1924	145	
1925	95	Pink bollworm and drought
1926	81	Pink bollworm
1927	53	Pink bollworm and disease
1928	39	Pink bollworm
1929	Closed season	
1930	95	
1931	118	
1932	249	
1933	70	Pink bollworm
1934	20	Pink bollworm
1935	Closed season	

[a] *Colonial Reports: Barbados* (1902–03 to 1936–37); *Reports on the Department of Science and Agriculture* (1936–34).

Barbadian planters, as well as frequent references throughout Barbadian history, support this.[4]

2. Winds.—The effects of winds have received frequent mention in Chapters III–VI. However, it is difficult, except in hurricane years, to determine how much the productivity of the island is affected by abnormal winds. Ordinarily, the northeast trade is steady during the harvest season and can be depended upon for operating the windmills. Occasionally, as in 1896[5] and 1931,[6] the winds failed, and the yield of the windmills was much reduced. Calms occur even in months when the average velocities are high, and, as the cane spoils within twenty-four hours after cutting, even a few hours without wind may cause considerable loss. This danger is one reason why the steam factories have tended to replace the windmills.

The danger of strong winds has discouraged or prevented the planting of many crops such as cacao, bananas, and citrus fruits. Other crops, such as cotton, have to be protected by windbreaks of Guinea corn or similar crops. Even sugar cane is occasionally blown down, especially along the roadsides.

Hurricanes are the most destructive aspect of wind, but hurricanes of moderate violence do not injure the productivity of the island so much as might be expected. Fortunately, the hurricane season occurs when nearly half of the cane fields are in catch or cover crops. Hence, unless the factories and other equipment are seriously injured by the storm (as in 1675 and 1780), the next

[4] For example, *Colonial Reports: Barbados* (1895), pp. 9, 12; *ibid.* (1903–4), p. 12; *ibid.* (1912–13), p. 24; *ibid.* (1920–21), p. 6; *Winthrop's Journal*, II 328; *Calendar of State Papers, Colonial Series*, 1669–74, May 17, 1671, etc.

[5] "127. I suppose the windmill process is very cheap—
(Mr. Pile) Very cheap, but very uncertain.
128. It does not involve much capital?
(Mr. Pile) But there is a constant expense in repairing the mills. As to their uncertainty, there are certain months during which the crops are reaped, and sometimes calm weather prevails and the windmills are unable to do much. For instance, in March last year during our crop season we had a terrible calm." Evidence in *Report of the West India Royal Commission* (1897), Appendix C, p. 156.

[6] *Report of Proceedings, Imperial Sugar Cane Research Conference, London, 1931*, p. 74.

crop may be planted without difficulty. Thus but one year's crop is lost. Furthermore, this loss does not extend equally throughout the island because considerable areas are sheltered locally by the relief during most of the hurricane.

The hurricane of 1898 reduced the sugar crop for 1899, but after allowance is made for the lesser amount of rainfall, the loss due to the hurricane seems to have been less than 10 percent of the crop. Circumstantial evidence indicates that the destruction of the catch crops was more serious. Despite a 25 percent increase in cereal imports over the preceding year, after the hurricane, dysentery and diarrhea, two diseases attributed, in Barbados, to food deficiency, were unusually prevalent from September 10 to the end of the year.[7] Although only eighty-five persons were killed and 260 were injured by the hurricane, the death rate jumped from twenty-six per 1,000 (1897) to thirty-nine per 1,000 (1898). Heavy rains accompanied the hurricane and washed the soil from plant roots, which together with injuries to the stems and leaves suffice to explain the widespread damage to catch crops implied by the facts above.

Nonclimatic factors.—In Figure 13 an attempt has been made to eliminate most of the effects of variable rainfall on the sugar production. Although the rainfall variable (especially as to monthly distribution) is not wholly eliminated, the graph does bring out clearly the principal fluctuations in production due to changes in methods of cultivation and manufacture, plant diseases and pests, new types of cane, and changing prices. Which of these factors accounts for each fluctuation of the curves, so far as can be determined from the evidence available,[8] is indicated at the bottom of the graph. In Table 15 a similar list of factors which affected the cotton crop has been included. Similar details for the ground-provision crops are often unobtainable;

---

[7] *Colonial Reports: Barbados* (1898), p. 23.

[8] Evidence from the *Barbados Blue Book* (1855–1934), *Colonial Reports: Barbados (1880–1936)*, *Reports on Barbados Department of Science and Agriculture*, or *Reports of the Dodds Botanic Station*.

where information is available, it will be included in the topical discussions which follow.

1. Pests and diseases.—This aspect of the environment is extremely unstable, for pests and diseases vary greatly, both in kind and destructiveness, from year to year. They are especially serious for several years after their initial appearance, or when the cane crop is in poor condition because of drought as, for example, in 1890–95, 1909, 1912, and 1920–21. The damage to the cane crop caused by them varies, according to most estimates, from 10 to 25 percent loss. For cotton and ground provisions the loss is much greater, possibly because these crops are more concentrated in certain parts of the island, and thus the whole crop is more readily infected.

The influence of pests is most clearly shown in the history of the Barbadian Sea Island cotton crop. In 1912, the crop was weakened by severe drought; insect pests and diseases became established, and continued to reduce the yields until 1915 when much of the cotton acreage was devoted to sugar. The cotton acreage increased again after 1922 when a better quality of seed was introduced. In 1925, the pink bollworm was accidentally introduced into the island. Its ravages were so severe that the cotton industry had almost disappeared by July, 1928, and a closed season was declared until July, 1929. In 1930, dates were established for cotton planting so that there would be a period of several months when there would be no cotton plants on which the pests could feed. Yields were high in 1932, but the pink bollworm again reappeared, and the cotton industry was again almost discontinued. Part of this last decline may be attributed to the low price of cotton which made its cultivation unprofitable.

There are three destructive diseases which attack Barbadian cotton, namely, angular leaf spot, black arm, and bacterial boll disease. There are also three important insect pests, the pink bollworm, the cotton leaf worm, and the corn ear worm. Only the pink bollworm is now of major importance in reducing the crop. The simplest remedy used for it, as well as for the other pests and diseases, is the burning of the old cotton plants, followed by

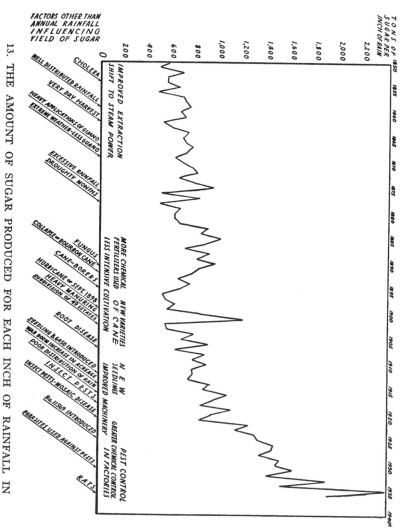

13. THE AMOUNT OF SUGAR PRODUCED FOR EACH INCH OF RAINFALL IN
BARBADOS DURING THE CALENDAR YEAR PRECEDING THE HARVEST

a closed season. Dusting with Paris green and lime is also practiced.[9]

Only from 1890–95 were pests and plant diseases as destructive in the cane fields as they were in the cotton fields. In 1891
the canes were attacked by the rind fungus (*Colletotrichum fal-
catum*), and were so weakened by the disease that they suffered
more severely than usual from the drought of 1894, and from
attacks of cane borers which accompanied the drought. The sugar
industry was not discontinued, but it was necessary to find a new
variety of cane to replace the Bourbon canes which were almost
universally used in Barbados during the nineteenth century. The
White Transparent canes were used until Barbadian seedlings
were developed which were equally or more resistant to the fungus, and at that same time more productive.[10]

The new canes resisted disease until 1908 and 1909, when
droughty periods "tended to induce the attacks of the sugar
cane root disease, *marasmius sacchari*." [11] The crops were only
slightly below the yield which the rainfall conditions alone would
imply. The droughty periods in 1912 and 1914 were accompanied
by attacks of the root borer, *Diaprepes abbreviatus*, which seemed
to have considerably reduced the 1913 and 1915 crops. The
drought of 1920–21 was likewise accompanied by attacks of the
root borer and also of the brown hard back beetle (*Phytalus
smithi*) which were so severe as to "make many 1919–21 sugar
experiments almost valueless." [12]

In November, 1920, the mosaic disease was discovered at Bank
Hall, St. Michael. This disease is attributed to an ultramicro-
scopic virus. When virulent, it may reduce the yield of cane by
as much as 80 percent. The Barbados Legislature acted promptly,
and passed the Mosaic Disease Eradication Act in 1921, which
provided for the inspection of the cane fields and the destruction
of the diseased canes. The act was allowed to lapse for a short

[9] *Cotton* (Barbados Department of Science and Agriculture, *Pamplet No. 4*
[1930]), pp. 5–10.
[10] *Colonial Reports: Barbados* (1894), p. 29; *Report of Proceedings, Imperial
Sugar Cane Research Conference, London, 1931*, p. 115.
[11] *Colonial Reports: Barbados* (1908–9), p. 11.   [12] *Ibid.* (1920–21), p. 14.

time before 1927, but the inspections were resumed in 1927, and the disease now seems to be under control.[13]

Insect pests were undoubtedly present in important numbers during the early 1920s, and some attempts were made to check them by collecting the insects by hand, by spraying, and by other methods. But no intensive effort was made to exterminate the pests until the sharp decline in sugar prices after 1925. The following note on the stem moth borer (*Diatraea saccharalis*) illustrates the former attitude of the planters toward insect pests:

Although . . . prevalent throughout the Island, the losses caused by it do not appear to have been fully realized, or else, until the last two years they have been accepted as a natural and unavoidable occurrence, attendant upon the growing of cane. No control measures were in operation in 1928 . . . and the pest has been in general assisted rather than combatted by prevalent agricultural practices.

The use of "borer gangs" to collect egg masses and to cut out dead hearts in young canes has been tried but has never been established in Barbados.

The soaking of plant cane to kill borer grubs and larvae prior to planting has been recommended, but is not practised, because proper facilities for adequate soaking of plants do not exist on most plantations nor has there been any universal or satisfactory hand selection of unbored cane, in order to avoid infesting plant fields from the time of their growth; it is only recently that the more progressive planters have paid serious attention to the latter method.

Further, under ordinary planting conditions it is necessary to intersperse blocks of young cane between blocks of unreaped cane, thus providing new fields in which the moths can carry on an unbroken cycle, and there are no huge unbroken stretches of cane planted at one time, as in larger sugar producing countries; a practice which tends to minimize borer damage.[14]

The Barbados government entomologist also notes that this pest is more common in the drier areas and in areas suffering from drought:

Experience during the drought of last season has shown that the borers are more successful in their attack when the growth and vitality of

---

[13] *Pamphlet No. 8, Agricultural Notes, July–December, 1930,* pp. 7–10; also *Reports on the Department of Science and Agriculture, passim.*

[14] *Report on the Department of Science and Agriculture* (1930–31), pp. 84–85.

the canes are weak; and that a uniform and satisfactory supply of moisture throughout the season, with resultant vigorous growth, is necessary for canes to withstand attack. The result of the drought appears to have been that moths were attracted to the fields of more normal, but nevertheless enfeebled growth, thus inflicting damage in such areas, whilst in the areas of sparse, short and unattractive cane growth, the lessened number of moths caused a relatively disproportionate damage. There is undoubtedly a relation between the vigour of the canes and the injury caused by a given number of moth borers.[15]

In 1927 the Department of Agriculture was reorganized and strengthened, so as to be able to carry on its work more effectively. Among its first measures was a concerted campaign to reduce insect losses. The stem moth borer was attacked by spreading its parasite, *Trichogramma minutum*. The success of this experiment was determined by sampling the infestation of cane joints at representative factories (Table 16).

TABLE 16

PERCENTAGE OF CANE JOINTS BORED BY THE STEM MOTH BORER
1929–33 [a]

YEAR	PERCENTAGE Bored	PERCENTAGE Badly Bored	PERCENTAGE Slightly Bored
1929	. . .	55.0	31.2
1930	. . .	19.0	53.7
1931	27.3		. . .
1932	17.4	. . .	. . .
1933	14.5	. . .	. . .

[a] *Report on the Department of Science and Agriculture* (1929–30), p. 110 (1932–33), p. 22.

Attempts were made to import parasites for the root borer (*Diaprepes abbreviatus*) and for the brown hard back (*Phytalus smithi*), but with little success so far. The collection of these pests by hand and the destruction of grubs in the soil by splitting or removing cane stumps and by thoroughly plowing infested fields, have proved effective and profitable.[16]

Gumming disease was discovered in Barbados in 1929, but al-

[15] *Ibid.*   [16] *Ibid.* (1933–34), p. 23.

though it has spread throughout the island wherever Ba. 11569 is planted, so far it has done little damage to the canes. Since this disease has been quite destructive elsewhere, the Department of Agriculture has tried to cope with it by recommending disease-resistant varieties of cane for use within the affected areas.

The Department of Agriculture has not been able to decide how much of the tremendous increase in cane yields since 1921 is due to pest and disease control. The planters of Barbados are satisfied that it caused a considerable part of the increase and they are willing to support further experiments along the same lines.

There is no doubt that pests have seriously reduced yields of other crops, although few exact records have been kept. At present, these crops are benefiting by the various methods being used to control cane and cotton pests. The distribution of pamphlets on methods of pest extermination is also educating the peasants, as well as the planters, concerning the most economical means of combating insect enemies.

2. Technical improvements in cultivation.—The variables discussed so far have been parts of the physical environment; the present section deals with variations in man's ability to use the Barbadian environment. These variables include changing manuring practices; the breeding, or importation, of improved plants; the development of dry-farming techniques; and other less important changes in cultivation, as in methods of weeding and spacing.

Until 1885 most of the manuring was based on the traditional methods of applying pen manure. However, enough guano (Figure 14) was imported after prosperous years to have a noticeable effect on the sugar yield. Thus, after four years with a very favorable balance of trade (1865–68), much larger amounts of guano were imported during 1869 and 1870; the result was that sugar yields in 1870 and 1871 were better than the rainfall would imply. Poorer trade conditions in 1869–71 caused a sharp decline in the guano imports in 1871 and 1872, and a crop disproportionately small in relation to the rainfall resulted in 1873. A tre-

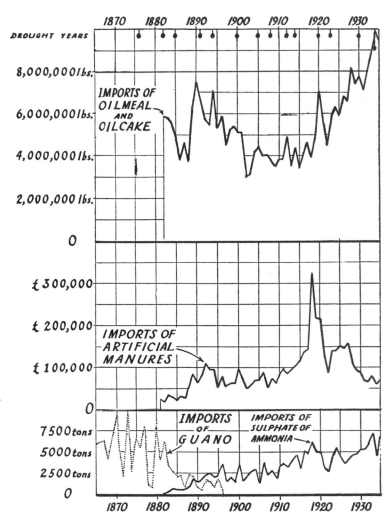

14. THE IMPORTS OF FERTILIZERS, OIL MEAL, AND OIL CAKE
INTO BARBADOS, 1865–1935

Sources: *Statistical Abstract for the Several Colonial and Other Possessions of
the United Kingdom* (London, 1877–1936), various numbers, *passim; Barbados
Blue Books* (1912–1935).

mendous import of guano in 1873 partially accounts for the better sugar yields in 1874 and 1875. Declining sugar prices after 1877 led to declining guano imports, and indirectly to lower yields in proportion to the rainfall until 1880 when a temporary upsurge of prices led at first to increased guano imports, and then to an interest in chemical fertilizers.

In 1885 Bovell and Harrison began experiments with varied types of fertilizer and determined that

. . . the application of certain compounds of nitrogen, phosphoric acid, and potash is advantageous, and that the most advantageous quantities of nitrogen to be applied depended on the rainfall. The greater proportion should be applied during the period of most active cane growth. . . . The total amount of nitrogen applied should not exceed the equivalent of 300 lbs. of sulphate of ammonia per acre.[17]

The results of these experiments were reflected in the sharp increase in the imports of sulphate of ammonia in 1888. This, together with the upward trend of all fertilizer imports since 1883, accounts for the bumper crops in 1888 and 1890 and for the fairly good crop in 1889.

The manurial methods worked out by Bovell and Harrison during this period were but slightly modified by their later experiments. These methods formed the basis of Barbadian practice up to 1930 when they were altered in some particulars to conform with the results of the more exact experiments of the investigators of the last decade.

The amount of manure applied from 1890 to 1927 depended on the prospects of the sugar industry and the credit of the planters rather than on any changes in technique. Thus the heavy imports from 1890 to 1895 were based on the desire of the planters to use their credit to apply the results of the manurial experiments. The failure of the 1895 crop led to a sharp decline in manure imports. Poor crops and the damage caused by the hurricane of 1898 kept the manure imports low until 1900 when the upset condition of the Cuban and Puerto Rican sugar industries made expansion profitable in Barbados. After a bumper crop, prices dropped, and

[17] *Report of the West India Royal Commission* (1897), Appendix C, p. 164.

manure imports declined until 1904. Prices declined again in 1907, and again the manure imports dropped. Improved prices from 1908 to 1912 were soon followed by increased manuring. Soon after came the war boom during which cultivation was forced to the limit. Then followed the decline of 1920–21 and the recovery of 1922, with the usual effect on manure imports in each case.

Sugar prices have declined since 1925, but since 1928 the manure imports have increased in spite of the almost steady decline in sugar prices. The experiments of the Department of Science and Agriculture have convinced the planters that the increased crop is worth much more than the additional cost of manuring. The results of these experiments have already been summarized on p. 37.

The breeding of cane seedlings has also been of great value, not only to Barbados, but to every cane-producing area. Many of its seedlings have

. . . found their way to other countries, and have become the standard canes of those countries. In Java, before that island had succeeded so remarkably in its cane-breeding experiments, 58% of the sugar area was planted with a Barbados cane. In St. Kitts, B. H. 10(12) and Sc. 12/4 are the most favoured canes; in Antigua B. H. 10(12) and B. 4507 are grown; in Trinidad B. H. 156 is the popular cane, and in Porto Rico B. H. 10(12) and Sc. 12/4 are grown in 90% of the fields.[18]

The actual breeding of seedlings started in 1887, but since careful records were not kept until 1903, it is only possible to surmise what was done. The parent canes used were two White Transparent seedlings, D. 74 and D. 95; also B. 208 and T. 24, both of unknown ancestry. "Most of the Barbados seedlings can be traced to those varieties." [19]

From 1887 to 1925, the

. . . seedlings were . . . obtained from arrows, the fertilisation of whose flowers was left to the results of chance pollination (referred to as open arrows). . . . From 1902–19, however, the above class of seedlings was

---

[18] *Report of the West Indian Sugar Commission* (London, 1930), Part IV, p. 33.
[19] A. E. S. McIntosh, "An Investigation into the Evolution of Sugar Cane Varieties by Breeding in Barbados, 1887–1925," *Agricultural Journal,* I (1932), 10.

supplemented by seedlings derived from one or more methods of controlled pollination.[20]

The results of this breeding were identified by numbers and letters. The numbers represented the individual seedling produced in its class; the letters classified the seedlings by method of fertilization: thus B or Ba (Barbados), B.H. (Barbados Hybrid), B.N.H. (Barbados Natural Hybrid), and B.S.F (Barbados Self-Fertilised). Sc. 12(4) was a Barbados seedling included in a consignment of seedlings sent to St. Croix and selected there.

The promising seedlings which were developed as the result of these experiments are shown in Table 17:

TABLE 17 [a]

PROMISING CANE SEEDLINGS DEVELOPED IN BARBADOS, 1904–25

YEARS	NUMBER OF "PROMISING" SEEDLINGS	SEEDLINGS USED BY THE PLANTERS [b]
Before 1904	32	B.208, B.3405, B.3412
1904–07	5	B.6388, B.6450, B.7169
1908–10	8	None
1911–12	8	Ba.6032, Ba.7924, Ba.8069, B.H. 10(12)
1913–14	10	Ba.11403, Ba.11569, Ba.12079
1915–16	8	B.117
1918–19	5	B.268, B.374, B.381, B.417
1920–22	2	None
1923–25	8	B.606, B.663, B.726, B.755, B.891

[a] A. E. S. McIntosh, "An Investigation into the Evolution of Sugar Cane Varieties by Breeding in Barbados, 1887–1925," *Agricultural Journal*, I (1932), 12–13.
[b] These seedlings were usually used commercially at later dates.

In 1928 a new system of sugar breeding was initiated which involved more careful and extensive experiments including the crossing of Barbadian varieties with imported varieties such as the Javanese P.O.J. One of the first accomplishments of the new system was the development of B. 2935 for use in the drier districts; it was planted with good results on 8,564 acres in 1937. It is too soon to predict the value of the other seedlings which have been

[20] *Ibid.*, p. 4.

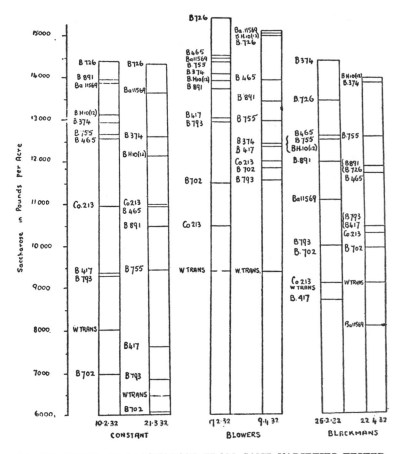

15. THE YIELD OF SACCHAROSE FROM CANE VARIETIES TESTED
IN BARBADOS DURING THE SEASON, 1930–32

Source: Reproduced from *Agricultural Journal*, I (July, 1932), facing p. 6.

developed. This work of the Barbados Department of Science and
Agriculture was recognized when Barbados was chosen in 1931
as the location for the British West Indian Cane Breeding Station.

As a result of these experiments, varieties that are sweeter, as
well as more pest-, disease-, and drought-resistant, have been developed. In addition, varieties have been developed which suit

the peculiar conditions of each part of Barbados, and, of these, five have survived the test of practical commercial planting. B.H. 10(12) seems well suited to the rainy districts for the second half of the crop; B. 726 does well in the rainy districts for the first half of the crop and is also suited to the moderately rainy areas. Ba. 11569 is the important variety in the drier districts, but it is being displaced by B. 891 and B. 2935 in districts which suffer from the gumming disease to which Ba. 11569 is only moderately resistant.

How much have these new varieties contributed to the increased cane tonnage of Barbados? Figure 15 shows that the yields of the new varieties (in terms of sugar per acre) are usually more than twice as high as the yields of the White Transparent canes. Figure 15 also shows that the new varieties are closely adjusted to certain environments. For example, Ba. 11569, which gave the highest yield when harvested on March 9, 1932, at the Blowers plantation, yielded even less than the White Transparent when harvested at the rainier Blackmans plantation on March 22 of the same year. B. 726 surpassed B.H. 10(12) at Constant (medium rainfall station in St. George's Valley), and at the early reaping at Blowers and Blackmans, but was surpassed by B.H. 10(12) at the late reaping at Blowers and Blackmans.

The change in cane varieties planted can be faintly traced in Figure 13. Thus the general upward trend of production per inch of rainfall from 1900 to 1910 coincides with the introduction of the first of the Barbados seedlings. The improved production after 1913 may be in part attributed to the introduction of B.H. 10(12) in the rainy districts and in part to the wider use of the drought-resistant B. 6450 in the drier districts.[21] The abnormally high production per inch of rainfall beginning 1924–25 has been attributed to the greater use of the drought-resistant Ba. 11569.[22] Soon after, a seedling of Ba. 11569, B. 726, was introduced and accounts for part of the heavier yields in the moderately rainy areas.

The production of cotton has not been sufficient to justify ex-

[21] *Colonial Reports: Barbados* (1912–13).   [22] *Ibid.*, p. 5.

tensive seed-raising experiments, and seeds have generally been imported. The only striking effect of the Department of Agriculture's efforts was in 1921 when the introduction of new strains of seed greatly increased the yield.

The ground-provision crop has become increasingly important to the Barbadian economy as the price of sugar has dropped. During the last decade, new varieties have been introduced, and some seedlings have been bred. The statistics for ground provisions are lacking, hence it is impossible to evaluate the practical results of these experiments. On the testing plots, at least, yields have been improved as much as 50 percent by the use of seedlings and imported varieties.

Yields have also been increased by the use of dry farming. Both mulching and the system of planting in holes rather than in rows are measures adapted to the conservation of soil water. Both methods have been used since the latter part of the seventeenth century. The application of pen manure also adds to the organic material in the soil and has a mulching effect. The experiments of the Department of Agriculture from 1928 to 1932 showed that "in a normal year, mulching will result in an increased yield of about 4 tons of cane per acre." [23] There is no specific evidence in Figure 13 that any of the increased cane yields were due to mulching, but since heavier cane yields mean more cane trash and since cane trash is used largely for mulching, it may be safely assumed that an increased amount of mulching has been done.

The methods of weeding and cultivating the land have changed but little during the period under review. Tests have been made of the spacing of sugar cane, cotton, and other crops, and slight but significant changes in the usual spacing have been recommended. For example, if the suggestions for spacing sugar cane are followed, increased yields of from two to five tons of cane per acre may be expected.[24] However, there is no evidence that any of the recent increases in yields are due to changes in weeding, spacing, or methods of cultivation.

[23] *Agricultural Journal,* I (1932), No. 4, 22.
[24] *Report on the Department of Science and Agriculture* (1933–34), pp. 10–15.

3. Economic factors.—In general, increasing prices have led to more intensive cultivation in Barbados. But the broad trends in Barbadian sugar production are influenced not so much by price as by the prospect of profits, actual or hoped-for, and profits are determined by comparing the value of the crop with the expenses. Thus the improvements in cane cultivation noted above have in some cases resulted in a decrease of costs at a faster rate than the decrease in prices.

At certain times, the situation of the sugar industry has been so desperate that increased production has been necessary to compensate for falling prices. At such times, retrenchment measures such as wage reductions and postponement of repairs have been practiced, but the intensive tillage has been maintained. At the same time, the planters have been adopting such measures as new varieties of cane, alternative products, and improved machinery in an attempt to maintain their incomes or, at least, to keep down their losses.

If the two generalizations just presented are considered in relation to Figures 2 and 13, their applicability to Barbados becomes apparent. Thus the declining prices from 1846 to 1876 were offset by approximately 50 percent increase in the production of sugar per inch of rainfall. From 1877 to 1879 prices declined sharply, and the weakened financial position of the planters forced such severe retrenchment that yields were affected. The better prices from 1880 to 1883 brought in some profits which reestablished the planters' credit and enabled them to intensify their methods and increase their yields during the price decline of 1883–86.

Even the combination of misfortunes which hit Barbados during the 1890s was met at first by increasing the applications of manure until the drought and the declining credit of the planters forced greater retrenchment after 1894. The downward trend was halted by the prospect of better prices due to the Spanish-American War. From 1903 until 1914 the trend of production was upward, for Barbados was then reaping the benefits of the scientific experiments which had been continued through the hard times of 1891–99. The World War boom caused not only a more intensive use of the land, but also a slight expansion of the area in cane; the depression of 1921 caused a reversal of both trends. After a brief recovery, a downward trend of prices started, but Barbadian planters combated this by increasing the efficiency of production with great rapidity.[25] Thus examples can be found of both decreasing and increasing intensity of cultivation as the result of declining prices. The former tendency is the more usual in most parts of the world; the latter tendency seems now characteristic in Barbados. The economic pressure which necessitates it has been well stated by the Director of Science and Agriculture:

What everyone should realise is that Barbados with its comparatively small rainfall, large population and small area must have increased sucrose in the cane and there is no other sugar research station in the world which is working on this problem. To combat the world depression we must either produce sweeter and heavier canes for all parts of the island and all periods of the crop or go out of sugar cultivation altogether.[26]

MANUFACTURING

By far the most important industry is the manufacture of sugar cane into muscovado, dark crystals, molasses, sirup, and rum. Much less important are those industries which supply the demand for certain simple manufactures in Barbados and, in some cases, in neighboring islands. These include the biscuit factories, tobacco factory, gas works, electric company, ice company, manure factory, and the Scotland district potteries. Both types of industry are closely related to the production of cane since it determines the amount of raw material available for the first group, and the probable market for the products of the second group.

Statistics for the sugar factories are difficult to obtain since many Barbadian planters do not keep separately the records of their factory and field operations. At least twenty-nine of the sugar factories handle cane from other estates as well as from their own estates. The owners of such factories may thus make

[25] *Barbados Official Gazette,* Supplement, February 27, 1936, pp. 11–14.
[26] *Report on the Department of Science and Agriculture* (1930–31), p. 11.

a profit manufacturing sugar even when their own cane fields are being harvested at a loss.

Three tendencies can be noted in the recent development of the sugar factories: (1) the substitution of steam factories for windmills; (2) the larger size of the factories; and (3) the greatly increased efficiency of the modern factories. The exact dates of these changes are uncertain. At the time of the visit of the 1897 Royal Commission, the following official reply was given to a printed question about the extent of improvements during the preceding fifteen years:

> Improvements in manufacture have not been extensive. Steam machinery has during the last 30 years been more extensively employed for crushing, and has no doubt effected some considerable saving by reason of the greater reliability of its operation as compared with wind power. In 1866 the number of steam mills in the island was 30; in 1875 it was 49; in 1884 it was 90; and in 1895 it was 102. The number of windmills is about 338. In the process of converting the juice into sugar, there has been no improvement in recent years. Eight plantations, aggregating some 5000 acres, have vacuum pans, but these were all erected prior to 1884. There is no triple or multiple effect on any estate in Barbados.[27]

Professor d'Albuquerque, Island Professor of Chemistry and Agricultural Science, testified before the Royal Commission that no double-crushing process was used and that all the mills were three-roller mills. He also pointed out that the muscovado factories produced 7.34 tons of sugar from 100 tons of cane, while central factories could produce 10.49 tons. Furthermore, the amount of sugar expressed in the juice was, according to experiments in 1884:

Factory	Percent
Gordon's (vertical windmill)	59.00
Bulkeley's (steam mill)	64.90
Bentley's (steam mill)	63.08

As these mills were above average, d'Albuquerque estimated that the probable average expression for the island was 55 percent. He

[27] *Report of the West India Royal Commission* (1897), Appendix C, Part III, p. 156.

estimated further that "for every 100 lbs. sucrose (crystallisable sugar) contained in the juice not more than an average of 75 lbs. ordinary Muscovado sugar is recovered." [28] This indicates that there was considerable room for increased factory efficiency in Barbados.

After the turn of the century, new and better machinery was installed in many of the factories as is shown by the high machinery imports in 1901, 1906, 1907, 1910, 1911, 1912, 1914–29, and since 1932. The greatest imports came during the war boom period. As the result of these changes in 1930, there was "every gradation from the windmill, through the three-roller steam plant, the eight-roller up to the factory equipped with a fourteen-roller mill." [29] For the years 1926–28, ten factories produced on the average 10.7 tons of sugar per 100 tons of cane, while the best factory produced 11.6 tons of sugar per 100 tons of cane. By 1934, the figure for the factories had been raised to an average of 11.8 tons of sugar per 100 tons of cane. It should be noted that the sweeter canes as well as the improved machinery and better chemical control contributed to these increases.

OTHER PRODUCTION

Other types of basic economic production in Barbados are mining (oil and building stone) and fishing. Only fishing has any relationship to variability of the environment, and this relationship is difficult to evaluate because of the lack of statistics.

The principal food fish is the flying fish, which is usually caught in large quantities from December to July. Sea eggs are next in importance as seafood ; they are obtainable from August to March since a closed season has been established during the rest of the year. Snappers and other deep-sea fish made up a relatively minor part of the total catch.

The supply of fish in the neighborhood of Barbados often fluctuates, possibly because of changes in ocean currents. No detailed

[28] *Report of the West India Royal Commission* (1897), Appendix C; Part III, p. 211.

[29] *Report of Proceedings, Imperial Sugar Cane Research Conference, London, 1931*, p. 74.

study has been made of this relationship, but some clews may be obtained from the following testimony:

One week fish may be scarce and the next they may be caught in abundance.[30]

Ever since the eruption of Pelee in 1902 the catch of flying fish has fallen off considerably. I remember flying fish used to be landed here in the old days and practically given away. . . . The fish is undoubtedly scarce; fishing boats go out fishing for 8 or 10 hours and bring back four, five or a couple of dozen fish sometimes. This is generally the work of two or three men. . . .

In 1902 we used to catch whales along this coast, but now we don't see them.[31]

There was remarkable unanimity by all the witnesses that the annual catch has fallen off considerably during the past ten years. . . .

It is the unanimous opinion of all the witnesses that the set of the prevailing ocean currents has changed. The most favorable currents, and those that formerly prevailed during the flying-fish season, are SE to NW and SW to NE. The former used generally to be met with during the early part of the season and the latter during the later months. For many years past the general complaint of the fishermen has been that the current sets day after day for prolonged periods from NE to SW.[32]

The change in the supply of local fresh fish affects especially the residents of the coastal districts. Since these districts are most subject to drought, this variable adds one more uncertainty to their food supply. The period of decline in the fishing industry coincides roughly with a period of below-average rainfall (1902–31), which suggests that changes in prevailing winds may control both the fish and rainfall resources.

EXCHANGE

Except for sugar products, ground provisions, pottery, and a few minor products, the goods consumed in Barbados are imported. These imports are paid for by the exports together with

[30] Testimony of Dr. Woolsey of St. Lucy, *Report of the West India Royal Commission* (1897), Appendix C, Part III, p. 174.

[31] Testimony of Mr. Thorne, mimeographed appendices to *Report of the West Indian Sugar Commission* (London, 1930), evidence on Barbados, I, 12.

[32] Report of the Fishing Committee in supplement to the *Barbados Official Gazette,* October 10, 1932, p. 2.

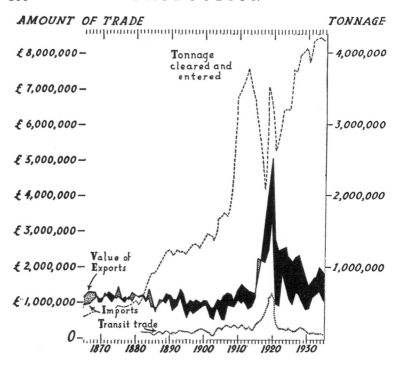

16. THE SHIPPING AND THE EXTERNAL TRADE OF BARBADOS
1865–1935

The black areas represent the amount of the unfavorable balance of trade;
the white areas represent the amount of the favorable balance of trade.

Source: *Statistical Abstract for the Several Colonial and Other Possessions of
the United Kingdom* (London, 1877–1936), various numbers, *passim*.

certain "invisible" items such as interest on foreign investments,
remittances from Barbadians living abroad, and a host of minor
items. These items account for the unfavorable balance of trade
which has existed for every year (except 1916) since 1885.

The exports of Barbados (excluding reëxports) consist mainly
of sugar (95 to 99 percent of the total). Since there is rarely any
large holdover, the quantity and value of the exports vary directly
with the size and value of the sugar production.

The imports of Barbados are roughly proportionate to the exports, but fluctuations in the value of the imports are rarely as

sharp as the fluctuations in the value of the exports. The steady flow of remittances from abroad, the use of credit in poor years, and the accumulation of foreign balances in good years tend to flatten out the import curve.

Less simple is the explanation of the fluctuations in the transit trade. It varies with the prosperity of the neighboring islands as well as with the ease of direct communication between the northern countries and these islands. The statistics are not sufficiently detailed or sufficiently accurate to evaluate the above factors. However, a few points are clarified by the graphs. In many years (for example, 1893, 1895, 1903, 1906, 1907, etc.), the transit trade varied with the imports of Barbados. This is because the same climatic and price fluctuations which influenced the Barbadian economy also influenced the neighboring islands. In two cases (1902–3, 1908–9), sharp declines in the transit trade resulted from quarantines imposed against Barbados—because of smallpox in 1902–3 and yellow fever in 1908–9. Partly as a result of the second quarantine, the Royal Mail Steam Packet ceased to use Barbados as a point of transfer after November, 1910, and thus caused a further decrease in the transit trade.[33] The sharp decreases in the transit trade after 1921 are due to price declines and the establishment of such direct shipping lines as the Canadian National.

Due to its strategic position and its entrepôt trade, Bridgetown handles an unusual amount of shipping in proportion to the size of its Barbadian hinterland. This shipping consists of three types: (1) liners which make Bridgetown a port-of-call; (2) tramp steamers which handle the excess cargo during the crop season; and (3) sailing vessels (schooners) which handle much of the interisland trade as well as some of the staples such as lumber. The liners account for most of the tonnage cleared, but many of them discharge and take on very little cargo. The upward trend of the curve showing clearances (Figure 16) is largely accounted for by the increased size and number of liners. The minor fluctuations (1881, 1895, 1902–3, etc.) represent changes in the trade

[33] *Colonial Reports: Barbados* (1910–11), p. 20.

of Barbados. The effect of the World War on shipping and the effect, also, of the depression of 1921 (which influenced the entire Caribbean trade) stand out conspicuously.

The internal trade of Barbados centers largely at Bridgetown. Most of the planters come to Bridgetown to make their purchases, as do also those of the Negro population who can afford the trip. Most of the island products which enter the internal trade are sold through Bridgetown markets. A few of the imported staples are sold through small stores which are spread throughout the island, but these stores cater mainly to the poorer class which can buy only minute quantities at a time. The internal trade can be measured only through the imports as no other statistics are available.

CHAPTER VIII

The Recent Barbadian Economy: Consumption

THE PRECEDING chapter has shown how Barbadian production has been largely controlled by a combination of three variables: physical environment, technology, and economic conditions. In a one-crop economy such as that of Barbados, production is rarely an end in itself, but rather a means of purchasing goods and services which will provide as much as possible the type of life the producers wish to live. This chapter considers how Barbadian production and the instability of the Barbadian environment have affected the life of the inhabitants.

CONSUMPTION OF COMMODITIES

The one-crop nature of the Barbadian economy makes it fairly easy to estimate the consumption by studying the customs returns. For the following analyses, certain commodities have been selected because returns were available for most of the period 1865–1935 and because these commodities represent the principal types of consumption.

In general, these returns represent goods to be consumed in the near future; but in some cases, the merchants may be building up their inventories in anticipation of a good year, while in other cases, the imports may be less than the consumption because the merchants are reducing their inventories. Rarely, however, are these effects sufficient to invalidate the conclusions based on the imports.

Food—The food supply of Barbados is in part locally raised (ground provisions, fruits, corn meal, some milk and mutton), and in part imported. Accurate figures for the local production are unobtainable, and fluctuations in local production can only be inferred rather than accurately determined. Sweet potatoes, yams, and eddoes are usually cheap just before the cane harvest, but may sell for half again as much during July and August. Their prices are also high in drought years and in years when high prices for sugar cause the canes to occupy an increased acreage. These price fluctuations probably reflect with fair accuracy the periods of large and small supplies of ground provisions.

The cereal imports supplement the ground provisions, and in droughty years may replace them. The cereal line in Figure 17 was obtained by adding together the net imports of rice, corn meal, wheat and other flour, oats, and breads. These staples are consumed by all classes, and a considerable import is necessary to maintain a reasonable standard of nutrition among the laboring classes. Fluctuations in these imports result either from a change in the demand for these articles due to a change in the supply of ground provisions, or from a change in the ability of the people to purchase cereals. Since these cereal imports are among the barest necessities of Barbadian life, a decline in cereal imports for the second reason indicates very hard times.

By comparing the cereal curve with the rainfall, sugar, wage, and other curves on Figures 2, 11, and 19, the following explanations of the major fluctuations are obtained. The high imports of 1868 indicate prosperity following large sugar crops from 1866–68, while the subsequent decline in 1870 reflects two poor sugar crops and declining sugar prices. The high imports in 1873–74 accompany two years of low rainfall and, probably, poor ground-provision crops. Improving rainfall conditions in 1875 accompanied a sharp decline of cereal imports. In 1877, an improvement in wages and in sugar prices and a fair sugar crop permitted an increased standard of living and consequently higher cereal imports.

To avoid the repetition of the same factors, the balance of this curve is interpreted in Table 18.

The imports of salt fish and meat are also used by all classes. These staples represent luxury foods for the laboring classes and cheap food for the middle and upper classes. In general, the curve follows the cereal curve and is affected by the same factors. In certain drought years (such as 1891 and 1912) when high cereal im-

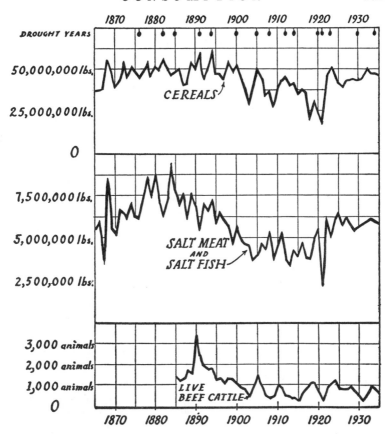

17. THE IMPORTS OF FOODSTUFFS INTO BARBADOS, 1865–1935

Source: *Statistical Abstract for the Several Colonial and Other Possessions of the United Kingdom* (London, 1877–1936), various numbers, *passim;* Barbados *Blue Books,* 1912–35.

ports were necessary to replace ground provisions, the imports of salt fish and meats were low because of low purchasing power. Also, whereas the general downward trend in cereal imports accompanied the decline of population, the downward trend in salt fish and meat imports started with the decline of the sugar prices in the 1880s. It is also interesting to note that in many economically difficult years, the decline in salt meat and fish imports was proportionately larger,

TABLE 18

CAUSES OF THE CHANGES IN THE AMOUNT OF CEREALS IMPORTED INTO
BARBADOS, 1879–1932

YEAR	CHANGE IN IMPORTS	PROBABLE CAUSES OF CHANGE
1879	Sharp decrease	Good ground-provision crop and poor prices for sugar
1880–82	Upward trend	Better sugar prices; lower flour prices
1883–88	Very sharp decrease	Sharp drop in sugar prices; labor economies on estates
1889–91	Very sharp increase	Bumper crops; higher sugar prices; labor economies abandoned
1892–93	Very sharp decrease	Collapse of Bourbon cane; more local foodstuffs
1894	Very sharp increase	Severe drought; very poor provisions crop; abnormally low prices for imported foods
1895–97	Sharp decrease	Poor sugar prices, reduced wages; more attention to local foodstuffs
1898–99	Moderate increase	Foodstuffs sent in to relieve hurricane sufferers; fair sugar prospects 1899–1900

The general downward trend after 1898 is in part due to the decrease
in population which probably began about this time.

Year	Change	Cause
1901–4	Sharp decrease	More attention to local foodstuffs due to poor sugar prices; unusually good local crops in 1903
1905–6	Sharp increase	Better prices for sugar; poor provision crops; increasing remittances from abroad
1907–10	Sharp decrease	Decline in sugar price; more emphasis on local foodstuffs
1911–12	Increase	Drought and poor local ground provisions
1913–21	Declining imports	Increased world provision prices; war restrictions on export of U.S. foods; prices of imported foods increased much faster than wages
1922–23	Very sharp increase	Unusual prosperity due to increase in sugar prices and drop in cereal prices

TABLE 18 (*Continued*)

YEAR	CHANGE IN IMPORTS	PROBABLE CAUSES OF CHANGE
1924–31	Somewhat lower	Declining sugar prices and slightly higher cereal prices; more attention to ground provisions
1932–	Gradually higher	Increasing population and slightly improved purchasing power

and occurred sooner, than the decline in cereal imports, for example, in 1869–70, 1882, 1885–86, 1891, 1899, 1909, 1912–13, and 1921.

The imports of live cattle are largely for slaughter, and therefore represent the fresh-meat consumption of the island. The bulk of this meat is sold to the middle and upper classes, and the imports therefore reflect the prosperity of these classes. Thus 1888–91, 1904–6, 1909–11, 1914–20, and 1922–29 were all periods when the planters and merchants were relatively prosperous; the intervening years were periods of depression or decline in business.

Textiles and clothing.—The textile curves (Figure 18) are not so satisfactory as the food curves because the items included in textiles have varied from period to period. Thus the curve up to 1899 does not include silk manufactures; after 1917 the only figures available include haberdashery and millinery. It should be noted that these figures are not net imports, and that they therefore include some reëxports.

In spite of the unsatisfactory nature of the textile figures, one generalization is clearly proved by the curve: textile and clothing purchases vary with the value of the Barbadian exports. When times are hard, it is easy for the Barbadian workers to make their clothes do for another year or two. When they can afford to buy clothes, as in good years, even the laborers purchase stocks of cloth and cheap clothing. Similar purchasing habits exist among the planters, although the yearly fluctuations in purchases among this class are probably not so great.

The planters' purchasing habits in clothing are probably reflected in the imports of leather goods since the laboring classes either have

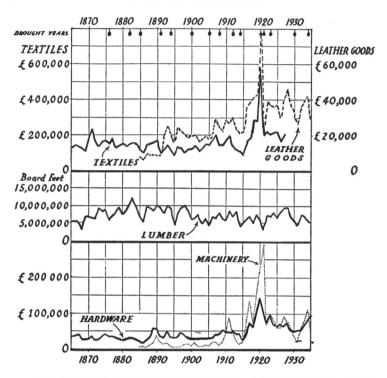

18. THE IMPORTS OF TEXTILES, LEATHER GOODS, LUMBER, HARD-
WARE, AND MACHINERY INTO BARBADOS, 1865–1935

Source: *Statistical Abstract for the Several Colonial and Other Possessions of
the United Kingdom* (London, 1877–1936), various numbers, *passim; Barbados
Blue Books,* 1912–35.

not worn shoes in important quantities, or else have worn rubber
shoes (sneakers). The curve of leather imports trends with the
textile curve and also with the curve of Barbadian exports.

Building materials and capital goods.—In general, the imports
in this group (Figure 18) fluctuate with the value of the exports of
Barbadian produce. In some cases, especially machinery and lum-
bering, there is a lag of one year which probably represents the
time necessary to order and receive goods from abroad after money
is received from the sugar crop.

The hardware curve, with a very few exceptions, follows the general rule stated above. The large imports of hardware in the poor years, 1897–98, were probably for dwelling improvements due to the extension of the water system. The large imports from 1907 to 1912 may represent similar improvements paid for by money earned abroad, especially in the Canal Zone.

The lumber curve also follows the general rule except in three cases. The extension of the water system and the repairs necessitated by the hurricane of 1898 account for the high lumber imports from 1897 to 1899. The prosperity brought about by "Panama money" is reflected in the imports of 1908, 1911, and 1913. Imports during the World War were low because lumber was expensive and hard to get. The generally low consumption since 1899 may be due to the declining population, and the consequent lessened demand for new houses.

The machinery curve shows the effects not only of high exports, but also of the current prospects of the sugar industry. A lag of one year is evident, for sugar machinery cannot be ordered on the spur of the moment. Thus the good prospects of the industry in 1889–90 resulted in heavy machinery imports in 1890–91. The improved prices in 1904–5 brought increased imports in 1906–7, and similar prices in 1910 resulted in higher imports in 1911.

Agricultural supplies.—This type of import includes two groups. The first consists of materials for containers including barrels, staves, sacks, bags, and the like. It is obvious that these imports vary approximately with the exports of the articles they are designed to hold. The second group consists of manures and feeds which directly or indirectly feed the crops.

Four curves have been plotted to represent the second group (Figure 14). The most complete curve is that of the value of artificial manure imports. This curve has the disadvantage of being affected by price fluctuations, especially after 1914. To supply quantitative data, two curves are provided: (1) guano imports, since guano was the principal manure until 1887; (2) sulphate of ammonia imports, since this chemical has been the leading imported fertilizer since 1887. The oil-meal (including oil cake) imports are appropriately shown with the manures, since these commodities are fed to the cattle, whose principal function is to produce pen manure.

Several general trends are apparent in these graphs. The trend of manure consumption was downward until 1887 when experiments showed the value of scientific manuring. Since 1887 the manure consumption has increased gradually, and the chemical manures have become more important than the guano. The downward trend of oil-meal imports from 1890 to 1915 suggests that less attention was being paid to cattle feeding, and hence to pen-manure production, during that period. This trend has been reversed since the World War.

The annual fluctuations in manure consumption have already been explained (pages 153–56). The prospects of a profitable sugar crop and the profits from the preceding year were in most cases the factors determining the increases and decreases in manure consumption.

The imports of oil meal also fluctuate with the prospects of the sugar industry. The shortage of locally grown fodder also influences these imports. In drought years, the harvest of sour grass and other hay crops is poor, and imported food must be used to supplement the pasturage. Thus, during the droughts of 1894, 1912, 1920, and 1930, the fodder imports increased although the planters were in a poor position to pay for them.

WEALTH

The analysis of Barbadian consumption of the staple commodities was not difficult. The factors analyzed in the balance of this chapter will be somewhat more difficult to measure. Nevertheless, there are sufficient indices available to make the analysis worth while. However, where data are lacking altogether or are impossible to evaluate, it has seemed better to omit the topic altogether rather than risk erroneous generalizations. Thus such important aspects of social life as religion, fraternal organizations, and amusements, are omitted. These factors may have some relationship to the fluctuations of the environment and its products, but the writer has not uncovered enough evidence to make any satisfactory statements.

The wealth of Barbados consists largely of land and of those things which are attached to the land: houses, windmills, barns, sugar machinery, and other improvements. Although it is impossible to give an accurate estimate of the value of estates for each year since the sales are not usually numerous enough to afford a fair sample, it can be safely stated that the exchange value of the land varies greatly according to the prospects of the sugar industry. The following facts (as well as the general opinion of Barbadian planters) support the above generalization. In 1881, when sugar sold in Barbados for $3.40–$4.20 per hundredweight the estimated total value of the estates was £5,558,680; in 1897, when sugar sold for $1.65–$2.30 per hundredweight, the estimated value of these estates was £1,973,025.[1] Real-estate values remained low until the war boom which culminated in 1920 when twenty-four estates sold for an average of £146 per acre.[2] After the crash, many of these purchases were "subsequently abandoned with the loss of large installments of the purchase price."[3] Some fortunate individuals retired from the sugar business during the boom; but most planters held on, and some of these were forced to sell at prices which barely covered their debts, for example, one estate was bought for £30,000 in 1920 and sold for £6,000 in 1930. Since 1930, prices have averaged about £35–£40 per acre.

Several trends have resulted from the declining values which have characterized most of the period since 1890. Absentee owners have

---

[1] *Report of the West India Royal Commission* (1897), Appendix C, Part III, p. 197. On p. 207, the average prices per acre from 1851–96 are given. These seem in most years to be influenced by the number and location of the plantations sold rather than by economic trends. In years when over twenty plantations were sold, the average prices reflect the influence of economic conditions. For example:

Year	Number of Estates Sold	Acreage Sold	Average Price per Acre
1888	12	1,329	£39
1889	36	5,629	42
1890	32	4,270	44
1891	7	1,442	26
1892	11	1,563	26
1893	23	4,899	35
1894	17	2,425	35
1895	5	522	28
1896	16	2,291	27

[2] *Colonial Reports: Barbados* (1920–21), p. 6.
[3] *Ibid.* (1921–22), p. 6.

found it increasingly difficult to manage their estates from abroad. A few have returned to Barbados, but most have sold out. Thus in 1897, 53 percent of the land was owned by absentee proprietors, but only 7.4 percent was thus owned in 1929.[4] In some cases, these estates were absorbed by neighboring estates; in many cases they were taken over, and continued as a unit under Barbadian management. A considerable number of the estates located near Bridgetown, or on marginal lands, were subdivided and sold as small peasant holdings.

As a result of consolidations and subdivisions, the number of sugar estates declined. The most rapid declines occurred during the periods of economic depression. The number of estates remained fixed at 508 from 1865 to 1890;[5] during the depressed period of 1890–96 the number declined to 441. A further decline to 388 occurred in 1902 when the *Blue Book* notes that forty-nine estates were sold or rented. In 1908, another count showed that the number of estates had been reduced to 332. In 1912 the number was 320, and in 1919, 305. The most recent figures are shown in Table 19.[6]

TABLE 19

NUMBER OF AGRICULTURAL HOLDINGS IN BARBADOS

ACRES	NUMBER OF HOLDINGS
Over 300	47
200–99	65
100–99	98
21–99	87
5–20	308
1–5	3,832
Under 1	13,899
Total	18,336

Homes play a much more important part in the wealth of Barbados than money values would seem to indicate. Barbadians

[4] *Memorandum of Information Prepared by a Local Committee* (West Indian Sugar Commission, 1929), p. 4.

[5] Figures on the estates are based on the *Barbados Blue Book* (1865–1934).

[6] From Department of Science and Agriculture estimate.

. . . have always striven for the privilege of living in their separate houses, however small the hut might be.

Wherever they are established in villages, they invariably take a pride in keeping, within the scope of their means, these small dwellings tidy. A large number of those working on plantations have been helped always by the plantation owners to keep their houses in repair by the credit of lumber repayable on the installment principle.[7]

The houses of the planters are generally of the local limestone, and are included in the valuations of the sugar estates. The bulk of the agricultural laborers own their homes but do not own the land on which they are placed. Their homes are generally of wood, and are constructed so that they may be taken apart and carried on carts to new locations if employment conditions necessitate such a move.

Although the value of the sugar estates has in general been declining, the demand for small homes has been so great that exorbitant prices have been asked for the small plots into which the estates have been subdivided. These prices were possible because large numbers of Barbadians were returning from the Canal Zone, Cuba, and the United States with large sums for real-estate investments. Thus 13,002 Barbadians returned between January, 1906, and December, 1910, and brought £102,456 with them.[8] As a result, prices such as £80 and £100 per acre prevailed, although plantations were selling at half that rate or less.[9]

The growing sugar crop is sometimes considered as a separate part of the wealth of Barbados, since it may be pledged as security for loans. Obviously, its value varies with the value of the sugar production and with the season of the year. The planters often carry fire and hurricane insurance on their canes as well as on their buildings; if they use these assets as collateral, the insurance is required.

Barbadians have also an important resource in foreign investments. Local bankers are unwilling to reveal the size of these investments, or to estimate the amount of income received from them. It is commonly admitted that both sums are high, and that the in-

[7] *Report on the Census of Barbados, 1921*, p. 42.

[8] *Census of Barbados, 1891–1911*, p. 8.

[9] "Evidence on Barbados," *Report of the West Indian Sugar Commission* (London, 1930), Appendix III, I, 59–63.

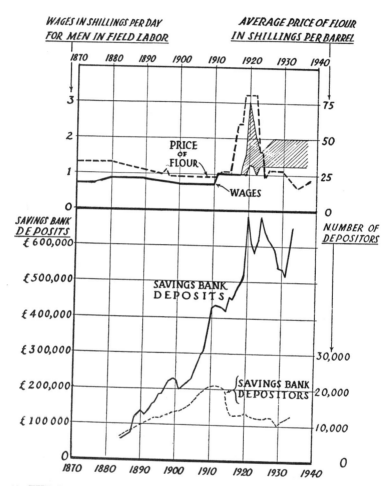

19. THE PRICE OF FLOUR, THE RATE OF AGRICULTURAL WAGES
THE SAVINGS BANK DEPOSITS, AND THE NUMBER OF SAVINGS
BANK DEPOSITORS, 1870–1938

These statistics considered together provide indices of the trends in the prosperity
of the working classes in Barbados.

Sources: *Barbados Blue Books,* 1870–1935; *Colonial Reports: Barbados* (1910–
37–38).

come received is an important part of the explanation of the unfavorable balance of trade (see below). The statistics of the Government savings bank represent a small part of these investments,
and provide the only index of the savings of the people. These figures (Figure 19) show a sharp upward trend until 1920, with breaks
in the trend in such depression years as 1891, 1901–2, and 1912–
14. A large part of these savings probably represent amounts re-
mitted from abroad by Barbadian emigrants. The sharp decline in
the number of depositors in 1915 probably represents the closing
of accounts by the poorer people whose wages advanced much less
rapidly than prices. Since 1920 the deposits follow the ups and
downs of prosperity of the island. If remittances from abroad have
been important during this recent period, they have been probably

OCCUPATIONS AND INCOME

The percentage of people in each occupational group has remained about the same since 1891 with the single exception of the
commercial group, which has greatly increased in importance.
Table 20 shows the distribution of people by occupations:
offset by withdrawals for land purchases and house construction.

TABLE 20 [a]

DISTRIBUTION OF BARBADIANS BY OCCUPATIONS, 1891–1921

PRINCIPAL OCCU-TIONAL GROUPS	1891		1911		1921	
	Per-cent	*Number*	*Per-cent*	*Number*	*Per-cent*	*Number*
Agriculture . .	24.8	44,995	21.9	37,692	21.9	34,157
Commerce . .	4.8	8,607	7.0	12,054	8.4	13,169
Domestic . .	12.4	22,229	15.3	26,762	16.2	25,255
Education . .	21.9	39,445	20.4	34,988	16.8	26,208
Industry . .	15.5	27,693	15.8	27,164	15.1	23,682
Other (including unemployed) .	20.6	37,337	19.6	33,323	21.6	33,841
Total . .	100.0	182,306	100.0	171,983	100.0	156,312

[a] *Report on the Census of Barbados, 1891–1911*, 1921.

Few figures are available as to the income of each group, and the following generalizations, which are based on a few statistics, and on the opinions of informed Barbadians, should be accepted with caution.

The agricultural group consisted in 1921 of 469 owners, 32,728 laborers, and 946 managers and other plantation employees. The incomes of the owners depend on the balance between the value of the crop and the expenses. Since the expenses (except harvesting and haulage) per acre tend to be the same in good seasons and bad, the cost of production per unit is much higher in poor years. Table 21 substantiates this statement:

TABLE 21 [a]

RAINFALL AND THE COST OF PRODUCING CANE IN BARBADOS, 1931–33

RAINFALL IN PRECEDING YEAR (INCHES)	YEAR OF HARVEST	AVERAGE COST OF PRODUCING CANE PER TON	
		Twenty-three Black-soil Estates	*Seventeen Red-soil Estates*
38.05	1931	$4.96	$3.11
71.45	1932	3.04	2.72
61.81	1933	3.45	2.77

[a] *Barbados Official Gazette,* February 27, 1936, Supplement, p. 13.

The profits or losses of the planters depend on the difference between these costs and the amount paid for cane at the various windmills and factories. The amount paid for cane varies considerably from year to year, and from factory to factory. No recent figures applicable to the entire island are available.

The managers and other plantation employees such as accountants are usually paid a fixed salary plus certain perquisites such as housing, garden produce, etc. Their incomes fluctuate only as the owners feel it necessary to cut expenses. In cases in which managers receive a percentage of the profits as part of their compensation, the occurrence of good and bad seasons influences them directly.

The incomes of the agricultural laborers are influenced by the size of the crop, by the amount of repair work performed, and by the rate of wages. Of these, the size of the crop seems most important. Thus the crops in 1932 and 1933 were large, and work was available to all laborers that wished it. Their earnings were high, although the profits of the planters were low or nonexistent because of the low price of sugar. The other factors, rate of wages, and amount of repair work, vary roughly with the condition of the sugar industry. Thus wages were reduced from 1865–70, from 1892–1902, and from 1920–24. According to the *Blue Books,* wages have not been reduced during the declining sugar prices since 1925; the laborers claim, however, that real wages have actually declined because larger tasks are expected for the standard rate.

The income of the commercial group cannot be stated. Many Barbadians expressed the opinion that it does not fluctuate so much as that of the planters since the merchants receive certain profits and commissions even in years when planters are selling at a loss. The same statements have been made concerning the industrial group including those engaged in the manufacture of sugar.

The people of Barbados receive important amounts of income from sources outside of the island, including tourists, commissions, foreign investments, and Barbadians working abroad and on ships. The amounts of these remittances are uncertain, and usually vary with conditions abroad rather than on the island. In 1930, accord-

TABLE 22

INCOME RECEIVED BY BARBADIANS FROM SOURCES OUTSIDE
OF BARBADOS

SOURCE		AMOUNTS
Remitted by Barbadians abroad		*(in £1,000s)*
Money orders	£78	
In letters	80 (est.)	
Through banks	100 (est.)	£258
Earnings of seamen (est.)		30–50
Commissions earned (est.)		50
Harbor fees		11
Tourists (est.)		30–55
Foreign investments (est.)		150–250
Total		£529–674

ing to the general opinion of informed Barbadians, the amounts in Table 22 were received.

If the smaller amount be accepted, these sources of income provided amounts equal to more than half the value of the exports of Barbadian produce during that year (£837,594). In a one-crop economy, such an extra source of income must have been an important "anchor to windward" during bad years; it may also explain why, although Barbados has repeatedly been on the verge of bankruptcy, it has, nevertheless, always had the resources to take advantage of the next upturn in business.

The income-tax statistics might be expected to give a good summary of the earnings of the planter and merchant classes. Unfortunately, the Barbadian Government is unwilling to reveal any information on these except the total amount paid each year. As the rates have varied, these figures are not comparable. Where possible, the amounts collected have been adjusted to present a comparable series (Table 23).

TABLE 23 [a]

INCOME TAX AND EXPORTS OF BARBADOS, 1921–27

TAX BASED ON INCOME FOR YEAR	INCOME TAX COLLECTED	TAX COLLECTED REDUCED TO 1926–27 RATE	TOTAL EXPORTS IN £1,000 (*First year 1921*)
1921–22	£18,244	£9,122	£1,467
1922–23	31,869	15,434	1,259
1923–24	121,314	60,657	2,189
1924–25	37,921	37,921	1,849
1925–26	21,508	21,508	1,421
1926–27	15,180	15,180	1,287

[a] *Barbados Blue Book* (1922–28).

It is apparent that the taxable income fluctuates with the value of exports.

VITAL STATISTICS

During most of the nineteenth century, the Barbadian population was increasing at a steady pace which was interrupted in only a few years, as during the cholera epidemic of 1854. About the beginning of the next century, this trend was reversed, and the population declined. No census has been taken since 1921, but it is generally agreed that the population has been increasing since 1921.

The principal cause of these trends has been changes in the rate of emigration and immigration. Emigration has been common since 1840, but the rate was not sufficient to do more than slow down the rate of population growth until about 1900. Accurate figures on emigration are not available (those in the official statistics are known to be incomplete), but since most of the emigrants are men, the ratio of men to women (Table 24) offers a clew to the rate of emigration.

TABLE 24 [a]

NUMBER OF WOMEN PER 100 MEN IN BARBADOS, 1844–1921

YEAR	WOMEN
1844	120
1851	118
1861	115
1871	121
1881	123
1891	125
1911	145
1921	148

[a] Barbados census reports.

These figures indicate that the rate of emigration declined from 1844 to 1861, increased slowly from 1861 to 1891, increased sharply from 1891 to 1911, and then continued at a high rate until 1921.

Poor economic conditions in Barbados and opportunities abroad for Barbadian laborers combined to encourage emigration. As a result, Barbadians worked on the Panama Canal, on the banana plantations of Central America, in the cane fields of Cuba and Santo Domingo, and in the seaboard cities of northeastern United States. Since 1921, immigration restrictions have been tightened in the United States and in some Latin-American countries, the Panama Canal offers little employment, and Cuba has contracted its sugar

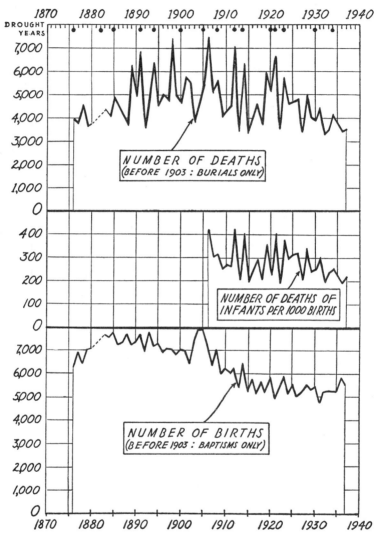

20. THE NUMBER OF BIRTHS AND DEATHS AND THE INFANTILE
DEATH RATE IN BARBADOS, 1881–1937

Sources: *Barbados Blue Books*, 1870–1935; *Colonial Reports: Barbados* (1880–1937–38).

acreage. No wonder the official figures have shown a surplus of immigrants (returning Barbadians) since 1921.

The number of births, obviously, influences the population. In turn, the number of births is influenced by the disproportion of the sexes which was caused by male emigration. Thus the downward trend of births (baptisms before 1903) started after 1893, or about the same time as the increase of emigration.

The variation in the number of births from year to year is small compared with the variation in the number of deaths. With one possible exception, the variation in births seems to be due to chance. The exception to be noted is the decline in births after a drought year. This occurred in 1892, 1913, 1915, 1921, 1931, and 1935.

Table 25 demonstrates that the Barbadian death rate is high largely because of an abnormally high infantile death rate.

TABLE 25 [a]

DEATH RATES AND INFANTILE DEATH RATES IN BARBADOS, BRITISH GUIANA, AND TRINIDAD, 1924–29

	DEATH RATE PER 1,000 INHABITANTS			DEATH RATE UNDER ONE YEAR PER 1,000 LIVING BIRTHS		
Year	Barbados	British Guiana	Trinidad	Barbados	British Guiana	Trinidad
1924	29.5	25.6	...	298	165	
1925	29.5	24.2	29.5	312	155	134
1926	29.6	25.5	28.8	314	159	143
1927	20.2	26.0	17.8	201	158	130
1928	30.1	27.9	18.7	331	185	129
1929	23.7	23.5	18.5	239	146	128

[a] *Report of the Acting Chief Medical Officer* (1929), p. 4.

The importance of the infantile death rate is further shown in Figure 20 where it will be noted that an unusually large number of deaths occurred during the years with a high number of births, for example: 1885, 1891, 1905, 1908, 1914, 1923, and 1928. In a few cases, as in 1894, 1901, 1905, 1921, the large number of deaths occurred one year after the unusual number of births.

There is little doubt that the high infantile death rate in Barbados is largely due to malnutrition and to diseases which result from it. The diet of the average Barbadian worker is so close to the minimum necessary for life that any food shortages are likely to have immediate repercussions on the health of the laboring class.[10] Young children seem most susceptible to such food deficiencies. In 1936, a committee was appointed by Governor Young to study nutrition in Barbados. This committee collected sample diets which are summarized in Table 26.

TABLE 26 [a]

TYPICAL DIETS OF BARBADIAN WORKING-CLASS ADULTS

COST PER ADULT PER DAY IN CENTS	COST PER ADULT PER WEEK IN CENTS	CALORIES PER DAY	MAIN FOODS USED
5.93	41.52	1,962	Rice, flour, sugar, potatoes, dried peas, salt meat and fish, cooking oil
10.85	75.93	3,065	The above plus more flour, milk, meat, and cooking oil
15.02	105.16	4,758	More of everything, especially meat and milk

[a] "Report of the Committee Appointed to Consider and Report on the Question of Nutrition in Barbados," *Barbados Official Gazette*, October 7, 1937, pp. 2–4.

---

[10] "The Committee consider that the diet of the average worker can be classed at the best only as a maintenance diet, and that the great shortage of milk, eggs, and fresh vegetables cannot be too strongly stressed, and there is no reason to doubt that many households live on the borderland of extreme poverty." ("Report of the Committee Appointed to Consider and Report on the Question of Nutrition in Barbados," *Barbados Official Gazette*, October 7, 1937, p. 5.)

"The above investigations have shown that the diets are deficient in fat, protein, and almost completely devoid of vitamins, and that the general health is bound to deteriorate. The poor physique of the average laborer, the abnormally high percentage of people with carious teeth, the prevalence of pellagra, the increase in the incidence of tuberculosis, and the lack of resistance in persons suffering from infectious diseases, provide sufficient evidence of the truth of this statement." (*Ibid.*, pp. 7–8.)

The best diet is perhaps typical of that of the skilled workers around Bridgetown; while the poorest diet is typical of that of the agricultural laborers in a large part of the island. These are representative diets—not minimum diets. Several of the diets cost less than thirty cents per week per adult.

During the last century, another factor, namely the unduly large proportion of children and old people in the Barbadian population, has contributed to the high death rate as well as to its variability. The healthy and more energetic workers are the group who emigrate; the men who remain behind are, on the whole, inferior in health and ambition. When the emigrants return, they have often reached at least middle age, and are especially subject to those diseases which accompany the approach of old age. Table 27 shows how emigration has removed a large part of the male population at the ages when their labor would have been the greatest asset to Barbados:

TABLE 27 [a]

POPULATION OF BARBADOS BY AGE GROUPS, 1921

AGE GROUP	NUMBER IN GROUP	NUMBER OF FEMALES IN EXCESS OF MALES
Under 10	35,229	363
10–19	36,523	1,953
20–29	24,925	8,167
30–39	16,944	7,542
40–49	16,617	5,253
50–59	12,786	3,120
60–69	8,397	2,123
70–79	3,774	1,288
80–89	976	468
Over 90	132	76

[a] *Report on the Census of Barbados, 1921*, p. 17.

An examination of the number of deaths [11] as shown in Figure 20 demonstrates the importance of nutrition in explaining the Barba-

[11] The graphs show the number of deaths and births rather than the birth rates and death rates because the population estimates on which these rates are based are known to be inaccurate.

dian death rate. The drought years, 1885, 1891, 1894, 1912, 1914, 1920–21, and 1923, stand out as years with unusual numbers of deaths. The hurricane year, 1898, was also a year of food shortage and, consequently, of many deaths. Other years of numerous deaths are due to difficulty in obtaining adequate food. Thus in 1901 many plantations began a policy of retrenchment which reduced the amount of work. From 1905 to 1908, the rains were extremely irregular, and the ground-provisions crops were poor. During 1909, the prices on imported provisions were high, and local provision crops were small because most of the land was used for sugar cane.

What part do epidemics play in explaining the fluctuation in the number of deaths? Apparently epidemics are the immediate cause, but the more basic cause is malnutrition. The years with a large number of deaths usually showed epidemics of dysentery, diarrhea, and enteric (typhoid) fever. But these diseases have been present in most years, and it is only when the food supply is poorer than usual that they cause abnormal numbers of deaths.

Until 1925 the law did not require the registration of the cause of death, and it 's therefore extremely difficult to estimate the influence of each disease.

Epidemics of smallpox (1902) and yellow fever (1908) have already been described (pages 128–29). An epidemic of malaria occurred in 1927 and caused deaths until 1930. All of these epidemics were due not so much to local conditions as to infection brought in by visitors. The epidemics were disturbing because of the quarantines they caused, and because of the fear of their spread through-

TABLE 28 [a]

Seasonal Distribution of Deaths from Diseases of the Digestive System, 1928–30

YEAR	JANUARY– MARCH	APRIL– JUNE	JULY– SEPTEMBER	OCTOBER– DECEMBER
1928 . .	106	118	493	475
1929 . .	88	84	282	237
1930 . .	85	80	268	323

[a] *Reports of the Registrar on Vital Statistics* (1928, 1929, 1930).

out the island, but their effect on the death rate was slight compared with the effect of the endemic diseases.

Table 28 shows that epidemics of diarrhea and enteritis occur each year during the rainy season. But it is evidently not the rains themselves which cause this seasonal distribution, for if this were the cause, the rainy years should have the highest death rate and the rainy parts of the island should suffer most severely. But neither of these corollaries is true. The deaths from diarrhea epidemics are highest in drought years. The following quotation dismisses the second corollary:

> The topographic analysis of the death-rate during this period is in- structive. From the highlands of St. John and St. Andrew it rose from 16.7 and 19.6 per 1000 respectively to 33.1 and 45.5 per 1000 in the low flat districts on the coast.[12]

A more probable explanation of the seasonal and yearly distribu- tion of deaths is found in economic causes which are related to rain- fall. The dry season is the harvest season, and work is plentiful; the rainy season is the slack period. Furthermore, if, due to a poor year, the planters are forced to economize on the use of labor, it is easier to do so during the rainy season. Another possible factor is the scarcity and high prices of ground provisions during the rainy sea- son, especially during the early part of the season (page 44). If the year is abnormally dry, those ground provisions which are harvested during the rainy season will be scarcer, and consequently higher in price, while at the same time the workers will have less money to buy the provisions. The scarcity of both ground provisions and of rainy-season employment is more acute in the drier districts, hence the higher death rates there.

In concluding this topic, attention should be called to the decreas- ing number of deaths since 1921. This trend is especially significant since it is believed that the population has been increasing during this period. The explanation is probably to be found in the greater amount of work due to larger crops; in the larger proportion of young and middle-aged males in the population; in the spread of knowledge of sanitation; and in the increasing concern of the Bar-

---

[12] *Colonial Reports: Barbados* (1894), p. 10.

badian people about the health conditions of the island. In the past, many Barbadians have been satisfied to consider Barbados as "the Sanitarium of the West Indies," and to neglect the evidence presented to them. Thus when in 1916, the International Health Board surveyed the conditions in Barbados,[13] its offer of assistance was refused. The recent report of the Committee on Nutrition and the tone of debates in the Barbadian Assembly indicate that this attitude has changed. Perhaps the most striking evidence of progress is that the droughts of 1930 and 1934 did not increase the number of deaths even one-quarter as much as the earlier droughts.

THE GOVERNMENT

Barbados has a representative government whose actions are limited by the veto power of the Crown and by a few minor restrictions. But the Barbadian Legislature does not represent the entire populace since only those males who have an annual income of £50 or the equivalent are eligible to vote. Approximately 18 percent of the adult male population can meet these requirements. Thus the legislature represents primarily the merchant, planter, and professional classes.

The functions of the Government are primarily to protect the interests of the upper classes by protecting property, aiding agriculture and commerce, and relieving the laboring class sufficiently to prevent disturbances. In performing these functions the Government has had to adopt numerous measures to offset fluctuations in the Barbadian environment and economy. Only the most important of these measures are presented below since a complete account would be more voluminous than informative.

Aiding sugar production and trade.—It is obvious that a sugar plantation loses much of its value as a working organism if creditors

[13] G. P. Paul, "Report on Ankylostomiasis Infection Survey of Barbados, from September 4 to November 16, 1916." The report shows the low standard of sanitation which prevailed in Barbados, including the lack of latrines and other sanitary conveniences. Hookworm infection was widespread; 69.1 percent of the population of St. Thomas were infected, but only 21–28 percent of the population of the drier parishes were infected. The prevalence of hookworm undoubtedly partially explains the poor resistance to other diseases.

are able to force the sale of any part of it. The chancery system is a legal device to prevent such dissolution. Let us suppose that the owner of a plantation is unable to pay the interest on the mortgages. A receiver is appointed by the court of chancery. This official has the right to raise money for working capital on the security of the plantation or its crops. At the end of a year, the plantation is appraised by a group of planters appointed for the purpose, and it is then put up for sale for the benefit of the creditors. If it is not sold, it continues to operate under a receiver. Reappraisements may be made from time to time at the request of the creditors. However, since the estate cannot be sold for less than the appraised value (except with the consent of all the creditors), the sale of estates at panic prices is prevented.[14]

A second means of keeping estates in cultivation is provided by the Agricultural Aids Acts. The first of these was passed in 1887 after a coincidence of poor crops and low prices in 1886 left many planters without any means of raising working capital.[15] These acts permit planters to borrow money for working capital with the growing crop as security. Such loans are first liens on the crop and rank ahead of the rights of mortgagees and other creditors. These loans are obtained either from commercial banks, from merchants, or from the Sugar Industry Agricultural Bank.

The third means of keeping estates in cultivation is the Sugar Industry Agricultural Bank. In 1902 the British Parliament gave the island £80,000 to tide over the planters between the time of the signing of the Brussels Convention and its coming into operation. Similar gifts to other British sugar-producing colonies were divided among the planters. The Barbadian share of the gift was used, instead, to form the capital of the Sugar Industry Agricultural Bank. This bank was so successful from 1903 until 1920 that it increased its capital out of earnings to £146,968 by 1920. It suffered severe losses in 1921 when nearly a quarter of a million pounds of loans remained unpaid. The prosperous years which followed resulted in

[14] For a complete explanation of foreclosures in chancery, see *Report of the West India Royal Commission* (1897), Appendix C, Part III, pp. 170–71.
[15] *Ibid.*, p. 157.

the repayment of most of these loans, and the bank again was able to make profits, and increase its capitalization to above £200,000.[16]

The Barbadian Government has aided the sugar industry through the work of the Department of Science and Agriculture (pages 150–60), through instruction in agriculture in the schools, and through the provision of transport facilities such as roads and wharves. The Imperial Government has aided through empire tariff preferences, grants, advice, and the development and protection of sea routes.

Protecting property.—The Barbadian Government must protect property both against the cupidity of man and against the destructive forces of nature. On the whole, the Government has been more successful in its regulation of man, for the island is remarkably free from major crimes, due as much to the character of the people as to the efficient police force.

Petty crimes, on the other hand, are quite common, and vary in number with the poverty of the laboring class. Praedial larceny and setting cane fires are the most significant of these offenses. The former offense consists of the theft of food or livestock from estates, and is especially common when the laborers are without means of purchasing food. The firing of cane fields may be motivated by revenge or by a need for immediate employment.

Figure 21 shows the number of cases of praedial larceny from 1874 to 1937. The larceny curve varies inversely with the prosperity of the working class in most years. Thus it resembles the curve of the number of deaths (Figure 20); both curves rise sharply in such hard years as 1886, 1891, 1894, 1898, 1912, 1914, the war years, 1920–21, and 1923. Both curves have declined during the last two decades when the huge increase in crops has provided plentiful work.

Increased agitation and riots among the laboring class have occurred during hard years, as during the "potato riots" of 1895. On the whole, such troubles have been few, for, in most cases, the laborers are quite aware of the difficulties of the planters and are sympathetic with them. The most recent riot occurred in 1937, and was

---

[16] "Evidence on Barbados," *Report of the West Indian Sugar Commission* (London, 1930), Appendix III, II, 44.

attributed to the improved machinery in the factories which caused "the reaping of the sugar crop to take place in 3 months compared with 5 months formerly, and a smaller number of workmen are employed." [17] Barbadian planters and officials have often stated that

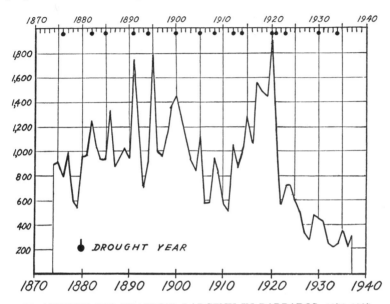

21. ARRESTS FOR PRAEDIAL LARCENY IN BARBADOS, 1874–1937

Sources: *Barbados Blue Books,* 1874–1935; *Colonial Reports: Barbados* (1930–31 to 1937–38).

the fear of reducing employment has prevented the introduction of more agricultural machinery.

The variability of the Barbadian environment is largely beyond human control, and the most that the Government can do is to find means of reducing the damage caused by unfavorable environmental conditions. The remarkable success of the Department of Science and Agriculture in reducing the losses due to drought, pests and diseases, and soil exhaustion have already been discussed. The problem of hurricanes is the environmental bugbear which remains to be treated.

[17] *The Crown Colonist,* February, 1938, p. 116.

Strongly constructed houses may protect the wealthy against the rigors of hurricanes, but such houses are not available to the poor. Insurance and reserves against hurricane damage must be used to lessen the effects of the damage. Until 1924, little was done by the Government to anticipate the arrival of hurricanes except to arrange a system of storm warnings, and to appoint a day for "special supplication to Almighty God for deliverance from storm." When hurricanes hit the island, contributions from more fortunate islands and from the British Isles were used to provide food and rebuild the homes of the poor. The damage from minor hurricanes, such as that of 1894, was taken care of by legislative appropriation.[18]

In 1924 the Government found that it had a considerable surplus on hand, and £100,000 was set aside as "a reserve fund to be drawn on only in cases of public calamity." [19] Although certain Barbadian politicians have been attempting to tap the fund ever since, it still remains intact, as a reserve in case of another hurriance. In 1929–30 it was stated:

. . . Progress has been made in the organization of hurricane relief arrangements during the year by the formulation of a scheme to give effect to relief measures and to indicate for the guidance of local committees what procedure should be followed.[20]

Each year the populace is reminded through the papers and schools of the system of storm warnings and of the relief arrangements. If a catastrophe should occur, each part of the island would be in charge of a committee of responsible citizens.

Other Government activities.—Medical and poor relief, water supply, and education are the other major items in the Barbadian Government budget. The medical and poor relief is supplemented by similar activities carried on by the parish vestries and paid for by real-estate taxes.

In a community with as low a standard of living as Barbados, and where a considerable part of the male population has emigrated, it is not surprising that a large proportion of the population

[18] £1,000 was appropriated in 1894 to take care of repairs to the wooden huts which were blown down. A similar "blow" occurred in 1918, and similar help was voted.

[19] *Colonial Reports: Barbados* (1924–25), p. 4.   [20] *Ibid.* (1929–30), p. 9.

should become community charges at some time or other. It is estimated that 32 percent of the whole population receive relief: 20 percent through the Poor Law and 12 percent through treatment at the General Hospital, the Mental Hospital, or the Lazaretto.[21] The amount of relief given increases slightly in depression years, and the total would be increased much more if the recipients were given relief adequate to maintain the health of the people. The need is not so much for more medical relief as for more and better food. This has been recognized in the recent report of the Committee on Nutrition which recommended that milk and two white biscuits be given out to the school children each school day. The Committee remarked:

> The proposal is certain to be received with derision by many. It would however be an attempt to remove the existing reproach that many of the working people live on the verge of extreme poverty and semi-starvation.[22]

Poor relief at present is largely medical, although some of the aged and infirm are supported in the parish almshouses.

Education is not compulsory, but it is free in the lowest grade of schools. A social stratification is maintained by charging a small tuition in the better Government schools. There are also high-grade private schools under Government supervision.

The availability of education has been both an advantage and a disadvantage to the island's economic system. Undoubtedly the people's knowledge of agricultural methods is increased, and they are able to learn still more because of their common knowledge of elementary school subjects. On the other hand, many of the laboring classes have become dissatisfied with field labor and, at times, there has been a shortage of field labor and a considerable surplus of clerks and artisans.

The extension of the water works accounts for most of the present indebtedness of the Government. An account of the early history of the water works has been given in pages 27–28. During

---

[21] Testimony of Dr. Hutson, "Evidence on Barbados," *Report of the West Indian Sugar Commission* (London, 1930), Appendix III, I, 65.
[22] "Report of the Committee . . . on . . . Nutrition," *Barbados Official Gazette,* October 7, 1937, p. 7.

the twentieth century the water works have been extended until today hardly any part of the island is more than a quarter-mile from a standpipe. The extension of the water works may have helped to account for the decreasing death rate in recent years. The earlier system tapped so little water that, in drought years, as, for example, in 1921, irking restrictions on the use of water, were necessary.[23]

Government revenue and expenditures.—About half of the revenue of the Barbadian Government is obtained from customs collections. The other important sources are excise taxes, water taxes, income taxes, and license fees. Almost all of these collections are influenced by the amount of business, and the years of depression can be identified on Figure 22 by the excess of expenditures, while the years of prosperity usually have a surplus of revenue. On the whole, the years with deficits are offset by the surpluses during prosperity. When prospects for future revenues are poor, the rate of taxation is increased; in good years the rates are decreased. Thus, in spite of its many economic booms and collapses, the Barbadian Government within the last century has never failed to meet its obligations or to maintain its sinking-fund payments.

The policy of increasing the rate of taxation in poor years undoubtedly increases the expenses of business when business can least afford such increases. Thus customs duties were increased in such poor years as 1883, 1895, 1896, 1900 and 1921. Income tax was also levied for the first time in 1922, and the rate was increased in 1929 and again in 1930 to compensate for declining receipts. Due to this policy of changing rates, the fluctuations in revenue are not so great as the fluctuations in exports.

Government expenditures shift with the prosperity of the island, but the fluctuations are not so great as in the value of the exports. Furthermore, the trend of these fluctuations is often opposed to the trend of business since emergencies make certain expenditures a matter of necessity. Thus the high expenditures after the drought of 1891 were due to the construction of public works to create employment; the high expenditures in 1899 represented repairs after the hurricane of 1898; those of 1902 represented the battle against

[23] *Colonial Reports: Barbados* (1921–22), p. 7.

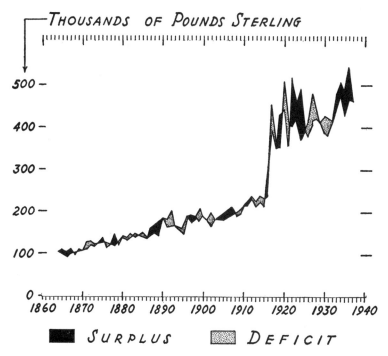

22. BARBADIAN GOVERNMENT SURPLUSES AND DEFICITS, 1864–1937

Source: *Statistical Abstract for the Several Colonial and Other Possessions of the United Kingdom* (London, 1877–1938), various numbers, *passim*.

the smallpox epidemic; those from 1926–31 were due to road improvements, sanitary improvements (including the anti-malarial campaign), and agricultural experiments. On the whole, there is only slight evidence of any retrenchment of Government expenses in poor years. Thus it would seem that the functions of the Barbadian Government are considered as absolutely necessary, and are therefore rarely curtailed.

COMMUNITY MORALE

It is evident to any visitor to Barbados that the morale of the island is influenced by the ups and downs of the sugar industry. The headlines of the newspapers feature news of sugar. Sugar conditions are a common subject of conversation, and reminiscences are often based on past boom years. Even good clothes, house improvements, and other major investments often date back to some profitable year. The present progressive spirit in the island may be attributed in part to the remarkable success of the sugar industry in increasing its production.

The present political and economic system of the island is fitted to the desires of the merchant-planter class. The laboring group is dissatisfied with the system, for they see little opportunity for advancement or, in many cases, even for a minimum healthful standard of living. The discontent of this group is expressed in the newspapers (owned by the mulatto middle class), and in the legislature by the colored and Negro members. In poor years, the reasons for discontent become obvious even to the defenders of the present system, and they resort to the plea that the economic condition of the island does not permit higher wages. It is to be hoped that bad hygienic conditions may eventually force rapid progress toward better living, just as bad economic conditions have forced improvement in the efficiency of the sugar industry. If the claims of local planters may be believed, the Barbadian sugar industry has been failing since 1650 due to droughts, pests, soil exhaustion, poor prices, and declining markets. But the industry today supports a large population on perhaps as high a standard of living as has ever existed in Barbados, and the trend of its production is upward. There are many environmental and economic reasons for its possible failure, and only one major reason for its probable continued success: there is no other industry which can support the present Barbadian population in Barbados. With this spur, Barbadians may be expected to continue to do as they have in the past, howl about their impending failure, and at the same time perform near-miracles to keep ahead of or up to their competitors.

CHAPTER IX

Conclusions

THE VARIABILITY of the Barbadian environment, especially of its rainfall, winds, vegetation, pests, and diseases, is significant because of the damage it has caused and because of its stimulation to activity and progress among the people of Barbados. The destructive effects of this variability are well known and have been illustrated frequently in the preceding chapters. Much less obvious is the stimulating effect which has encouraged a more thorough exploration and exploitation of the Barbadian environment.

This environmental stimulation supports the theory that "Civilization is the product of moderate adversity." [1] The monotonous climate of the tropical rain forest provides little stimulus; its even heat discourages work, while the reliability of its rains makes the quest for food relatively easy. On the other hand, the great variations found in climates such as in Central India have overwhelmed man. Barbados lies between these two extremes. Its oceanic climate provides pleasant living conditions which in normal years present few problems, while the frequent variations from these conditions provide that moderate adversity which keeps man out of a rut.

However, variability of the environment has not been the only factor accounting for Barbadian progress. Changes in man's use of the environment have also been of major importance. These changes were often stimulated by environmental abnormalities; for example, the droughts of 1891 and 1894 hastened the development of the water works. Such changes in man's relationships to the environment, together with variations in that environment, have played a much more important part in Barbadian development than has hitherto been recognized.

[1] J. Russell Smith, *Industrial and Commercial Geography*, p. 6.

Undoubtedly, other factors than variability of the environment have been important in Barbados. Otherwise how can one explain the slower progress in islands such as Antigua which are relatively similar in environment and environmental variability? Density of population, the accidents of history, the presence of outstanding leaders, and many minor factors have also played their parts. However, the evidence presented earlier seems to indicate clearly that, all other factors remaining the same, Barbadian progress would have been slower had the Barbadian environment been more stable.

The Barbadian environment is pleasantly tropical, but making a living in Barbados is by no means so easy as it is in the sparsely settled parts of the tropics. Even in the best years, man must work, and often work hard, to obtain enough on which to subsist. As in the densely populated parts of the East Indies, in Barbados the laborers appear more willing to work than in most tropical lands. Thus the overpopulated condition of Barbados has contributed to its progress.

In the opinion of the writer, the following quotation from Griffith Taylor suggests why Barbados has made an unduly large contribution to civilization in proportion to its size and population.

> In the past it has been usual to explain national progress in terms of military power, religious beliefs, and sagacious rulers. . . . It would be foolish to deny the great influence of these factors, but there is a growing school of thinkers who believe that the environment is at least of equal importance. . . . Further than this, many scientists are coming to the conclusion that it is the *variation in the environment* which is the most potent factor of all in influencing human evolution, whether social or biological.[2]

The facts indicate that it is the moderate adversity caused largely by variations in the Barbadian environment which explains an important part of the island's progess.

How has this moderate adversity operated in stimulating Barbadian development? Certainly it has not operated directly, for there is no evidence that the Barbadian environment provides the type of

[2] Griffith Taylor, *Environment, Race, and Migration,* p. 4.

climatic stimulation described by Ellsworth Huntington in his *Civilization and Climate*.[3] Instead, each variation in the environment has had a long series of repercussions through chains of relationships such as were illustrated on page 141. Economic, political, and social factors have often been integrated with these environmentally stimulated impulses, and have thus modified the final outcome. But in many cases these modifications have been insufficient to obscure the effect of the initial environmental variation. Thus the effect of drought on the death rate is apparent in spite of all the intermediate links pointed out on page 141. The indirectness of the relationship may sometimes mask the effect of the environmental variable, but this does not necessarily lessen its importance.

As these generalizations oversimplify the actual relationships, it is advisable here to summarize the relationships which were demonstrated in Chapters VII and VIII, and to note to what extent they coincide with similar relationships which appeared in the historical evidence in Chapters III–VI.

AGRICULTURE

The amount of ground water in the soil is the most important factor in determining the size of the sugar crop. The amount of rainfall during the year preceding the harvest has the greatest influence on the amount of ground water. The amount of rainfall during the two years preceding the harvest and the seasonal distribution of the rainfall are also important.

The amount of rainfall has not had sufficient influence on the cotton yield to be apparent in most years above the influence of such factors as pests.

Ground-provision crops are exceedingly sensitive to a drought of even a short duration. The shortage of home-grown provisions in drought years has been frequently referred to from the earliest times, as in 1629, 1647, 1663, 1669, 1670, and 1703.

Winds have supplied the power of the windmills and through them have influenced the amount of sugar manufactured. This factor has been important ever since about 1660, when windmills

[3] Ellsworth Huntington, *Civilization and Climate,* Chap. X.

were introduced, but its importance is declining with the increasing predominance of steam factories.

Hurricanes have frequently damaged the crops, but with the exceptions of 1675 and 1780, the damage has been no greater than that caused by a drought. The damage done to the mills and the ground provisions often has been more important than the damage to the sugar crop.

Pests and diseases have always been a major cause of reduced crop yields. The resulting losses have been especially serious when drought has already reduced the yield. Good examples are found in 1650, 1663, and 1670, and in many later years.

The soil deteriorated during approximately the first forty years of Barbadian history. Since then heavy manuring has either maintained or improved soil fertility with two exceptions: in poor years when fertilizers could not be afforded; and on small peasant holdings. Whenever the prospects of the sugar industry were good, the amount of manuring has been increased and larger crops have resulted. Only in recent years have planters realized that it is economical to spend large amounts on manuring even when economic conditions are poor.

At frequent intervals since 1890 improved varieties of cane have been introduced which have greatly increased the yield.

Mulching and other dry-farming techniques have been important since the end of the seventeenth century. The larger amount of cane trash available, as the result of heavier yields, has increased the amount of mulching.

Until recently, increasing prices have led to the more intensive cultivation of sugar cane. Declining prices caused the planters to turn to ground provisions and other crops. Recently, planters have tried to compensate for declining prices by increasing their production.

MANUFACTURING

The improvements in the technique of manufacturing sugar usually occurred during periods of declining prices, as from 1652–70, 1732–39, and 1845–55. More recently it has been in the years of relatively high prices that most of the machinery has been bought. Possibly this has been because of the large amounts of capital needed to purchase modern sugar machinery. Hence such capital investments are difficult in years of depressed prices even though the need for them is then most clearly recognized.

FISHING

Changes in the winds and currents seem to have made fishing less productive since 1902.

EXCHANGE

The exports of Barbados vary closely in amount with the production of sugar, and in value with the production and price of sugar. The imports vary with the exports, but do not vary so much because some of the imports are paid for from savings or from receipts from abroad. In slavery days, the imports were much steadier because the planters had sufficient credit to maintain their purchases through depression periods. The balance of trade was then favorable,[4] whereas during most of the last century it has been unfavorable.

The shipping which visits Bridgetown depends on the development of transport services which serve the Caribbean area. Minor fluctuations are caused by changes in the amount of exports.

Some transit trade has been carried on almost since the first settlement. The amount varies with the prosperity of the surrounding region, with the lack of direct services to the smaller islands, and, occasionally (because of quarantines), with health conditions at Barbados.

CONSUMPTION

Consumption, except for locally grown provisions, varies with the imports. The cereal imports vary both with the purchasing power of Barbadians and with the need for foodstuffs to supplement local ground provisions. On the other hand, the meat and fish

[4] See graph facing p. 244 in Frank W. Pitman, *The Development of the British West Indies, 1700–1763.*

imports are affected largely only by changes in purchasing power. The imports of textiles and clothing vary also with the purchasing power. The imports of capital goods and agricultural supplies vary with the prospects of the sugar industry. So far as can be determined from very uneven evidence, these generalizations apply throughout Barbadian history.

WEALTH

The wealth of the island has varied with the prospects of the sugar industry since most of it consists of real estate used directly or indirectly in the sugar business. In the first century of the island's history, the less efficient and the smaller planters were often forced to sell out to the larger (and usually more efficient) planters. This increased the yields of the land, and hence the productivity of the island. In recent years, many more estates have been subdivided than consolidated. The resulting small subsistence plots have declined in productivity, but the increasing productivity of the remaining estates has more than offset the decline of the peasant holdings.

OCCUPATIONS AND INCOME

The commercial and artisan classes seem to have been increasing in importance since 1700. The income of these classes is influenced by the prosperity of the sugar industry, but it does not fluctuate as greatly as the profits of the planters. The merchants often bought estates from planters who were forced to emigrate. This suggests that the merchants were more prosperous than the planters in hard times. Absentee landlordism, which was so important until the present century, probably developed because certain merchants got control of the estates and later retired to conduct their trade in England.

The incomes of the laboring class today seem to be influenced largely by the size of the crop. Under slavery, the prosperity and generosity of the master were more important in determining the goods received by the slaves.

Incomes from abroad play an important part in the Barbadian economy. These are derived from savings accumulated by planters and merchants when the balance of trade was favorable and during occasional years of high profits. During the last three-quarters of a century, remittances from colored and Negro emigrants have been important.

VITAL STATISTICS

The trends in population reflect the opportunities each class has had to make a living in Barbados as compared with other accessible places. Thus from 1650 to 1750 the white population decreased because many found emigration necessary and advantageous. During the same period, the slave population trended upward due to heavy slave imports. Thereafter, the slave population remained static until the abolition of the slave trade, when an increase started. The white population remained static after 1750, the surplus apparently being eliminated by a slow but inconspicuous emigration. After Emancipation the Negro population increased rapidly, and Negro emigration started. After 1900, emigration was so great that, for a quarter of a century, it exceeded the natural increase, hence the population decreased. Recently emigration has slowed down, and the Barbadian population is thought to be increasing.

Within these general trends, the numbers and health of the populace have been affected from year to year by environmental and economic fluctuations. In poor years the death rate increases rapidly, especially because of the high infantile death rate. Malnutrition seems to be the ultimate cause, although diseases are listed as the immediate cause. These fluctuations in the death rate date back to at least 1647. In the early years, epidemics were much more serious, perhaps because of poorer medical care.

GOVERNMENT

From the earliest days of the colony, the Government has catered to the planters. The history of the island is replete with special legislation designed to aid the sugar interests.

COMMUNITY MORALE

The planter aristocracy has experienced numerous boom periods interspersed with collapses and periods of depression. During or just after each economic crisis, the economically weaker planters have lost out, and have been forced to seek employment or to emigrate. These eliminations of the planters have been especially large when a hurricane or a bad season has coincided with poor economic conditions.

After a crash, the planters have usually appealed to the British Government for relief. Assistance has often been forthcoming, but usually not in sufficient amounts to solve the problem. After outside sources have failed, some of the planters have usually discovered some way of increasing their crops or of otherwise increasing their incomes. Thus the survivors of each crash become better established to benefit by the next boom.

The periods of progress in Barbadian history almost invariably have arrived soon after conditions have just been described as "hopeless." Necessity has provided a strong incentive, and in times, of stress, the planters have always fought the crisis "with their backs to the wall." New methods have been discovered, or old, rarely used methods have been more widely adopted under the goad of economic necessity. When the emergency was over, the desire for progress has often been replaced by self-satisfaction, and the planter aristocracy has reverted to a conservative policy.

To document this important relationship between hard times and progress in Barbados, Table 29 has been prepared. It is based on the data already presented in Chapters III–VIII.

If the intervening periods of relative prosperity be examined, it will be found that, with almost no exceptions, they were lacking in the initiation of improvements. Where progress has been made in such periods, usually it has consisted of a continuation of some trend started during the preceding difficult period. Thus during the war boom (1915–20), while many improvements were made in the factories, they were not new in type, but were rather extensions

TABLE 29

A COMPARISON BETWEEN THE PERIODS OF HARD TIMES AND THE
PROGRESSIVE MEASURES ADOPTED IN BARBADOS, 1647–1931

YEARS	NATURE OF THE DIFFICULT CONDITIONS	PROGRESSIVE MEASURES ADOPTED DURING OR IMMEDIATELY FOLLOWING HARD TIMES
1647–51	Drought; epidemics; declining prices	Consolidation of small properties; replacing of horse mills by cattle mills; first windmills.
1660–70	Soil exhaustion; droughts; caterpillars	Establishment of one-crop system; heavy manuring
1675	Hurricane	Replacing of wood houses by brick and stone houses
1691–94	Epidemics; hurricane	Attempts to increase white population; harbor and sanitary improvements
1700–1705	Droughts; epidemics; price decline; trade restrictions due to war	Economic makeshifts; smuggling and other illegal trades; claying of sugar; use of slaves in responsible positions
1715–23	Declining prices; epidemics affecting livestock	Completion of shift from cattle mills to windmills
1731–39	Hurricane; drought; epidemics	Improvements in sugar extraction; protection of certain home industries
1765–87	Sugar ant; hurricanes; upset trade due to American Revolution	Partial shift to cotton; improvements in processing of cotton and sugar; better layout of plantations; more crop rotation
1800–14	Decline in prices; wartime trade interruptions; abolition of slave trade	Formation of agricultural societies; more crop rotation and self-sufficiency in raising provisions; introduction of Bourbon canes; plowing; careful spacing; guano imports

TABLE 29 (*Continued*)

YEARS	NATURE OF THE DIFFICULT CONDITIONS	PROGRESSIVE MEASURES ADOPTED DURING OR IMMEDIATELY FOLLOWING HARD TIMES
1831–34	Hurricane; Emancipation; poor prices	Houses rebuilt to suit the climate; plainer and healthier habits of life; better methods of cultivation
1846–50	Reduction of British protective duties on colonial sugar; sharp price declines	Advances in almost every phase of cultivation and manufacture
1854	Cholera; serious competition from beet and East Indian sugar	Plans for water works (started 1859); increased exports to U.S.
1880–86	Price decline; irregular weather	Increased manuring; scientific experiments; Agricultural Aids Act
1890–95	Exhaustion of Bourbon cane; droughts; caneborers; plant diseases	White Transparent cane; scientific experiments; extension of water works
1903–13	Poor prices; droughts; smallpox and yellow fever	Seedlings introduced; cotton and other crops tried; Sugar Industry Agricultural Bank established
1920–22	Drought; poor prices; pests and mosaic disease	Seedlings introduced; reserve for calamities; economies of all kinds; great increase in yields due to scientific work
1928–31	Drought; poor prices; malaria	Continued improvement of yields due to applied science; improved sanitary conditions

of the type of improvements which the more progressive factories had made earlier. Free spending for proved benefits rather than experiments along new lines have been characteristic of the progress, if any, during boom periods.

The Barbadian environment has been well worth exploiting. Its inhabitants have used many of its potentialities, but in many cases utilization of these has been stimulated by problems arising from environmental variability or economic change. In solving these problems, the leaders in the Barbadian culture have discovered new ways of utilizing the environment which might forever have been ignored were the problems less pressing. To this fortunate combination of environmental potentialities and problems may be attributed much of the economic development of Barbados.

Bibliography

Acts of the Privy Council, Colonial Series. 6 vols., London, various dates.

Agricultural Reporter, The. Bridgetown, 1846–53.

Alexander, Sir J. E., Transatlantic Sketches. Philadelphia, 1833.

Andrews, Charles M., The Colonial Period. New York, 1912.

Aspinall, Algernon, The Pocket Guide to the West Indies. New York, 1931.

Barbados, Assembly, Acts and Statutes of Barbados. London, 1656.

—— Assembly, Acts of Assembly Passed in the Island of Barbados from 1648–1718. London, 1721.

—— Assembly, Laws of Barbados. Vols. I–VIII. Bridgetown, various dates.

—— Botanical Station, Occasional Bulletins, Nos. 1–10. Bridgetown, 1891–98.

—— Colonial Secretary, Barbados Blue Book. Bridgetown, 1850–1935.

—— Colonial Secretary, Colonial Reports: Barbados. London, 1881–1938.

—— Colonial Secretary, Report on the Census of Barbados, 1921. Bridgetown, 1921.

—— Comptroller of Customs, Annual Report on the Customs Revenue, Trade, and Shipping of the Island.

—— Department of Agriculture, Annual Report. Bridgetown, 1890–1925.

—— Department of Science and Agriculture, Agricultural Journal. Quarterly, Bridgetown, 1932–38.

—— Department of Science and Agriculture, Pamphlets, Nos. 1–9. Bridgetown, 1929–31.

—— Department of Science and Agriculture, Report on the Department of Science and Agriculture. Annual since 1926–27; included in *Agricultural Journal* since 1932–33. Bridgetown, 1927–31.

—— Harbour and Shipping Department, Annual Report, 1928–37.

—— Medical Department, Annual Report of the Chief Medical Officer, 1928–37.

—— Medical Department, Annual Report on Poor Relief, 1928–37.

—— Police, Annual Report, 1925–37.

—— Post Office Department, Annual Report, 1905–37.

—— Registrar, Annual Report on the Vital Statistics, 1928–31.

Barbados, Sugar Commission, Final Report. Bridgetown, 1932.
—— West Indian Cotton Conference. Bridgetown, 1932.
Barbados Advocate. Daily, Bridgetown.
Barbados Advocate Weekly. Bridgetown.
Barbados Museum and Historical Society, *Journal.* Quarterly, Bridge-
town, 1933–38.
Barbados Official Gazette. Bridgetown, 1880–1938.
Bayley, Frederic, Four Years' Residence in the West Indies during the
Years 1826, 7, 8 and 9. London, 1833.
Beer, G. L., The Old Colonial System. New York, 1912.
—— The Origins of the British Colonial System. New York, 1908.
Bell, Herbert C., Studies in the Trade Relations of the British West
Indies and North America, 1763–73, 1783–93. Philadelphia, 1917.
Benns, F. L., The American Struggle for the British West Indian Carry-
ing Trade, 1815–30. Bloomington, Ind., 1923.
Bovell, J. R., Notes on Rotation and Catch Crops. *West Indian Bulletin,*
I (1899), 204–11
Bowman, Isaiah, Geography in Relation to the Social Sciences. New
York, 1934.
Boyce, Sir Rupert W., Health Progress and Administration in the West
Indies. London, 1910.
Bruhnes, Jean, Human Geography. New York, 1920.
Buttenshaw, W. R., Barbados Woolless Sheep. *West Indian Bulletin,*
VI, No. 2 (1905), 187–94.
Calendar of State Papers, Colonial Series (America and West Indies).
London, various dates.
Caribbeana. 2 vols., London, 1741.
Chester, Greville J., The Shell Implements and Other Antiquities of
Barbados. *Archaeological Journal,* XXVII (1870), 43–52.
Coleridge, Henry Nelson, Six Months in the West Indies in 1825. New
York, 1826.
Colonial Office 28, Barbados, Original Correspondence with the Board of
Trade. MSS.
Commons Journal, Vol. VI (1650).
Crown Colonist, The. London, 1931–38.
Cundall, Frank, Bibliography of the West Indies Excluding Jamaica.
Kingston, 1909.
Cutteridge, J. O., Geography of the West Indies and Adjacent Lands.
London, 1931.
Davies, John, The History of the Caribby Islands. London, 1666.
Davis, N. Darnell, Cavaliers and Roundheads in Barbados. George-
town, 1887.

Davis, William Morris, The Lesser Antilles. New York, 1926.

Davy, John, The West Indies before and since Slave Emancipation. London, 1854.

Deerr, Noel, Sugar and the Sugar Cane. Manchester, 1905.

Donnan, Elizabeth, Documents Illustrative of the History of the Slave Trade to America. 2 vols., Carnegie Institution, Washington, D.C., 1931.

Edwards, Bryan, The History, Civil and Commercial, of the British Colonies in the West Indies. Philadelphia, 1806.

Ellis, Ellen B., Introduction to the History of Sugar as a Commodity. Philadelphia, 1905.

Empire Marketing Board, Report of Proceedings, Imperial Sugar Cane Research Conference, London, 1931. London, 1932.

Fassig, O. L., Hurricanes of the West Indies. Washington, 1913.

Fewkes, J. Walter, Archeology of Barbados. Proceedings of the National Academy of Science, I (1915), 47–51.

Fisher, R. S., Statistical Account of the West India Islands. New York, 1855.

Foster, Alice, Barbados. *Journal of Geography*, XXII (1923), 205–16.

Garriot, E. B., West Indian Hurricanes. U.S. Weather Bureau, Bulletin H.

Guppy, H. B., Plants, Seeds, and Currents in the West Indies and Azores. London, 1917.

Hall, Richard, Acts of Barbados. London, 1764.

Hardy, F., Some Aspects of the Flora of Barbados. *Agricultural Journal,* Vols. I and II (1932–33), *passim.*

Harlow, Vincent T. (ed.), Colonizing Expeditions to the West Indies and Guiana, 1623–67. London, 1925. Hakluyt Society, Series II, Vol. LVI.

—— A History of Barbados, 1625–85. Oxford, 1926.

Harrison, J. B., and A. J. Jukes-Browne, The Geology of Barbados. Bridgetown, 1890.

Herskovits, Melville J., Life in a Haitian Valley. New York, 1937.

Hillary, William, Observations of the Changes of the Air and the Concomitant Epidemical Diseases in the Island of Barbados. London, 1759.

Historical Manuscript Commission, Tenth Report, Appendix, Part VI.

—— The Manuscripts of the House of Lords, New Series, 5 vols., London, 1887.

Hughes, Griffith, Natural History of Barbados. London, 1750.

Huntington, Ellsworth, Civilization and Climate. 3d ed., New Haven, 1924.

Jukes-Browne, A. J., and J. B. Harrison, The Geology of Barbados. *Quarterly Journal of the Geological Society,* XLVII (1891), 197–248; XLVIII (1892), 170–226.

Ligon, Richard, A True and Exact History of the Island of Barbados. 2d ed., London, 1673.

Loven, Sven, Origins of the Tainan Culture. Göteborg, 1935.

Lyttleton, Edward, The Groans of the Plantations. London, 1688.

McKinnen, Daniel, A Tour through the British West Indies in the Years 1802 and 1803. London, 1804.

Madden, R. R., Twelve Months' Residence in the West Indies during the Transition from Slavery to Apprenticeship. Philadelphia, 1835.

Massachusetts Historical Society Collections. Boston, 1806–1927.

Mathieson, W. L., British Slave Emancipation. London, 1932.

Matley, C. C., Old Basement of Barbados. *Geological Magazine,* LXIX (1932). 366–73.

Mayo, William, A New and Exact Map of the Island of Barbados. London, 1722.

Memoirs of the First Settlement of Barbados. Bridgetown, 1741; reprinted, 1891.

Morrell, W. P., British Colonial Policy in the Age of Peel and Russell. Oxford, 1930.

Moxley, George Joseph H. S., An Account of a West Indian Sanitarium and a Guide to Barbados. London, 1886.

Narrative of General Venables, ed. by C. H. Firth. London, 1900.

New Map of the Island of Barbados, A. London, 1890.

Newton, Arthur Percival, The European Nations in the West Indies, 1493–1688. London, 1933.

Oldmixon, John, The British Empire in America. Vol. II. London, 1741.

Pares, Richard, War and Trade in the West Indies. Oxford, 1936.

Parsons, Commander J., Admiralty Chart No. 2485: Barbados. Surveyed 1869; reprinted with slight alterations, 1927.

Paul, G. P., Report on Ankylostomiasis Infection Survey of Barbados from September 4 to November 16, 1916. International Health Board, 1916. MS.

Pinckard, George, Notes on the West Indies. London, 1806.

Pitman, Frank W., The Development of the British West Indies, 1700–1763. New Haven, 1917.

—— Slavery on the British West India Plantations. *Journal of Negro History,* XI (1926), 584–668.

Poey, Andrés, A Chronological Table of the Cyclonic Hurricanes Which Have Occurred in the West Indies and in the North American Waters from 1493 to 1855. London, 1856.

Porter, George R., The Nature and Properties of the Sugar Cane. 2d ed., London, 1843.

Poyer, John, The History of Barbados. London, 1808.

Prinsen Geerligs, H. C., The World's Cane Sugar Industry, Past and Present. Manchester, 1912.

Public Acts in Force Passed by the Legislature of Barbados, 1762–1800, The. London, 1807.

Ragatz, Lowell Joseph, The Fall of the Planter Class in the British Caribbean, 1763–1833. New York, 1928.

—— A Guide for the Study of British Caribbean History, 1763–1834. Annual Report of the American Historical Association, 1930, Vol. III.

—— Statistics for the Study of British Caribbean Economic History, 1763–1833. London, 1927.

Rawson, Governor R. W., Report upon the Population of Barbados, 1851–71. Bridgetown, 1871.

Reed, W. W., Climatological Data for the West Indian Islands. *Monthly Weather Review*, LIV (1926), 156–57.

Report from the Committee on the Commercial State of the West India Colonies. London, 1807.

Report from the Select Committee on the West Indian Colonies. London, 1843.

Sauer, Carl O., The Morphology of Landscape. *University of California Publications in Geography*, II, No. 2 (1925), 47.

Schomburgk, Sir Robert H., The History of Barbados. London, 1848.

Schuchert, Charles, Antillean-Caribbean Region. New York, 1936. "Historical Geology of North America," Vol. I.

Sessional Papers, 1831–32. Vol. XX. London, 1832.

Sewell, W. G., The Ordeal of Free Labor in the British West Indies. New York, 1861.

Sinckler, Edward G., The Barbados Handbook. London, 1914.

Skeete, C. C., Barbados Rainfall. Pamphlet No. 9, Department of Science and Agriculture, Bridgetown, 1931.

—— The Condition of Peasant Agriculture in Barbados. Bridgetown, 1930.

—— Weather Observations and Weather Records in Barbados, 1924–33. *Journal of the Barbados Museum and Historical Society*, I (1934), 115–36.

Smith, Captain John, The First Planting of Barbados. Works, 1608–31. London, 1884.

Smith, J. Russell, Industrial and Commercial Geography. New York, 1925.

Southey, Thomas, Chronological History of the West Indies. 3 vols., London, 1827.

Sturge, Joseph, and Thomas Harvey, The West Indies in 1837. London, 1838.

Sugar, a Handbook for Planters and Refiners. London, 1888.

Taylor, Griffith, Environment, Race and Migration. Chicago, 1937.

Thomas, Sir Dalby, An Historical Account of the Rise and Growth of the West-India Collonies. London, 1690. Reprinted in *Harleian Miscellany,* Vol. IX, London, 1810.

Thome, James A., and J. H. Kimball, Emancipation in the West Indies. New York, 1838.

Tracts and Other Papers, collected by Peter Force. 4 vols., Washington, 1836–46.

Trechmann, C. T., The Uplift of Barbados. *Geological Magazine,* LXX (1933), 19–47.

Tucker, R. W. E., Control of Field Crop, Garden and Fruit Pests in Barbados. Pamphlet No. 7, Department of Science and Agriculture, Bridgetown, 1931.

—— Notes on Insect Pests of the Sugar Cane. Pamphlet No. 3, Department of Science and Agriculture, Bridgetown, 1930.

United Kingdom, Board of Trade, Statistical Abstract for the Several Colonial and Other Possessions of the United Kingdom. (The title varies.) London, 1877, and annually.

—— Department of Overseas Trade, Report on Economic and Financial Conditions in the British West Indies. London, 1921, 1922, 1923, 1924, 1928, 1930, 1932, 1935.

United States, Hydrographic Office, Chart No. 2319: Barbados.

—— Hydrographic Office, Chart No. 5253: Carlisle Bay.

—— Hydrographic Office, *West Indies Pilot.* Vol. II, 1929.

—— Weather Bureau, Climatological Data, West Indies and Caribbean Service (monthly and annual). San Juan, 1921–38.

Wagemann, Ernst F., Britische-westindische Wirtschaftpolitik. Leipzig, 1909.

Watts, Arthur P., Une Histoire des colonies anglaises aux Antilles (de 1649 à 1660). Paris, 1924.

West India Royal Commission, Report. London, 1897.

West Indian Sugar Commission, 1929, Memorandum of Information Prepared by a Local Committee.

West Indian Sugar Commission, Report (Cmd. 3517). London, 1930.

—— Report (in continuation of Cmd. 3517, Colonial No. 49). London, 1930.

—— Mimeographed Appendices to the Report of the West Indian Sugar

Commission, Appendix III: "Evidence on Barbados." 2 vols., London, 1930.

White, Father Andrew, Narrative of a Voyage to Maryland. *Maryland Historical Society Fund Publication,* No. 7. Baltimore, 1874.

Winthrop's Journal, 1630–49. Ed. by James Kendall Hosmer. 2 vols., New York, 1908.

Yearbook of the Bermudas, Bahamas, British Guiana, British Honduras and the British West Indies. Annual, 1926–27, 1928, etc. Montreal, 1927, etc.

Index

Abolition Movement, 110
Absentee landlordism, 69, 100, 118, 177
Adversity as cause of progress, 202
Africa, flora and fauna derived from, 24
African cultural influence, 7
Agricultural Aids Act, 193
Agricultural Reporter, The, 119; excerpt, 120
Agricultural societies, 111, 118
Agriculture, variation in factors influencing, 141-62, 203-4; climate, 141; pests and plant diseases, 148; improvements in methods of cultivation, 153; economic factors, 161; imports of supplies, 175 f.; occupations and income, 182 f.; government aid and protection, 192-94, 207; *see also* Sugar, production
Agriculture, Department of, *see* Science and Agriculture
Albuquerque, d', Professor, 163
American Revolution, effects of, 100 ff.
Amusements, 97
Animals, indigenous, 42; domesticated, 42-43, 55, 62; distemper, 88, 89; *see also under names, e.g.,* Cattle; Horses; etc.
Ants, sugar, 101, 103
Apprenticeship of former slaves, 116, 118
Arawak Indians, 7, 51, 53
Area, 3
Atkin, Governor, quoted, 78, 79
Attorneys, 118
Ayscue, Sir George, 65

Banks, 47; Sugar Industry Agricultural Bank, 127, 133, 134, 193; loans, 133, 134, 193
Barbadoes Gazette, 97
Beaches, 28
Beet sugars, 121, 123, 132; export bounties, 126, 127, 129
Birth rate, 68, 70, 105, 186; effect of drought upon, 187

Black-soil districts, 48, 49; map, 34
Bligh, Captain, 109
Bollworm, 145, 148
Boom periods, 57, 58, 88
Borers, 150, 151, 152
Bovell, John, experiments with sugar cultivation, 125, 135, 155
Bowman, Isaiah, quoted, 12
Braithwaite, John, 98
Breadfruit, 109
Bridgetown, location, 4, 5, 45; port, 4, 14, 46, 96, 167; trade center and metropolis, 4, 45, 168; surrounding area, 5, 45, 178; population, 45, 122; fire, 76; about 1750, 95 f.; desire of Negroes to live near, 118; mentioned, 16, 24, 40, 56, 62, 75, 79, 82, 107, 127, 189
British Government, *see* England
British West Indian Cane Breeding Station, 136, 158
Brunhes, Jean, quoted, 11
Buildings, materials, 4, 43, 73, 79, 105, 174 f.; location in relation to topography, 30; *see also* Houses; Huts

Camels, 59, 62
Campos, Pedro a, 51
Canada, 6, 100; trade with, 124, 129
Cane Breeding Station, West Indian, 136, 158
Carib Indians, 7, 51
Carlisle, Earl of, 54, 61, 64, 77n
Carlisle Bay, 4, 45, 46, 54, 56
Cattle, 36, 43, 89, 94, 104, 173; legal provisions, 91
Cattle mills, 36, 60, 73, 89, 95
Cereal imports, 170, 171 f.
Chadbourne Plan, 136
Chancery, 123, 193
Child health and mortality, 117; infantile death rate, 134, 186, 187; causes, 188
Cholera, 122, 185

Smuggling, 71, 86, 105
Social life, 47
Soils, 33-37; exhaustion first noted, 76; water-absorbing capacity, 143
Sour grass, 41, 42
Spanish, the, 7, 51, 52, 72, 76
Speights Bay, 4, 59, 103
Speightstown, 49, 59, 75
Steam factories, 121, 123, 146, 163
Stem moth borer, 151
Stores, retail, 46, 84, 168
Storm warnings, 196
Stream system, 30; gullies, 30 f., 95
Structure and relief, 5, 25-29, 30
Suffrage, 192
Sugar Act, of 1739, 92; 1764, 100; 1846, 121
Sugar industry: beginning of sugar economy, 57, 58; as legal tender, 64, 66, 86; prices, 66-68, 107-9, 112, 121, 126, 133, 135, 136, 161 f.; duties, 78, 79, 91, 100, 112, 113, 114, 116, 121; exports, 84, 90, 102, 166; insurance, 87, 92, 93, 100, 179, 196; expansion of world supply, 89; direct trade with Europe, 91, 92; preference on imports into United Kingdom, 112, 136; effect of beet sugars upon, 121, 123, 126, 127, 129, 132; investigation and recommendations of Royal Commissions, 126, 136; government aid and protection, 126, 192 ff., 207; World War period, 132 ff.; report of Barbadian committee, 136; causes of success analyzed, 139; determination of profits, 161; loans on, 179, 193; community morale influenced by, 199; *see also* Plantations; Planters
manufacturing, 162-64, 204; windmills, 30, 36, 73, 89, 121, 146, 163; cattle mills, 36, 60, 73, 89, 95; earliest factories, 60; patents for improvements, 91; steam factories, 121, 123, 146, 163; average expression of mills, 163; machinery, 164
production: manuring, 36 f., 42, 61, 95, 112, 126, 153-56, 160, 176 methods of cultivation, 38 f., 61, 80, 111, 119, 125, 135, 153-60; crop yields, 61, 73, 80, 92, 109, 113, 119, 139, 144, 155; cane fires, 75, 194; patents for improvements, 91; production in-

creased, 119 ff., 135; reasons for increase, 120; experiments by scientists in cane production, 125, 135, 155; relation between rainfall and production, 125, 141-44, 149, 159, 161; between other factors and production, 147, 149, 150 ff.; pests and plant diseases, 148, 149-53; yield of saccharose from cane varieties, *chart,* 158; contribution of new varieties to increased tonnage, 159; rainfall and the cost of production, *chart,* 182
products: clayed sugar, 86 f., 92; muscovado, 86 f., 121, 164; molasses, 105, 112, 124, 131; sirup, 130
varieties: Bourbon cane, 108, 124, 126, 150; Brazilian, 108; Otaheite, 108; seedlings, 125, 126, 135, 150, 156 f.; White Transparent cane, 126, 150, 156, 159; drought resistant varieties, 132; terms by which distinguished, 156, 157
Sugar Industry Agricultural Bank, 127, 133, 134, 193
Sunshine, 16, 17

Tariffs, *see* Customs duties
Taxation, levied in commodities, 64; "enumeration dues," 78; tariff preference given West Indian colonies, 112, 136; income tax, 134, 184, 198; government revenue, 198; *see also* Customs duties
Taylor, Griffith, quoted, 202
Temperature, 5, 15-17, 20, 48, 141
Terraces, 4, 5, 27, 28; bottoms, 32, 35
Textile imports, 173 f.
Thomas, Sir Dalby, 95; quoted, 80, 81
Thorne, Mr., quoted, 165
Timber, 73, 174 f.
Tobacco, 53, 55, 58, 64, 66, 86
Topography, 5, 25-29, 30
Tourist trade, 131, 183
Trade, transit, 46, 63, 167, 205; New England, 63, 72, 73, 78, 85, 92, 99, 103, 105, 124; change to slave-sugar economy reflected in, 63; with England prohibited, 64; illegal practices, 71, 86, 105; trend to Empire trade, 71 f.; cessation of, with Spanish Caribbean, 85; direct trade with Europe, 91, 92, 103; with U.S., 108, 113, 123 f.,